Manchester and São Paulo

Manchester and São Paulo

Problems of
Rapid Urban Growth

Edited by
John D. Wirth and Robert L. Jones

STANFORD UNIVERSITY PRESS

Stanford, California 1978

Publisher's Note

The chapters of this book were initially papers given at a conference held at Stanford University in April 1977 under the sponsorship of the university's Center for Latin American Studies. They have been edited for publication by the *Stanford Journal of International Studies* editorial board, composed of 35 Stanford Law School students.

Particular credit for carrying the conference to fruition belongs to John D. Wirth, Frederick Stout of Stanford's Urban Studies program, and Leonor Gaston Motta, former Editor-in-Chief of the *Journal*. Primary financial support for this project was provided by the Dickinson Symposium Fund, Hills Brothers Coffee, and the Tinker Foundation. Generous help came as well from the Bechtel Corporation, the Fundação Biblioteca Patricia Bildner, the United States Information Agency, and the Ford Foundation.

Stanford University Press
Stanford, California
© 1978 by the Board of Trustees of the
Leland Stanford Junior University
Printed in the United States of America
ISBN 0-8047-1005-8
LC 78-55321

Contents

Introduction

JOHN D. WIRTH*

Manchester during its period of most rapid urban growth (1790-1850) and São Paulo after 1890 can be seen as paradigm cities. Each in its own way exemplifies the unprecedented changes brought on by industrialism. Manchester was the first great industrial city: contemporaries saw this former market town in the English Midlands as a phenomenon of world significance. São Paulo is the premier industrial city of the Third World. If current trends continue, by the year 2000 this former coffee service center on the Brazilian plateau will be the world's largest urban complex.

In relating the two cities thematically, certain shared structural similarities become clear. Neither is a port, or a national capital; both are linked to port cities and each depends on its nation's capital city for a wide range of political, financial, and cultural functions. Both were market towns that rapidly outgrew their role as regional distribution points to become great hubs of capitalist manufacturing and commerce. Indeed, it is as industrial cities that they are known best.

But that Manchester and São Paulo underwent broadly similar phenomena is a riskier proposition. Can we in fact compare two capitalist industrial cities at different points in time, in divergent national contexts, with different roles in the world economy?

Yes and no. Paulistas are certain they face something new. Like Mancunians in their day, they are greatly preoccupied with the fact and meaning of their city. But São Paulo is no replica of Manchester: the growth stages pioneered by the nineteenth-century city are not being followed sequentially by its twentieth-century counterpart. São Paulo's industrialization began late, after strategic points in the international economy were already occupied by others; and it proceeded more quickly because foreign capital, technology, and knowhow were available to it. Unlike Manchester, whose population growth peaked

* Professor of History and Director of the Center for Latin American Studies at Stanford University.

1

in the 1810's at 3 percent a year, São Paulo grows at a 5 percent rate, adding 600,000 people each year, more than the entire population of Manchester in 1850. Manchester had the world as a market and Britain's overseas empire as an outlet for its surplus population; São Paulo sells primarily to Brazil and absorbs millions of Brazilians who cannot emigrate abroad. Manchester in the end achieved stability; São Paulo may someday do the same, but its current problems are staggering.

Rates of capital accumulation, the mix of technologies, the sources of finance, the incorporation of labor—all are different. Indeed, it can be argued that what is interesting is precisely the differences between the two cities, which, as Florestan Fernandes remarked at the conference that gave rise to this volume, "stem from the consequences of Manchester developing in the earlier phase of industrial capitalism, whereas São Paulo is developing in the phase of monopoly capitalism." But there are analogies worth looking at, too, if one is careful to specify what is different and why. These are some points of legitimate comparison:

—Changing city-hinterland relationships, including migration.

—Spatial organization problems caused by rapid, unplanned growth.

—Changing patterns of production and corresponding changes in the organization of labor.

—Problems of adapting to city life.

—Changing political strategies of city elites.

—Intellectuals' and artists' perceptions of phenomena without precedent.

The papers in this collection, which address all these points and others, cluster logically in three sets: cognition, city-hinterland relationships, and governance and adaptation.

Intellectuals in Manchester and São Paulo came to grips with rapid social change in similar ways. For artists in both cities, the problem was that of creating what we now think of as modernism: making an art and a literature that would do justice to the new urban and industrial reality. The effect of Manchester on Coleridge, Dickens, and others is well known. In São Paulo, as Richard Morse and Iumna Maria Simon point out, there were more basic problems, the first of which was to create an adequate vocabulary. Morse and Simon salute the poet Mário de Andrade for blending the rhythms and idioms of popular speech with vivid new images of the metropolis.

Thinkers in both cities grappled with the central problem of intellectuals who confront the modern: what elements of the past can be saved and made to serve, what should be discarded?

In Morse's view the English had an easier time of it than the Brazilians, since the English could draw on a generally agreed view of nationality in which all classes played an honorable part. The Paulistas, by contrast, on the periphery of the Western world, had to create a new concept of nationality from the unpromising beginnings of slavery and plantation agriculture. Why did they find sociology a more adequate cognitive apparatus than economics? Morse's thesis is provocative: Manchester went for economics because it already had a working theory of society; São Paulo chose sociology because it had to start from scratch.

What appears most forcefully in Valdo Pons's account of Mancunian bourgeois thought is its diversity. Yet it was the fumbling bourgeois reformers, not the clear-sighted Engels, whose vision prevailed. Pons also makes the point in passing that working-class popular literature lacked a sense of the city as a system. This suggests some very important questions about class identity, a phenomenon which from Engels to E.P. Thompson has engaged observers of the capitalist city. Not until Florestan Fernandes's seminal work on the Negro in São Paulo was there a penetrating Brazilian study of how a class society can develop in an environment of fragmentation, isolation, and particularism.[1]

In the first essay on city-hinterland relationships, Bryan Roberts finds that the process of capitalist transformation in the countryside around Manchester was virtually complete when that city "took off" as a dynamic industrial city in the late eighteenth century. São Paulo State, by contrast, has yet to complete these profound changes in work and production. Consequently, São Paulo city industrialized from the center outward, and the patterns and consequences of rural to urban migration there were different. Roberts concludes that there is no single path of urban capitalist development. He notes further that Manchester, far from representing the classic path, was atypical because it lacked an agricultural frontier.

Martin Katzman, an economist, and John Sharpless, an economic historian, contribute complementary papers. Katzman sees São Paulo as a rare case of industrialization coming out of tropical export agriculture, a genesis that led to very different growth rates and patterns from those of Manchester and the American Midwest. Another rarity was the success of São Paulo, a regional city, in overtaking the primate city of Rio de Janeiro in both population and size of industrial park. Sharpless examines the relationship of Manchester to Liverpool, its port, and concludes that the two cities were interdependent but coequal. By contrast, São Paulo early achieved clear dominance over its port, Santos.

Finally, the last three papers focus on aspects of governance and adaptation. Robert Shirley, in a path-breaking paper, finds that the elites of São Paulo, a pre-existing agricultural export center, were much better organized to handle the early problems of social unrest caused by industrialization than the Manchester elites, who responded haphazardly to crisis. Comparative analysis of the police and legal systems shows how tough-minded, repressive elites helped shape the development of labor. In Manchester, labor organized to compete for a share of the social product; in São Paulo, corporatist controls and benefits were "bestowed" on workers from the top down.

Peter Fry discusses the two fastest-growing religions among the lower classes in São Paulo: Protestant Pentecostalism and Afro-Brazilian Umbanda. It might be expected that capitalist São Paulo would embrace Protestantism, just as Manchester turned to Methodism in its time. In fact, Pentecostalism and Umbanda offer very different beliefs. The intense activity of these two antithetical competitors for the soul of urban man suggests much about the fluidity of class structure, the plasticity of intergroup relations, and the choices available to residents.

Lincoln Allison examines the social role of British football, with comments on the incorporation of labor and the development of local solidarities based on team spirit and pride of place. Brazilian football followed a similar, rapid pattern of diffusion from elites to middle classes to masses. All three authors touch on the importance of national culture. Though such observations are unfashionable today, there is something very Brazilian about the informal and eclectic scenario Fry describes. British team football is characterized by its tight structure and collective effort, whereas Brazilian soccer is noted for a looser, more individualistic style of play. In counterpoint to the religious theme, some Brazilians think their teams should tighten up!

These are some of the insights, as often as not surprising, that a comparison of the two cities reveals. From these papers it is also clear there was no single, cumulative crisis of the system in either city, let alone any single identifiable crisis of rapid urban growth. As Charles Tilly pointed out in his summary remarks at the conference, the concept of crisis must be rejected. Rapid capitalist urban development reveals no course from stress through decay to breakdown.

In *Engels, Manchester, and the Working Class*,[2] Steven Marcus reminds us that the shock of Manchester can still shock. But the explanation for crime, riots, and upheaval is more likely found in the specific types of prevailing property relationships and the patterns of repression and control, as Tilly pointed out. Jorge Wilheim noted that the existence of exploitation does not by itself reveal very much: it is with the specific facts and context that administrators like himself must deal. Finally, there are classes of related problems that crop up as cities grow rapidly: crime, crowding, sewage, and pollution.

Many questions raised by the comparison are not easily answered. Why did workers organize themselves effectively in Manchester and not in São Paulo? (At the conference, Juarez Brandão Lopes noted that only now, it seems, are São Paulo workers beginning to organize effectively at the level of the factory committee.) Was it good or bad that Manchester developed stable working-class neighborhoods and labor-management relations that eventually inhibited technological innovation? Can the putting-out system in nineteenth-century Manchester and its satellite towns be equated, as Roberts suggested at the conference, with putting-out arrangements in Latin American cities today?

What about family structure, since migrants to Manchester and São Paulo both maintained kinship ties? Much needs to be known about collective action and self-help activities in the neighborhoods, topics raised in documentary films at the Stanford conference. What about the migrant's view of the city as opportunity? Jorge Wilheim remarked at the conference that for a migrant to São Paulo, owning a house is tantamount to having a piece of the urban dream; it is a sign that he is "making it" and will not slip back into rural obscurity. Was that the way it was in Manchester?

And what of other cases? What does the history of Chicago, for example, have to tell us about rapid urban growth? The novels of Dreiser, the poetry of Sandburg, the sociology of the so-called Chicago school, which developed an American analysis of the city—all these are grist for our cognition mill. Chicago's role as a distribution point and processing center for the Midwest offers insights on the city-hinterland relationship. Governance and adaptation in Chicago are topics that need no introduction to American readers. Or one could start with the pace and feel of a neighborhood—something these papers do not do—and work outward to the districts, zones, and suburbs, using perhaps Studs Terkel's *Division Street: America*[3] and recreating similar environments for Manchester and São Paulo.

Having started with questions, this collection ends not with answers but with different and deeper questions. Manchester and São Paulo are different in some ways, analogous in others. It is not just an intellectual exercise to examine the parallels and differences. The promise of area studies is to generate well-documented case studies and concepts that can be used in other contexts. To mix British Studies with Latin American Studies so that each case and the research on each could be suggestively and legitimately related was the rationale of this undertaking. It is time, from every point of view, to achieve a better understanding of what has happened, and is happening, in the industrial cities of the capitalist world.

NOTES

1. FLORESTAN FERNANDES, THE NEGRO IN BRAZILIAN SOCIETY (NY: Atheneum, 1971).

2. STEVEN MARCUS, ENGELS, MANCHESTER AND THE WORKING CLASS (NY: Vintage, 1975). For socioeconomic conditions in São Paulo, *see* CÂNDIDO PROCÓPIO FERREIRA DE CAMARGO *et. al.*, SÃO PAULO 1975; CRESCIMENTO E POBREZA (São Paulo: Edições Loyola, 1976).

3. STUDS TERKEL, DIVISION STREET: AMERICA (NY: Pantheon, 1966).

Manchester Economics and Paulista Sociology

RICHARD M. MORSE*

THE TWO CITIES under consideration in this collection of papers are logical subjects for comparison because both were loci for unexampled bursts of industrialism with all its concomitants: Manchester for the West, and São Paulo a century later for the Third World. The demographic, institutional, and economic realms all yield obvious approaches for this challenging inquiry. Yet in comparing structural features of early and late development, I find myself drawn to the cognitive realm and to the question of how the mind in each case came to grips with phenomena without precedent. When one examines products of the mind one may favor esthetic versions of experience that are relatively free of self-conscious intellectualizing.[1] Or one may deal with assumptions and modes of analysis that attach to more instrumental sorts of mental exercise.[2] In any event the split is arbitrary, for, as this essay suggests, intellect takes effective grasp of social issues only when it feels itself in easy, affective communion with the traditions of a national or cultural community. In the formulation of Alfred North Whitehead, to whom we shall later return, generalization requires a prior stage of "first apprehension," or "immediate cognizance."

The unwieldy comparison of mental responses to industrialism needs a focus. It would, after all, be foolhardy to attempt to canvass the full intellectual panorama in both Manchester and São Paulo. Thus, the comparison will be organized around the Manchester School of Economics and the Paulista "school of sociology." Coupling these "schools," neither of them properly a school, is admittedly a marriage of convenience. A safer analogy would be between the lobbying activities of the Manchester School and those of the Brazilian interest groups studied by the economic historian Nícia Vilela Luz.[3] Or, one could reasonably inquire why Marxist thought, inspired in part by Engels' reflections on Manchester, failed to shape social out-

* Professor of History at Yale University.

7

comes in England while later versions of it, despite its precarious applicability to Brazil, assumed importance for Paulista sociologists.

Although these more targeted issues will not be dismissed, I prefer to stay with the elusive juxtaposition of the "schools." They confront us with a large question in the sociology of knowledge. By the mid-nineteenth century, a broad array of intellectual gambits was available in the West for coping with conditions of rapid social change. Why, if we ascribe a kernel of symptomatic wisdom to the designation of our "schools," did economics become conspicuous in Manchester and sociology in São Paulo? Economics and sociology must here be taken not as curricular specialties or disciplines, but as matrices for a broad range of perceptions of "the social question." The point at issue is how two different constructions of social reality were required for achieving intellectual control.

I. MERRIE OLDE ENGLAND AND SAD BRAZIL

São Paulo is equipping itself to be a great industrial center, something like Chicago and Manchester combined.

Report of the Prefect of São Paulo, 1914

A. *The Historical Contexts of Development*

Although the two cities developed almost a century apart, the historical contexts offer many parallels. In both cases we witness industrial and population surges, starting about 1780 for Manchester and about 1880 for São Paulo. It slackened in the second half of the nineteenth century for Manchester, but still continues unabated for São Paulo. In the early decades of the critical period, São Paulo's demographic growth was more intense than Manchester's, although its selective import substitution produced less massive industrial concentration. In both these modest agrarian centers the industrial explosion had a shock effect that would have been diluted in an urban panorama that already included a numerous preindustrial proletariat.

In England, the new industrial centers, removed from London, largely inspired the Combination Acts of 1799–1800 that suppressed trade unionism and were designed to contain the spread of continental Jacobinism. In Brazil, while Rio's industrial workers were dispersed in a large city, in São Paulo they seemed compact and threatening.[4] Longer-term outcomes differed. Manchester's Peterloo Massacre of 1819 was followed in five years by the repeal of the Combination Acts. Thenceforth workers found a measure of semiautonomous accommodation within English industrial society—whether by the "collective self-consciousness" that E. P. Thompson stresses or simply because, as Bryan Roberts vouchsafes in a quaintly Ricardian vein, Lancashire eventually found itself with an undersupply of labor for an overindustrialized city.[5] In São Paulo, the 1917 general strike was soon followed by anti-anarchist repression and eventually—at the moment when European immigration had dropped off and internal migration of "docile" workers had begun—by state co-optation of the labor movement. Thus, the supply of industrial labor continued to outrun demand. In recent decades it has become commonplace to remark that São Paulo's industrialization departs from the English "model."

We need not review the array of circumstances that differentiate the two cases. They would include broad historical and cultural considerations; the economics of industrial markets, technological multipliers, capital formation, and the like; socioeconomic institutions inherited from the preindustrial period; the respective political cultures; and demographic factors. What claims attention here is that those who witnessed the two industrialization processes in the early phase, who saw trees and not forests, reacted in similar ways. They convey a sense of immense unpreparedness and piecemeal improvisation.

Manchester, the "mere village" described by Defoe in 1727, had not yet, by the early nineteenth century, developed a local government competent to guide the city's change or to cope with social unrest. Remedies for transportation, poor relief, control of labor, or rising prices were devised not by a government concerned with common welfare but by pressure groups claiming powers under specific local acts.

> The absence of adequate channels of communication between the people at large and the oligarchical elite sitting in Parliament insulated government from the pressures of urbanization and made it slow to take appropriate action with regard to the exploitation of the laboring class by the factory owners, child labor, and the wretched conditions in the new factory districts.[6]

This situation obtained as well in Brazil, although São Paulo's city government was perhaps more "efficient" than Manchester's: not because it drew on lavish resources and community spirit at the municipal level but because it received privileged attention as seat of the provincial government in a patrimonial system of administration.

In the 1870's, when the western coffee boom was under way and the agro-urban elite began to favor urban residence, nearly one half the annual budget of the province (1872 population, 837,000) was spent on the capital city (population, 31,000). Yet urban improvements featured chiefly those services and cosmetic projects that made life more amenable for the well-to-do in their places of residence, business, and sociability.[7] Middle groups were crushed by inflationary pressures, and the lower classes were relegated to mushrooming slums (*cortiços*). Given the city's meteoric growth (reaching 14% per year in the 1890's), the hauteur of its ruling groups, the heavily skewed allocation of income and political voice, weak ties of social solidarity, and the speculative, improvised character of its physical expansion—given all this—the municipal unit was in no position to make rational use of public services that had become available since the boom days of Manchester.[8] A report of 1891 alerted the state president to haphazard construction and street layout, grave hygienic deficiencies, faulty public services, and pestilential swamplands.[9] The following account of Manchester in the 1820's applies without a scintilla of change to São Paulo of the 1890's:

> No attempt whatever was made to control individual developers. Each piece of land within the town was built upon according to the whim of its owner, with no limitation on use except potential marketability. The result was an incredible hodgepodge of land uses that, through a process of natural selection, managed to assume a rough order on a town-wide basis, while remaining chaotic at the neighborhood level.[10]

B. *Two Visions of National Experience*

For all their similarities, one broad difference in the two sets of contemporary accounts deserves notice. As early as the 1780's observers of Manchester described a "growing gulf" between rich and poor. After Peterloo and into the 1840's, social critics, politicians, and travelers across the political spectrum found here the seedbed for a new society of "classes" or, in Disraeli's phrase, of "two nations."[11] They offered widely divergent explanations and therapy for the phenomenon. Some called for "corrective" attitudes, action, or legislation. Others announced the advent of a new society, whether a prosperous industrial-urban regime or, in Engels' classic diagnosis, a new proletarian order. Yet whatever the discrepancies of intent, analysis, and recipe, commentators agreed on one or another version of social polarization and on the prophetic role of Manchester. In the margin of his travel diary Tocqueville wrote: "Separation of classes, much greater at Manchester than at Birmingham. Why? Large accumulations of capital, immense factories."[12] Had Engels lived in Birmingham and not Manchester, Briggs grandly conjectures, his notions of the historical role of classes might have been quite different, and Marx might have been not a communist but a currency reformer.[13]

The English, in short, shared an implicit vision of an inclusive national society that had evolved for centuries, producing institutions, legal arrangements, social philosophies, leadership, and compelling national symbols as each historic occasion required. Under modern pressures of industrialism, some took cues from bygone eras of imagined *communitas*, others placed faith in remedial rationalism, still others sensed a large dynamic of historical transformation at work. But all shared the image of a coherent national society persisting through time.[14]

In Brazil matters were different. There was little by way of a "national experience" available through literature, historiography, and shared memory of heroic episodes.[15] The country, wrote Sílvio Romero, lacked the philosophy, science, or grand poetry of the Europeans: "Youth has scarcely any inspiration of its own, national and Brazilian." Joaquim Nabuco blamed slavery for the country's "moral anarchy" and impotence for "social transformation."[16] Brazilians found in their past no equivalent to the mythic "merrie England" that Mancunians were wont to evoke. Indeed, one intellectual produced a "portrait of Brazil" in 1928 that was subtitled an "essay on Brazilian sadness."[17] The past society that Brazilians recollected was grounded in slavery and thus, from its origins, more severely "polarized" than even nineteenth-century England. Instead of experiencing what the English perceived as organic evolution from "feudalism" to industrialism, Brazil was riven from the start by capitalist and seigniorial economic structures. Against this backdrop, the plight of São Paulo's enclave of immigrant factory workers was almost an epiphenomenon.

A second great Brazilian fragmentation was of the national polity. From origins, again, the discontinuity between the state apparatus and local command structures could not comfortably be mediated by that characteristically English invention, "evolution." Political theorizers of the early twentieth century, like Alberto Tôrres and Oliveira Viana, were less concerned with the welfare of the society than with consolidating and legitimizing central mechanisms for its management. Indeed, at the very moment of São Paulo's early industrial burst, federal power was decentralized to favor the most economically advanced states. Paulistas saw their own state not as a modernizing pole for the nation but as a locomotive reluctantly trailing empty and useless cars. In his ironically titled short story, *Evolução* (Evolution, 1884), Machado de Assis satirized his compatriots' view that industrialism mean new sorts of commodity imports rather than a shift in the national social and political calculus.[18]

How indeed could industrialization be translated into societal terms if most Brazilian citizens were simply invisible? The pen of a Nabuco or a Euclides da Cunha (in his classic *Rebellion in the Badlands*) might occasionally spotlight the black man or backlander, but with little hint of the systemic determinants of his condition. What was true for squatters, sharecroppers, plantation hands, and ex-slaves across the face of the land was only slightly less so for the largely foreign work force of São Paulo. To be sure, there is an official record of proletarian "problems" in the municipal survey of *cortiços* of 1893 and in data assembled for the bulletin of the State Department of Labor in the 1910's and 1920's. But such "problems" represented more a nuisance to be controlled than a social presence to be conjured with. Even in the 1910's, the golden age of labor militancy, workers showed relatively weak capacity for developing class identity vis-à-vis vested interests that were considerably more repressive and less accommodating than those of the English: "Here was . . . a proletariat largely formed by foreign workers, whose radius of action did not exceed the boundaries of the factories and the struggle for the most basic demands. At no point did it manage to influence 'global politics' or obtain more elaborate social legislation."[19]

One may instructively compare the critical reflections of Frenchmen who visited Manchester—Tocqueville, Buret, Faucher—with the breezy comments of their latter-day compatriot, Georges Clemenceau, on his visit to São Paulo in 1910. Clemenceau's travel account gives no hint that São Paulo was an industrial center. The city's "universal language," he remarked, was French (not, of course, the Italian of the proletariat). He had only praise for the French-trained police force, whose troops "would figure creditably at Longchamp." He excused Brazil's lack of protective laws for factory and farm labor, remarking that they would have been ineffectual under the nation's "imperfectly centralized" political organization. As it was, large employers had "done their best to improve the material condition of their hands without waiting to be compelled to do so."[20] Such were the impressions of a long-time radical warhorse of French politics, oppo-

nent of Ferry's colonial policies, and supporter of Zola in the Dreyfus affair.

Latin American *pensadores* are often accused of elitism and cloudy, derivative theorizing. This puts the cart before the horse. An object of scrutiny that is only vaguely discernible necessarily provokes personal, erratic shafts of exploratory vision. The case of Luís Pereira Barreto (1840-1923), perhaps São Paulo's most original thinker in its early industrial period, illustrates the point. As a practicing physician trained in Belgium, a campaigner for economic and educational reforms, a polemical philosophizer in touch with European thought, Pereira Barreto gave only glancing attention to the "social question" of industrialism, in large measure because its historical context was uncertain. The society he saw around him was a giant invalid (*um grande doente*), not because of the localized traumas of factory life but because the whole historical trajectory of the nation was enigmatic. The races of Brazil, he wrote, were not yet a "people." The rural squatter eked out a lethargic existence of closed horizons while foreigners were imported to produce the colonial monocrop. Intellectual life was sterile and pedantic (*bacharelesca*) because it had unfolded in quarantine from the social and moral development of the people.[21] If reference points for the national society and its origins were obscure—here is the implicit question—how could one take grasp of current "problems"?

The exercise in comparative intellectual history we have set, then, involves the following considerations. First, the industrial phenomena of Manchester and São Paulo occurred in two divergent national contexts. Second, Paulista intellectuals who addressed social issues had access to a century of Western thought that was unavailable to Englishmen in the heyday of Manchester yet was of problematic relevance to Brazil. Third, despite the fresh juxtaposition of industrial circumstance and intellectual paradigm, there is a sense in which São Paulo had, all along, accompanied Western development *pari passu*. Not only had it kept abreast of European thought, even if selectively and at a distance, but its institutions had progressively internalized Western rationalization.[22] Given these considerations, how did the respective urban societies institutionalize means for developing corrective social theory and praxis?

II. MANCHESTER ECONOMICS

Britain—alone of major Western societies—never produced a classical sociology.

—Perry Anderson, 1968

A.   *The Statistical Movement*

Today we look to universities as an institutional base for social inquiry and, less confidently, as a source of strategies for social reform. Universities of early nineteenth-century England were ill-suited for such missions. Oxford and Cambridge molded rather than educated the governing class and did little to sharpen critical faculties of mind. University College with its utilitarian emphasis was not founded in London until 1828 and Owens College, the future University of Manchester, not until 1851.[23] A national intelligentsia, therefore, that was destined to launch from outside university precincts such "world-historical" bodies of doctrine as classical economics, utilitarianism, and evolutionism—to say nothing of Marxism—needed unusual institutional inventiveness. Exemplary was the Manchester Statistical Society founded in 1833, first of the provincial societies and the only one to survive throughout the early decades. Established by Liberal, reform-minded, second-generation members of the commercial and industrial aristocracy, the Society proposed to examine social and economic issues without partisanship. For this purpose it assembled data on industrial production, prices, demography, public health, schools, and transportation, and tried to explain statistical correlations between newspaper readership and frequency of riots, and between the spread of education and increased criminality. The Society was concerned to show that urbanization, not the factory system, was responsible for social evils, and that humanitarian employers shared common interests with a work force that had a proper "moral" education. Cullen observes a tension between the Society's moralistic condemnation of the workers' laziness and improvidence and its environmentalist recognition of the deleterious effects of ignorance and squalor.[24]

The rage for statistics was linked to prevalent assumptions about the rationality of the social order. The accepted image of the invisible hand implied that conflicts of interest were not implacable but arose from misunderstandings about "real interests," that is, from ignorance or unreason. "In a curious mirror-image anticipation of Marx," Philip Abrams has said, "the political economist saw conflict as a form of false consciousness." The ideal, then, was neither laissez-faire nor interventionism, but a government possessing sufficient "facts" to permit judicious application of accepted principles of political economy. Thus "the proper response to doubt and dissension was to mobilize empirical information," and the statistical movement "was

institutionalized under direct patronage of the British political elite."[25] Only by the 1850's was it widely apparent that opinions of the most divergent sort influenced the collection, presentation, and interpretation of numerical "facts."

B. *The Manchester School*

The Manchester School of Economics, a diversely composed movement for political action rather than a data-gathering and debating group, yields even richer clues than does the statistical movement to the premises and processes of English political life.[26] The School was one of several dissident or reformist movements—including consumer cooperativism, the campaign for improved factory conditions, and Chartism—that found a central locus in Manchester as the heart of the English export industry. Although one associates the School with the crusade for free trade, it was no mere practical arm of the classical economists. In fact no true economists were affiliated with it, and its spokesmen felt obliged to challenge certain reservations that professional economists held regarding the desirability of unrestricted free trade. Far from recapitulating the Ricardian synthesis, the School's collaborators analyzed and interpreted a series of discrete issues, especially the effect that free trade in grain might have on its price and hence on production, employment, wages, and rents. Only from 1838 to 1846 was the Manchester movement coherently mobilized in pursuit of repeal of the corn laws; and only in retrospect did Disraeli scornfully baptize it a "school." Thenceforth the Manchester crowd was united mainly in its admiration for Bright and Cobden and in selective endorsement of their policies.

The Manchester program went well beyond a bourgeois apologia for rapacious textile manufacturers. The School's component groups, as Grampp identifies them, were practical businessmen who predicted that free trade would increase textile production and lower factory wages; "humanitarian" businessmen of the sort who had founded the Statistical Society and exemplified *noblesse oblige*; pacifists like Bright and Cobden who believed that free trade would promote worldwide economic interest in peace; Philosophic Radicals who espoused utilitarianism and various forms of government intervention; and middle-class radicals, perhaps the most important group, who advocated broad social and political reforms. This array of spokesmen addressed a similarly diverse audience of landlords, manufacturers, tenants, and farm and factory workers. Thus the School's assumption had to be, first, that English society, however heterogeneous, was in fact a coherent system functioning according to general principles; second, that one might design reformist measures to benefit all constituencies; and third, that one could demonstrate these benefits with logical arguments adapted and convincing to each constituency affected.

The Manchester School and its audiences, then, assumed a nation to which all "belonged" and a socioeconomic system by which it was articulated. Circumstances were not felt to require abstruse theorizing and research or tendentious communitarian appeals. A few "self-evident" economic principles, some statistical "facts," and common-sense reasoning sufficed to diagnose and prescribe for the whole range of social tensions and dysfunction.[27] When Peel learned of the 1848 Revolution in France, he ventured that he had saved England from a similar fate by yielding to the sober arguments of Manchester.

C.   *A Defective Sociological Imagination*

For our purposes a central point is that the Manchester School was concerned with social distress yet offered precious little by way of social analysis—at the very time, moreover, when foundations for a science of society, or "sociology," were being laid on the continent. Of thirty-one European sociological thinkers whom Robert A. Nisbet examines, only four are English (Burke, Coleridge, Maine, Spencer), and of these only one, perhaps, a *bona fide* sociologist.[28] The sociological vision inspired by Engels' study of Manchester found its praxis on the continent. Stung by the "betrayal" of English workers, Engels withdrew his dedication to them from the English translation of his book. Not until the London School of Economics created a chair for L. T. Hobhouse in 1906 was sociology formally professed in England.

In explaining why pre-Comtian and Comtian sociology found such fertile soil in France, Gouldner calls it an "N plus one" science answering social needs that were neglected by middle-class political economy with its focus on private utility. He interprets French positivist sociology as a product of dispossessed aristocrats (de Bonald, de Maistre, Saint-Simon) that was of interest to new strata not yet possessed of property. By de-emphasizing property rights and pointing scientistic or technocratic paths toward social reconstruction, French sociologists offered a road map for the marginalized rather than an agenda for insiders. The English middle classes, alarmed by the example of French Jacobinism, reached accommodation with the upper class to form a "composite" ruling group. In the absence of a threat from socialism, the dominant classes were not forced to produce a comprehensive countersystem of social thought.[29]

The German comparison is also illuminating. Nineteenth-century Germany, Hawthorn has said, was a country without an empiricist tradition, political coherence, or sweeping social change, while England had all three.[30] The English empirical temper allowed men to trust their senses and come to similar impressions of the world. The nation's political coherence, taken for granted since the eighteenth century, turned minds from probing social premises to devising social strategies. The gathering speed of social change made it clear that men, for all their Lockean individualism, were becoming interdependent. Under such conditions utilitarian political economy could thrive. In Germany, by contrast, the central characteristic of national thought was, in Santayana's words, "that it is deliberately subjective and limits itself to the articulation of self-consciousness."[31] The Englishman asserted and defended himself against society; the German had to define the society. The Englishman measured himself against his experience of others; the German had to constitute himself from within. English society was so secure that it was taken for granted; German society was so chaotic that it monopolized attention. In these respects nineteenth-century Germany had much in common with the societies of Latin America. It is no accident that German philosophy strikes deeper resonances in the Latin American mind than do English and French.

III. PAULISTA SOCIOLOGY

> . . . *Political Economy, incongruous and abstruse, hobby of bombastic pedants, whose reputation consists in creating obstacles to human progress*
>
> —*Sílvio Romero, 1873*

A. *European Social Science in the Brazilian Setting*

If the sociological imagination was expendable for the earlier industrial civilization, why, we now ask, did it assume intellectual prominence in the later one? And, the corollary question, why was full implantation of economic training and research delayed until the 1960's in an urban society that had for several decades epitomized modern industrial development in Latin America? These questions return us to the historic tension between Brazil's accompaniment of ideas as they emanated from Europe and the inner logic of the nation's own intellectual development.

The record shows a valiant Brazilian effort to keep pace with European, and especially English, economic thought. The *Principles of Political Economy* of José da Silva Lisboa, owing much to Adam Smith, was published in 1804, the very year that Say's *Treatise* appeared in France. Political economy was taught in the new law faculties established in São Paulo and Recife in 1827. Writings of the proto-socialists Sigmondi and Godwin were prescribed as well as the standard texts for classical economics. After 1870 the work of Marshall, Jevons, Walras, and MacLeod became known in São Paulo. Eventually political economy was taken up by engineering and commercial schools, where applied aspects were stressed and classical precepts were often qualified by a dose of Listian protectionism. Not until the founding of the Faculty of Philosophy, Sciences, and Arts of the University of São Paulo in 1934 (followed in 1946 by a separate Faculty of Economics and Administrative Sciences) did economics find its place as a social science. Even then, practice of the discipline lacked a strong research base and was characterized by econometrics, rarefied Keynesian analysis, and an attempt to reconcile protectionism with economic individualism. The clues for an economic analysis fitted to Brazilian needs were more likely to be gleaned from the institutionally oriented economic history of Caio Prado Junior than from the economics lecture hall.[32]

Sociology appeared in São Paulo long after economics. The local "patriarch" of the discipline was Paulo Egídio de Oliveira Carvalho, who popularized Spencer via the *Correio Paulistano* in the 1870's, and, at the end of the century, offered public lectures to expound Durkheim's criminology and sociology of law. Although Paulo Egídio had a few important disciples, it was not until the 1930's that sociology took root in São Paulo as an accepted field of teaching and research, and not until the 1950's that we can discern the beginnings of a Paulista "school." The reasons, Antônio Cândido finds, were a general lack of interest in the subject and a lack of context for the social roles required by the profession.[33] To this end one might add that Paulo Egídio's attempt to reconcile Durkheim's objectivity toward the "social fact" with his own ethical convictions as a jurist has a curiously formalistic flavor. His reading of Durkheim, one presumes, failed to capture the powerful moral imperative that infuses the treatment of division of labor, suicide, and sociological method.[34] How, indeed, could Durkheim's brooding Old World concern with anomie and loss of community have retained its force in the raw-boned, parochial Paulista society of 1900, still hostage to the structure of—by Parisian terms—a primitive plantation economy?

One could at this point sketch the career of sociology in São Paulo from Paulo Egídio through the educational sociology of the 1920's and the descriptive and statistical research of the 1930's to the formation of the Paulista school in the 1950's. This, however, would leave us with the familiar treatment of Brazilian intellectual history as delayed reflex to a foreign example. If the flowering of the sociological imagination was a *prise de conscience*, not an academic appendage to economic "development," we must be prepared to find inspiration for it outside the realm of the "social sciences" narrowly conceived. To an important extent, I feel it derives from the Modernist movement in arts and letters of the 1920's.

B. *The Modernist Quest for Premises of Nationhood*

In stressing the novelty of industrialism in the setting of Manchester and São Paulo, we observed that Brazilian intellectuals were less prepared than the English to deal with the phenomenon. Their best writing, to be sure, abounds in *aperçus* and significant intimations; yet in their reliance on systems of "out-of-place" ideas, they produced no comprehensive mapping of the society and polity.[35] Much of the nation's diverse population was, as we have said, "invisible." The prerequisite for rendering perceived experience was even lacking, namely, a supple and shared mode of discourse, a "Brazilian language," fitted to national circumstances.[36] What the case initially required was not painstaking empiricism or judicious fine-tuning of imported methods and systems but a pulverization of vision, vocabulary, and *idées reçues* for fresh reconstitution. This mission was assumed by the Modernists in the 1920's.

Born in the 1890's, the Modernists had never known the quiet, sedate agrarian town of the early coffee years. Theirs was the commercial and industrial boom city, more hospitable to Italians and Syrians than to rural squatters and ex-slaves, a young metropolis seemingly oblivious to tradition. Yet for all of São Paulo's hustle and bustle, urban society was suffused with vigorous "patriarchal" survivals while, at its upper reaches, it paid parochial homage to the routine products and *politesse* of French culture. São Paulo was a "Gallicism yelping in the wilderness of America," wrote Mário de Andrade, in 1921 in the first poem of his *Hallucinated City*.[37]

Modernist verse and manifestoês are best known for their imagistic splintering of an anachronistic environment. What merits attention here is not the demolition of clichés—which, taken in itself, assimilated the Modernists to new sensibilities in the Western world—

but the search for a viable point of departure. The phrase is bad. It was less a search than an intuitive appropriation, while the point of departure was not a set of propositions but an analogous cultural moment in the distant past. Consider these examples.

In 1762 Rousseau commenced his *Social Contract* with the sentence, "Man is born free; and everywhere he is in chains." What followed was a political agenda for a new institutional order. In 1928 Paulo Prado, a São Paulo litterateur and scion of a vigorous entrepreneurial family, commenced his *Portrait of Brazil* with the sentence, "In a radiant land lives a sad people." He then diagnosed a moral condition or state of soul that sapped volition and blocked political action. Historically, Brazilians had been prey to the deadly sins of covetousness, lust, and above all sloth or sadness. Sadness (*tristeza*) here is not a euphemism for the effects of miscegenation or schistosomiasis. It applies to the whole people and is akin to medieval *tristitia* or *acedia*, a state of spiritual dryness, desolation, and inner coldness.[38] Its cure is what a later generation of Brazilians would hear of as "conscientization."

The "hallucinated" São Paulo of Mário de Andrade's early verse was not an economic reality but an arena for the quest of self. Not precisely an arena, perhaps, for city and self interpenetrated. In decomposing his world, in effacing boundaries of self, the poet was posing Montaigne's old question, "*Que sais-je?*" In the ensuing cascade of verse, fiction, studies, chronicles, and correspondence, Mário held to his quest for both Brazilian and self identity. The arts, popular and highbrow, were of persistent fascination, as were ethnicity, sexuality, language, and speech. The quest was not for formulae and systems but for the social, cultural, and psychological grammar of life. Yet beneath the inquisitive, skeptical Montaigne lay a Rabelais. Just as Gargantua was not a literary invention but a real giant inhabiting the lore of French country folk, so Mário's tale of Macunaíma was a methodical if inspired composite of Brazilian folk belief drawn heavily from Koch-Grunberg's thesaurus of legends. For all of Mário's policed, bourgeois, twentieth-century conscience, he could still glimpse what Rabelais had gazed squarely upon, "the secret folly at the heart of the universe, the wild uncertainty, the abyss of lunacy that underlies our rational constructions."[39]

In presenting himself as sensualist and *enfant terrible*, Oswald de Andrade seemed the real Rabelaisian. Yet his early verse and manifestos have a spare, reductive quality; they strip appearances to stark essentials. Beneath the Oswaldian Rabelais lies a Montaigne.

The poems of his *History of Brazil* recover the fresh unmediated view of the early chroniclers: Vaz de Caminha, Gandavo, d'Abbeville. In the "Poems of Colonization" a few lines suffice to evaporate official myths overlaying the facts of slavery, race, violence, and control. For example:

> feudal lord

> If Pedro II
> Comes around
> With his boilerplate
> I'll throw him in the slammer

In four lines, a new agenda for future decades of "research." Then, Oswald's Anthropophagic Manifesto: Brazil's Indians were never catechized but became somnambulists. Replacing logic with Carnival, Brazil garbed the Indian as a senator of the Empire who pretended he was Pitt or else inserted him in Alencar's operas with their robust Portuguese sentiment. What, after all, could Europe offer? In its golden age Brazil had already enjoyed communism and surrealism, a society without the oppression, complexes, and prostitution inventoried by Freud. The cannibal Indian revealed "natural man" to Europe, making possible the French Revolution, Bolshevism, and Surrealism. In moving Brazil from periphery to center, Oswald sought his own center in Montaigne: "So we may well call these people barbarians, in respect to the rules of reason, but not in respect to ourselves, who surpass them in every kind of barbarity." Oswald's *jeu de mots*, "Tupi or not Tupi," was in dead earnest: conscientiousness or sloth.[40]

What the Modernists, or *these* Modernists, did was to recover points of moral reference in the critical transition from Middle Ages to Renaissance, a transition that England had negotiated smartly enough but the Iberian world had rather bungled. Sheer instinct—what else can one call it?—turned certain Brazilians to delve deep into their collective memory and reenact a historic moment of blockage.

Modernism was catalytic but left no blueprints. It validated implicit queries without yielding explicit answers. When the post-Modernist generation was questioned in 1943-44 as to its agenda, an authorized and articulate spokesman, Antônio Cândido (b. 1918), called the 1940's a time of social disorganization, of nervous enthusiasms and feverish inquiry. The Modernist forerunners, he said, were a sacrificial generation, overwhelmed by success. The artist had won his freedom, but at the cost of virtuosity, hedonism, wrangling, and political obscurantism. The new generation was "critical." It condemned narcissism and pursued intellectual activity as an instrument for living—a less inspired generation, less improvisational, but one committed to steady maturation. Small wonder that Oswald called them the *chato-boys* (roughly, the "little squares"), or that in later years Antônio Cândido found his own early essays on Oswald to reveal an "aggressivity marked with condescension."[41]

In his deposition, Antônio Cândido did mention one precursor as an intellectual link: poet and critic Sérgio Milliet whose "analytic intelligence" and "sociological orientation" produced pioneering essays in social history. He compared Milliet's capacity for "intellectual systematization" favorably to Gilberto Freyre's functionalist "cultural sociology," which he was early to recognize as a lapse into "social and historical sentimentalism, into conservatism and traditionalism."[42] Antônio Cândido, then teaching sociology and preparing his outstanding study of rural society (*Os parceiros do Rio Bonito*), eventually resumed his primary vocation as literary critic and historian. Although the story of his distinguished intellectual and pedagogical career fully exemplifies the theme of this essay, it is Florestan Fernandes, his fellow teaching assistant in the 1940's for the Chair of Sociology II at the University of São Paulo, who is more centrally identified with the Paulista school of sociology and to whom we shall shortly return.[43]

The prominence of "sociology" in Antônio Cândido's early statement takes added significance from the fact of its advocacy by a foremost literary scholar. He had in mind, of course, not cultivation of an academic "discipline" but self-critical, research-oriented intellectual endeavor that would engage Brazilian society in many dimensions: historical, political, economic, and cultural. The institutional bases for such an enterprise had existed since the founding of the Free School of Sociology and Political Science (1933) and the Faculty of Philosophy, Sciences and Letters (1934). The former had an Anglo-American orientation, while the latter, a component of the new public University of São Paulo, was under heavily continental influence. Created in the wake of São Paulo state's military defeat by the central government in 1932, both centers, particularly the Free School, reflected a "certain intellectual mobilization of the dominant classes, who were seized at that moment by the idea of forming leaders, real technicians in public matters, with intellectual training that could give them positions of economic and political leadership in the State and the Nation."[44]

A related initiative of the modernizing elite was the creation of a multi-faceted municipal Department of Culture in 1935. Just as the

Faculty became the Trojan horse for critical, leftist sociology, so the Department was designed by intellectuals associated with the moderate-left of the Democratic Party: Paulo Duarte, Sérgio Milliet, and the first director, Mário de Andrade. Mário was one of the few of the Generation of 1922 who seriously attempted the "routinization of Modernism," in Antônio Cândido's felicitous Weberian phrase. One central function of the Department was precisely that of the Manchester Statistical Society just a century earlier, namely, to collect data on urban living standard, social mobility, nutrition, ethnicity, demography, and illegitimacy. After inspecting the Department's findings, a visiting Frenchman exclaimed, "Why . . . it's a city seen under a microscope!" This empirical research was published in the Department's *Revista do Arquivo Municipal*; but unlike the reports and transactions of the Manchester Society, the *Revista*'s pages were open to studies in history, ethnography, folklore, and sociology. Moreover, Brazilian contributors shouldered visiting or resident foreign scholars like Paul Arbousse-Bastide, Claude Lévi-Strauss, Roger Bastide, Emílio Willems, Samuel Lowrie, Horace B. Davis, and Donald Pierson.[45]

The *Revista*, the Society of Sociology (1934), the Society of Ethnography and Folklore (1937), and the journal *Sociologia* (1939) all served to ventilate diverse approaches—thematic, disciplinary, European, North American—to the national "reality." Several reasons existed for this favorable climate. First, unlike their Manchester counterparts, the modernizing elite (with rare exceptions like Simonsen[46]) did not become partners in the intellectual inquiry made possible by their largesse. The institutionalization of social research and the involvement of distinguished foreign professionals divorced the academic agenda from the intent of the patrons. Second, the confluence of intellectual traditions, none of which neatly answered the complex needs of the case, called for selective syntheses that none of the mature generation, Brazilian or foreign, was sufficiently disencumbered to manage. Third, those who *would* meet the challenge were still students, bewildered by an unexampled university experience, by intellectual multiplicity, and by discontinuities between ideas and the still shadowy "issues" of time and place. Writing of his professorial stint at the University, Lévi-Strauss recalled with characteristic complacence that while the foreign mentors were accustomed to respecting only fully matured ideas, they were besieged by students who thirsted for the latest novelty, who had neither taste nor methods for learning, yet who felt bound to include in every essay an evolutionary survey from the apes to our times. Looking back, he paradoxically observed that the subsequent thirty years produced an intellectual advance in São Paulo that might well have taken generations. The upheavals that history books claim to result from "the play of nameless forces in the heart of darkness," he concluded, "may also be brought about, in an instant of lucidity, by the virility and set purpose of a handful of gifted young people."[47]

C. A Sociology "Made in Brazil"

By the 1940's it was clear that urban-industrial fact-finding in the British manner, even modernized by American methods, did not yield a firm handle on the problems of São Paulo. Sheer statistical inquiry was soon assigned to public functionaries as the young social scientists turned toward anthropology and social psychology, finding research interests in Amerindian and Afro-Brazilian studies, assimilation of foreign and domestic migrants, and rural community studies. Georges Gurvitch even complained that the Brazilian sociologists' gravest omission was their failure to exploit São Paulo city as a unique social laboratory.[48] His reproach is a representative homily from a routinized academic establishment. What escaped him was that the sociologist, no less than the Modernist poet before him, required a point of cognitive leverage if his contribution were not to be simply mimetic. Even in denouncing the poets' narcissism and political ingenuousness, the social scientists revisited the Modernists' topics of early fascination. The initial research of Florestan Fernandes features several themes from the Modernist repertoir. Not only did he share Mário de Andrade's consuming interest in folklore and in the European immigrant, but, like Oswald de Andrade, he extracted leading ideas from intellec⁺ual engagement with the Amerindian and African presence in Brazil. His first two major works were on the Tupinambá, and, just as Oswald had reread the sixteenth-century chroniclers to compose his poetic "History of Brazil," so Fernandes scrutinized their contributions to ethnography.[49]

In the early 1950's, few would have selected black-white race relations as the starting point for an inquiry into the foundations of a new industrial society. Blacks were a small percentage of the population of the industrializing south, and even those who discredited the Brazilian "myth of racial democracy" tended to subordinate race to the issue of class. Yet Fernandes testifies that the three chapters he contributed to the UNESCO-Anhembi race-relations project, codirected by Roger Bastide, forced him to reconstruct the economic history of São Paulo and its transition to capitalism; to construe abolition as a revolution of "whites for whites" that hastened consolidation of the urban, industrial economy; to juxtapose the phenomena of racial and social stratification, yielding the hypothesis of a transition from a society of "estates" (*sociedade estamental*) to a society of classes, creating a "bourgeois revolution"; to identify mechanisms of control applied to all disinherited social groups; to perceive "black protest" movements of the 1920's and 1930's as harbingers of populist politics. "I had arrived at a large panorama of Brazil and, within it, the relations among economy, society, and state disproved the various conventional images constructed until then about 'our land' and 'our people.' "[50]

In his autobiographical essay, "In Search of a Critical and Militant Sociology," Fernandes gives his indispensable version of how there arose "what some, for lack of imagination, call 'the Paulista school of sociology.' "[51] He describes his boyhood "apprenticeship" in an urban society which, from his lower-class position, seemed composed of sharks and sardines. Once ensconced in academe, he resolved to build an intellectual position from which to confront the inhibitions and hegemonic bourgeois ideology of "a society as oppressive and repressive as the Brazilian." He in effect gave notice that the ascendancy of Kay-Shuttleworth, Samuel Smiles, or their trans-atlantic heirs had far different implications in a society that had had its Cromwell than in one that had not. The foreign teachers whom Fernandes encountered as a student were, he suggests in a complement to Lévi-Strauss' reminiscence, "less concerned with the organism of the patient than with the brilliance of the operation." For them it must have seemed an "attempt to pour good wine in a bad barrel. We leaked on every side." The Faculty was a transplant. The professors made unfulfillable cultural demands and presented an eclectic panorama of ideas that seemed unrelated to Brazil. Their charges wondered what they might do with a training that required random ingestion and threatened to substitute "intellectual artificialism" for "cultural parochialism." Still, there were advantages to an academic bill of fare that was too heterogeneous to be "copied," that forced consumers to make their own syntheses. From the Faculty one could learn, if not the "right" system, at least some architectonic principles for building one. From the Free School one could learn how the "Chicago school" had used the metropolis as a sociological laboratory. The intellectual "periphery," then, had become a "center" because of interpretive and integrative needs forced upon it.

As substitute for Roger Bastide in the Chair of Sociology I after 1952 and as its occupant after 1955, Fernandes resolved to create a "greenhouse" for engendering a counterinstitution inside the establishment. The intent was to develop a sociology "made in Brazil" (as distinct from a "Brazilian sociology") and to open a "political space" from which to influence the sources of academic power. A glance at Fernandes' list of two dozen or more coworkers over the years shows that the group was scarcely solidary on doctrinal or even personal grounds. But to a degree they shared the commitment to construct a sociology for developing lands from "a descriptive, comparative, or historico-differential perspective." They would not "compete with" sociologists of the "central nations," yet would break with the eclecticism of foreign mentors. Fernandes soon concluded that one could not reconcile Marx, Durkheim, and Weber in simple additive fashion. The Modernists who preceded him had advocated ingesting foreign ideas anthropophagically, internalizing the "parental" authority. More cautiously, Fernandes proposed developing an agenda, methods, and syntheses within a situation of "dependency" (a term he advanced in 1956) or "heteronomy" (a term he attributes to Marx but which derives ultimately from Kant). The task was to revisit the old questions, using familiar techniques and perspectives, but isolating what Marx called "specific differences." The original inquiry into slavery and race opened research areas in entrepreneurship, labor, education, the state, political participation, and international relations.

We do not propose here to complement Fernandes' personal reminiscence with a rounded intellectual history of the "Paulista school" during the past quarter century.[52] It may well be that Fernandes' long-term objective of fusing what was useful in several traditions of inquiry within "a specifically Engelsian materialist position" was not fully apparent to his protégés in the early years.[53] What bears on our argument is that the original excursus into ethnohistory and race relations led in the 1960's to a cluster of themes relating directly to the dilemmas of political action in an urban-industrial society. The Manchester-style inquiries by American sociographers of the 1930's—statistical documentation of the plight of the urban poor—had not illuminated political realities. Of what use was proof of socioeconomic asymmetry when the consciousness of "class" (no less evident in Manchester to Disraeli and Kay-Shuttleworth than to Engels) was still dormant? Thus the prior need to explain the failure of syndicalism, the polyclassist appeal of "populist" politics, the patrimonial attitudes of entrepreneurial groups, the social selectivity of schooling, and the inhibiting effects of international "dependency." In short, the Mancunians addressed a political situation. The Paulistas addressed (in an extended sense of Hobsbawm's term) a prepolitical one. This required reinterpreting, even upending, received categories and scouting fields of empirical research appropriate to the task. In England sociology was a handmaiden to political economy. In Brazil economics serves the sociological imagination or else, as has widely occurred since 1964, is condemned to be an instrument of technocracy. In Pascalian terms, the English managed with an *esprit de finesse* (as, in large part, they still do) while Brazilians were forced to cultivate the *esprit géométrique*.

IV. AND MAYBE THE TWAIN SHALL MEET . . .

Tous les géomètres seraient donc fins s'ils avaient la vue bonne, car ils ne raisonnent pas faux sur les principes qu'ils connaissent; et les esprits fins seraient géométriques, s'ils pouvaient plier leur vue vers les principes inaccoutumés de géométric.[54]

—*Pascal, 1670*

Perry Anderson's essay, "Components of the National Culture," must surely be the most relentless argument we have for the feebleness of the sociological tradition in England.[55] In lieu of a sociology of knowledge he proposes a sociology of ignorance to account for the "absent center" of British culture created by the lack of a comprehensive or, in his aggressive word, "totalizing" explication of the society. England, he insists, never produced a Weber, Durkheim, or Pareto (whom he petulantly identifies as bourgeois counter-Marxian synthesists) nor, much less, a Marxian continuator like Lenin, Lukács, or Gramsci. The flaccidity of sociological thought left a breach that was largely filled in the twentieth century by "white" or "counter-revolutionary" émigrés like Wittgenstein, Malinowski, Namier, Popper, and Berlin who "systematized the refusal of system" and gave intellectual cachet to England's "slovenly empiricism." Anderson summarizes English achievements in nine realms of inquiry from philosophy and political theory to psychoanalysis and literary criticism, concluding that all the disciplines underwent "structural distortion" for lack of a common center of sociological reference. If some literary critics decried Victorian capitalism, their commentaries fell short of a conceptual system. If Keynes smashed the equilibrium framework of classical economics, he still accepted capitalism (though without "zeal or sanctimony"), and no successor was able to restore economics to the matrix of political economy. If Malinowski, Radcliffe-Brown (who did a stint in São Paulo), and the anthropologists developed integrated visions of primitive societies, they were in effect converting the tribal victims of British imperialism into a surrogate object for "totalizing" theory that was proscribed at home. Moreover, functionalism failed to deal with structural contradictions created by the very fact of British presence.

Anderson accounts for the "absent center" of English intellectual life with his claim that the industrial bourgeoisie was checked by a prior capitalist class, an agrarian aristocracy that controlled a state formed in its image. Fearing working-class organization and the example of the French Revolution, industrial groups avoided confrontation with the older elite and thus produced no revolutionary ideology. Strong sectoral disciplines advanced, such as economics and biology, but the hegemonic ideology was a piecemeal utilitarianism with strong components of traditionalism and empiricism. Thus the English bourgeoisie "renounced its intellectual birthright. It refused ever to put society as a whole in question." This bourgeois acquiescence ultimately deprived "the left of any source of concepts and categories with which to analyze its own society, and thereby attain a fundamental precondition for changing it."[56]

What strikes one in Anderson's analysis is its seeming applicability to the vastly different case of Brazil. Here too it is commonplace to speak of a composite agrarian-industrial elite, united in defense of a congenial state apparatus and in a determination to short-circuit the effects of unwholesome foreign examples—whether the Haitian slave revolt or the "Bolshevist" Revolution—on the laboring poor. Further, there is research to show the ideology of Brazilian industrialists as being even spongier and less consistent than that of their English counterparts on such issues as the role of the state, foreign investment, and labor policy.[57] Yet, as we have seen, the Paulista sociologists eventually managed to adumbrate comprehensive—even, loosely, "revolutionary"—diagnoses under the noses and at the expense of elite patrons. Two circumstances help explain why this was so, and why the argument of "hegemonic bourgeois ideology" must be accepted with caution. First, Brazil's Catholic, Roman-law tradition had created a secular predilection for grand systemic matrices to which problematic social issues can be casuistically referred. Anderson himself reminds us in a footnote of Weber's observation that the English common-law tradition was not conducive to "general concepts" derived from cases but favored movement "from the particular to the particular." Second, in nineteenth-century England there was publicly available a plausible set of assumptions about the composition of the national society, the institutions by which it was articulated, and the strategies available for reform. These assumptions, even if "incorrect" from Anderson's corner, were consensually verified and, it seemed, empirically verifiable. They functioned as a system even if they did not intellectually comprise one. In the Brazil of *circa* 1950, no comparable set of assumptions existed.

This essay, then, has been less concerned with how class interest conditions social science than with how social scientists get foothold when ideas, in Roberto Schwarz' phrase, are "out of place." Neither a "hegemonic ideology" nor a "critical sociology" is a mere cerebral reflex. Their elaboration requires a point of purchase, both affective and cognitive, in the phenomena addressed. They also require minimal conformance, configurational if not doctrinal, with a people's habitual, informal ways of construing experience. In the first instance, therefore, the achievement of the Paulista sociologists is better explained by Whitehead's theory of intellectual development than by a neo-Marxist one.

In *The Aims of Education*, Whitehead distinguishes phases of romance, precision, and generalization in the acquisition of intellectual mastery. Romance is the stage of first apprehension when the subject matter has the vividness of novelty, holding within itself mysterious connections and half-glimpsed possibilities. Immediate cognizance of fact takes precedence over systematic procedure. Romance is the ferment of mind without which education cannot occur. At the stage of precision "width of relationship is subordinated to exactness of formulation." The grammar of language and of science assumes priority; analytic powers are trained; the facts acquired are those dictated by the logic of analysis. Finally, generalization is a return to romance with the new advantage of "classified ideas and relevant technique." General principles triumph and are available to orchestrate any variety of details.

From my treatment of São Paulo it is apparent that I associate "romance" with the Modernists of the 1920's, "precision" with the sociographers and foreign methodologists of the 1930's and 1940's, and "generalization" with the Paulista sociologists since the 1950's. As Whitehead insists, however, the sequence is not a mechanical one but a stylization of the "rhythmic claims" of freedom and discipline. All mental development contains "cycles of such cycles." Mário de Andrade, for example, worked steadily toward "precision" in his studies of folklore and the arts, and in *O movimento modernista* (1942), he in effect apologized for not having attained "generalization." Oswald de Andrade, on the other hand, leaped to generalization in his Utopian theses. By the same token, the young sociologists, even while rebelling against what they took to be the anarchic self-indulgence of the Modernists, reproduced their predecessors' "romantic" search for origins in the ever-seductive realm of ethnicity.[58] The next step, Fernandes tells us quite in Whitehead's vein, was to turn to systematic empirical research into regional problems within "a descriptive, comparative, or historico-differential perspective." Relying on the formal or theoretical science of the "central nations," such inquiry would illuminate Marxian "specific differences" and awaken a "critical conscience" of the effects of underdevelopment and external domination.

At first glance the agenda of Fernandes seems to thwart Whitehead's cycle at the threshold of "generalization," precluding the synthesis of freedom and discipline. This impression is conveyed by his distinction between theory and specific research and his transfer of center-periphery terminology to the intellectual realm. What Whitehead intended by the transition to "generalization," however, was not deliberate, self-conscious movement from ordered fact-finding to grand theory but, rather, a quantum jump, or psychic shift, by which an observer advances from heteronomy to autonomy in his conceptual management of observed experience. This is all we can mean by intellectual maturity. Some, at least, of the Paulista sociologists have negotiated the transition. We may ask, moreover, why a Brazilian's transatlantic reliance on Gramsci or Lévi-Strauss should place him in a more acute state of "dependence" than a modern Englishman's intracultural reliance on Hobbes and Bentham.

Whitehead's three stages are not specific to culture or situation. He defined them with explicit reference to the English school and university system. I apply them to the intellectual development of the nation's community. My point is that the Brazilian poet or sociologist could not address industrialism until he had come to terms with the national society. In England, industrialism from the start fully engaged the spectrum of sensibility. There was no necessary "progression" from romance (Dickens) to precision (statistical societies) to generalization (classical economics). Consensus on the national context was such that issues were smoothly accommodated to inherited views of person, polity, and society. So pervasive was this consensus that the "critical and militant" sociology of Engels and Marx could be relegated to other nations—even, eventually, "underdeveloped" ones that escaped its original premises. In early industrial São Paulo there was no prevailing consensus, whether rooted in knowledge or hitched to ideals. Hence the priority requirement for a comprehensive vision of person, polity, and society that the sociologists have done their best to provide. Their inquiries, in fact, pose fresh queries to modern Englishmen about their own industrial past.

NOTES

1. *See* Simon, *Poetic Evolution in the Industrial Era: The Brazilian Modernists*, 13 STANFORD J. OF INT'L STUDIES, this volume at 35 (1978).

2. The complex interaction of "exhibitive" and "manipulative" orientations is traced in JUSTUS BUCHLER, NATURE AND JUDGMENT (NY: Columbia U. Press, 1955).

3. NÍCIA VILELA LUZ, A LUTA PELA INDUSTRIALIZAÇÃO DO BRASIL, 1808 À 1930 (São Paulo: Difusão Européia do Livro, 1961).

4. BORIS FAUSTO, TRABALHO URBANO E CONFLITO SOCIAL 62 (São Paulo: Difusao Editorial, 1976).

5. E. P. THOMPSON, THE MAKING OF THE ENGLISH WORKING CLASS 830 (NY: Vantage Books, 1966); and Roberts, *Agrarian Organization and Urban Development*, 13 STANFORD J. OF INT'L STUDIES, this volume at 77 (1978).

6. FRANÇOIS VIGIER, CHANGE AND APATHY, LIVERPOOL AND MANCHESTER DURING THE INDUSTRIAL REVOLUTION 35, 92 (Cambridge, MA: M.I.T. Press, 1970).

7. *See* Marcus, *Provincial Government in São Paulo: the Administration of João Teodoro Xavier, 1872-1875* (unpublished Ph.D. dissertation, Yale U., 1973); and Shirley, *Legal Institutions and Early Industrial Growth*, 13 STAN. J. OF INT'L STUDIES, this volume at 157 (1978).

8. The exploitative, unplanned introduction of public transport to São Paulo is examined in Greenfield, *Algumas notas sôbre a história de viação urbano em São Paulo*, 99 REVISTA DE HISTÓRIA 117-43 (1974). An interesting contrast ·is Los Angeles, usually considered a paradigm of sprawl and disorder, yet where by the 1880's, "[c]ommercial and civic associations exerted pressures on municipal authorities and private enterprises and negotiated with governmental officials and corporate interests in an effort to make them more responsive to community sentiment." ROBERT M. FOGELSON, THE FRAGMENTED METROPOLIS, LOS ANGELES 1850-1930 36 (Cambridge, MA: Harvard U. Press, 1967).

9. *Relatorio dos estudos para o saneamento e aforestamento das varzeas adjacentes á cidade de S. Paulo . . .* (manuscript in the Biblioteca Municipal de São Paulo, 1891).

10. VIGIER, *supra* note 6, at 137.

11. ASA BRIGGS, VICTORIAN CITIES 86-94 (London: Oldhams Press, 1963). *See also* Pons, *Contemporary Interpretations of Manchester in the 1830's and 1840's*, 13 STAN. J. INT'L STUDIES, this volume at 51 (1978).

12. ALEXIS DE TOCQUEVILLE, JOURNEYS TO ENGLAND AND IRELAND 105 (New Haven, CT: Yale U. Press, trans. George Lawrence & K.P. Mayer, ed. J. P. Mayer, 1958).

13. BRIGGS, *supra* note 11, at 113.

14. The enlargement of the effective political community through the mobilization of "public opinion" is shown in LEON S. MARSHALL, THE DEVELOPMENT OF PUBLIC OPINION IN MANCHESTER, 1780-1820 (Syracuse, NY: Syracuse U. Press, 1946).

15. In contemporary Brazil cultivation of a "social memory" is acknowledged as an objective of government policy.

16. The best panorama of *fin-de-siécle* intellectual life is by a contemporary: MARTÍN GARCÍA MÉRÓU, EL BRASIL INTELECTUAL (Buenos Aires: F. Lajouane, 1900).

17. PAULO PRADO, RETRATO DO BRASIL, ENSAIO SOBRE A TRISTEZA BRASILEIRA (Rio de Janeiro: Jose Olympio, 6th ed., 1962).

18. MACHADO DE ASSIS, OBRA COMPLETA 703-08 (Rio de Janeiro: Jose Alguilar Editora, 2nd ed., 1962).

19. LEÔNCIO MARTINS RODRIGUES, TRABALHADORES, SINDICATOS E INDUSTRIALIZAÇÃO 112 (São Paulo: —, 1974). Rodrigues explicitly contrasts Brazil and Europe. *See also* Hall, *Immigration and the Early São Paulo Working Class*, 12 JAHRBUCH FÜR GESCHICHTE VON STAAT, WIRTSCHAFT UND GESELLSCHAFT LATEINAMERIKAS 393-407 (1975); Maram, *Labor and the Left in Brazil, 1890-1921: A Movement Aborted*, 57 THE HISPANIC AM. HISTORICAL REV. 254-72 (1977).

20. GEORGES CLEMENCEAU, SOUTH AMERICA TO-DAY 258-60, 268-74 (London: T. Fisher Unwin, 1911).

21. ROQUE SPENCER MACIEL DE BARROS, A EVOLUCÃO DO PEN-SAMENTO DE PEREIRA BARRETO (São Paulo: Editorial Grijalbo, 1967); and LUIS PEREIRA BARRETO, 10 BRAS FILOSÓFICAS (São Paulo-Editorial Grijalbo, 1967).

22. The "rationalization" of life in early nineteenth-century São Paulo is a central theme of GILBERTO LEITE DE BARROS, A CIDADE E O PLANALTO (São Paulo: Livraria Martins Editora, 1967), especially 207-30, 335-68.

23. Gillespie, *English Ideas of the University in the Nineteenth Century*, THE MODERN UNIVERSITY 27-55 (Ithaca, NY: Cornell U. Press, ed. Margaret Clapp, 1950).

24. M. J. CULLEN, THE STATISTICAL MOVEMENT IN EARLY VICTORIAN BRITAIN 104-17 (NY: Barnes & Noble Books, 1975); and T.S. ASHTON, ECONOMIC AND SOCIAL INVESTIGATIONS IN MANCHESTER, 1833-1933 (London: P.S. King and Son, Ltd., 1934).

25. PHILIP ABRAMS, THE ORIGINS OF BRITISH SOCIOLOGY: 1834-1914 8-30 (Chicago: U. of Chicago Press, 1968).

26. For information on the Manchester School I rely on WILLIAM D. GRAMPP, THE MANCHESTER SCHOOL OF ECONOMICS (Stanford, CA: Stanford U. Press, 1960).

27. The working class Chartists built a platform on political rather than economic prescriptions, but like the Manchester School, they assumed a national "system" that could be properly articulated by applying a handful of axioms.

28. ROBERT A NISBET, THE SOCIOLOGICAL TRADITION (NY: Basic Books, 1966).

29. ALVIN W. GOULDNER, THE COMING CRISIS OF WESTERN SOCIOLOGY 125-26 (NY: Basic Books, 1970).

30. GEOFFREY HAWTHORN, ENLIGHTENMENT AND DESPAIR: A HISTORY OF SOCIOLOGY 35-37 (Cambridge, England: Cambridge U. Press, 1976).

31. GEORGE SANTAYANA, THE GERMAN MIND: A PHILOSOPHICAL DIAGNOSIS 12 (NY: Thomas Y. Crowell Co., 1968).

32. Nogueira de Paula, *Brasil*, EL PENSAMIENTO ECONÓMICO LATINOAMERICANO [Latin American Thought in Economics] 70 (Mexico City: Fondo de cultura económica, Luis Gondra, *et al.*, 1945); Hugon, *A economia política no Brazil*, 2 AS CIÊNCIAS NO BRASIL 299 (São Paulo: —, ed. Fernando de Azevedo, 1955); Franken, *Ciências econômicas no Brasil*, working paper for Financianora de Estudos e Projetos (Rio de Janeiro, 1976); and CAIO PRADO JR., HISTÓRIA ECONÔMICA DO BRASIL (São Paulo: Editôra Brasiliense, 7th ed., 1962).

33. Cândido, *Informação sôbre a sociologia em São Paulo*, ENSAIOS PAULISTAS 510-14 (São Paulo: Editora Anhambi, 1958).

34. PAULO EGÍDIO, ESTUDOS DE SOCIOLOGIA CRIMINAL (São Paulo: —, 1941); this critique of Durkheim in 1900 won Egídio entry to the International Institute of Sociology on the recommendation of Gabriel Tarde and René Worms. *See* A. L. MACHADO NETO, HISTÓRIA DAS IDÉIÁS JURÍDICAS NO BRASIL 51-57 (São Paulo: Empresa Graphica Revista dos Tribunaes, 2d ed., 1969).

35. *See* Schwarz, *As idéias fora do lugar*, 3 ESTUDOS C.E.B.R.A.P. 149 (1973); also appearing in ROBERTO SCHWARZ, AO VENCEDOR AS BATATAS 13-28 (São Paulo: Livraria Duas Cidades, 1977).

36. *See* BARBOSA LIMA SOBRINHO, A LINGUA PORTUGUESA E A UNIDADE DO BRASIL 99-158 (Rio de Janeiro: Jose Olympio, 1958).

37. MÁRIO DE ANDRADE, HALLUCINATED CITY, translated by JACK E. TOMLINS (Kingsport, TENN: Vanderbilt U. Press, 1969).

38. *See generally* SIEGFRIED WENZEL, THE SIN OF SLOTH: ACEDIA IN MEDIEVAL THOUGHT AND LITERATURE (Chapel Hill, NC: U. of North Carolina Press, 1967). Paulo Prado's cultural inquiry is given a familial context in Levi, *The Prado Family, European Culture, and the Rediscovery of Brazil, 1860-1930*, 104 REVISTA DE HISTÓRIA 803-23 (1975).

39. THOMAS M. GREENE, RABELAIS: A STUDY IN COMIC COURAGE 10 (Englewood Cliffs NJ: Prentice-Hall, 1970).

40. OSWALD DE ANDRADE, DO PAU-BRASIL À ANTROPOFAGIA E ÀS UTOPIAS (Rio de Janeiro: Civilização Brasileira, 1972); OSWALD DE ANDRADE, POESIAS REUNIDAS (Rio de Janeiro: Civilização Brasileira, 3rd ed. 1972).

41. *See* ANTÔNIO CÂNDIDO, VÁRIOS ESCRITOS 33-92 (São Paulo: Livraria Duas Cidades, 1970).

42. MÁRIO NEME, ed., PLATAFORMA DA NOVA GERAÇÃO 29-40 (Pôrto Alegre, Brazil: Livraria do Globo 1945). For responses of the previous generation, *see* EDGARD CAVALHEIRO, ed., TESTAMENTO DE UMA GERACÃO (Pôrto Alegre, Brazil: Livraria do Globo, 1944).

43. A scrupulous concern with tensions between private vision and public context, between esthetic integrity and social commitment, is shown explicitly in ANTÔNIO CÂNDIDO, LITERATURA E SOCIEDADE (São Paulo: —, 1965). Antônio Cândido and Fernandes are discussed in CARLOS GUILHERME MOTA, IDEOLOGIA DA CULTURA BRASILEIRA 1933-1974 (São Paulo: Editora Atica, 1977); Mota's interest in intellectual history, however, inclines more toward manifest ideology than toward latent morphology.

44. Cândido, *supra* note 33, at 514. For statements from the 1930's on leadership training, "the task of the elites," and "the illusion of equality," by an industrialist and economic historian closely associated with the Free School, *see* ROBERTO C. SIMONSEN, EVOLUÇÃO INDUSTRIAL DO BRASIL E OUTROS ESTUDOS 459-69 (São Paulo: Companhia Editora Nacional, 1973).

45. *See* PAULO DUARTE, MÁRIO DE ANDRADE POR ÊLE MESMO (São Paulo: Edart-São Paulo Livraria Editora, 1971); and Dassin, *The Politics of Art: Mário de Andrade and the Case of Brazilian Modernism*, (unpublished Ph.D. dissertation, Program of Modern Thought and Literature, Stanford University, 1974).

46. SIMONSEN, *supra* note 44.

47. CLAUDE LÉVI-STRAUSS, TRISTES TROPIQUES (NY: Criterion Books, trans. John Russell, 1961).

48. Cândido, *supra* note 33, at 516–20.

49. *See* Fernandes, *Um balanço crítico da contribuição etnográfica dos cronistas*, A INVESTIGAÇÃO ETNOLÓGICA NO BRASIL E OUTROS ENSAIOS 191-289 (Petrópolis, Brazil: Editora Vozes, 1975), which is a reprinted study of 1949; his analysis of the sociological function of war among the Tupinambá informed Fernandes' reflections on São Paulo's "constitutionalist revolution" of 1932, an essay of 1949 reprinted in MUDANÇAS SOCIAIS NO BRASIL 250-65 (São Paulo: Difusão Européia do Livro, 1960).

50. FLORESTAN FERNANDES, A SOCIOLOGIA NO BRASIL 198 (Petrópolis, Brazil: Editora Vozes, 1977). The prospectus for the UNESCO-Anhembi project appeared as *O preconceito racial em São Paulo*, 11 INSTITUTO DE ADMINISTRAÇÃO (U. of São Paulo, 1951). *Relações raciais entre negros e brancos em São Paulo*, co-ordinated by Bastide and Fernandes, was published by Editora Anhembi, São Paulo in 1955. Subsequent publications of the project included studies of race in Rio Grande do Sul and Santa Catarina by F. Cardoso and O. Ianni, and a study of the integration of blacks in Paulista society by Fernandes. The project challenged the received image of Brazil just as the earlier study of blacks in the United States by the Myrdal group had laid under question the "American creed."

51. FERNANDES, *supra* note 50, at 140-209. *See also* the inquiry into Fernandes' intellectual formation and current positions published as an "Entrevista" ["Interview"] in 2 TRANS/FORMAÇÃO, REVISTA DE FILOSOFIA 5-86 (1975).

52. *See* MARIA ISAURA PEREIRA DE QUEIROZ, ed., 1-3 INTRODUÇÃO AO ESTUDO DA SOCIOLOGIA NO BRASIL (São Paulo: U. of São Paulo, Instituto de Estudos Brasileiros, 1971).

53. In a recent symposium a well-known disciple recalled that "Florestan had been a Marxist before, but when he was my professor [in the early 1950's] he was a functionalist, and a very good one. Then again he became a Marxist or something like that, but this is the personal history of Florestan." *See generally* FLORESTAN FERNANDES, FUNDAMENTOS EMPÍRICOS DA EXPLICAÇÃO SOCIOLÓGICA (São Paulo: Cia. Editora Nacional, 1970), and FLORESTAN FERNANDES, ELEMENTOS DE SOCIOLOGIA TEORICA (São Paulo: Cia. Editora Nacional, 1970).

54. The Krailsheimer translation of the epigraph runs as follows: "All mathematicians would therefore be intuitive if they had good sight, because they do not draw false conclusions from principles thàt they know. And intuitive minds would be mathematical if they could adapt their sight to the unfamiliar principles of mathematics."

55. Anderson, *Components of the National Culture*, 50 NEW LEFT REVIEW 3 (1968).

56. Anderson is taken to task for his frequently doctrinaire and invariably humorless style of analysis in Thompson, *The Peculiarities of the English*, THE SOCIALIST REGISTER 1965 311-62 (NY: Monthly Review Press, Ralph Miliband and John Saville, eds., 1965).

57. *See generally* FERNANDO HENRIQUE CARDOSO, EMPRESÁRIO INDUSTRIAL E DESENVOLVIMENTO ECONÔMICO NO BRASIL (São Paulo: Difusão Européia do Livro, 1964).

58. Brazilian intellectuals had for a century nursed the theme of ethnicity, less in the morbid spirit of "racism" that supercilious North American historians ascribe to them (perhaps projectively) than in a quest for the foundations of nationhood—an agenda prescribed by the German scientist Martius in 1843.

Poetic Evolution in the Industrial Era: The Brazilian Modernists

IUMNA MARIA SIMON*

Poetry and progress are two ambitious entities which instinctively hate one another, and, when they meet along the way, one must serve the other.[1]

Charles Baudelaire

I. THE CRISIS OF MODERN POETRY

EVER SINCE THE EMERGENCE OF INDUSTRIAL CAPITALISM, its effect on cities has been a dominant theme of modern literature. The shock of urbanism and industrialization gives rise to a new sensibility which seeks fresh modes of expression. The first reactions of artists to the new environment are often negative, yet they gradually incorporate the techniques and processes developed by industrial civilization into the structures of their works. This article will discuss the thematic and stylistic response of poetry to urban industrial growth as exemplified by the work of the Modernist poets of Brazil during São Paulo's rapid expansion in the 1920's.

The cycle in poetry of antagonism to and incorporation of the reality of urban industrial growth coincides with, or possibly determines, what has been called the "crisis of poetry" in modern civilization. As the Brazilian poet and critic Decio Pignatari best expressed it:

> [The crisis of poetry] is itself a part of an even vaster crisis: the survival of the crafts in face of the Industrial Revolution (economic, social and ideological). . . . The crisis of crafts in the nineteenth century is that of the artist who no longer finds a function in utilitarian society. He internalizes the crisis and displays it in the act of making his art.[2]

* Assistant Professor of Brazilian Literature at the Institute of Letters, History and Psychology of Assis — State University of São Paulo.

The face of this urban and industrial exigency was first described by the Romanticists.[3] William Blake's visions of the city of London are well known: confusion and chaos, but also organization and a systematic state of mind.[4] Wordsworth's first impression of the capital was one of admiration as well as anxiety. He accused the urban masses of being the incarnation of confusion and a threat to identity, but he also sensed that they represented the historial forces of liberation and the possibility of new order and union.[5] It was, however, the poetic experience of Charles Baudelaire—the "poet of modernity" *par excellence*—which affords the better example of the nineteenth century's internalization of the crisis of poetry and its manifestation in the form of art.

When Baudelaire used the word modernity in 1859, he apologized for the neologism, while explaining that he needed to express that special capacity of the artist to look towards the "desert of a "metropolis" and see not only the "decline of mankind" but also feel a "mysterious beauty" not yet discovered.[6] Walter Benjamin stresses the importance of the motif of the crowd in Baudelaire's poetry by explaining that the metropolitan masses were so much a part of the poet's experience that it is rare to find a description of them in his poems. His most important subjects—especially the theme of the crowd—appear in the construction of his poems as "hidden figures." The possible meaning of these "hidden figures" is explained by Benjamin in his analysis of Baudelaire's well-known poem, *Le Soleil*: "[I]t is the phantom crowd of words, the fragments, the beginnings of lines, from which the poet, in the deserted streets, wrests the poetic booty."[7] Benjamin raises such issues in order to discuss the concept of modernity in a poet who questioned whether lyric poetry could exist in a modern world.[8] How could lyric poetry have as its basis the "experience of shock" encountered in large cities, an experience that demands a high level of consciousness? How could the poet transform the characteristics of loss and decadence, and their negative connotations, into something fascinating?

> Poverty, decay, evil, the nocturnal, and the artifical exert an attraction that has to be perceived poetically. They contain secrets that guide poetry on to new paths. In the refuse of urban centers, Baudelaire smells a mystery, which his poetry depicts as a phosphorescent shimmer. In addition, he approves of anything that banishes nature in order to establish the absolute realm of the artificial.[9]

Baudelaire's aesthetics are essential to understanding the responses of modern poets to the changes caused by the advance of civilization. Two problems involved in those responses are of greatest importance. First, there are *thematic* ambivalences in the literary images of the city which reveal a dual impulse of both rejection and acceptance. Second, there are *stylistic* dissonances in the poetic process which gradually appropriate the techniques and resources of a civilization that rejects poets and is in turn rejected by them.[10]

Modern poetry, although characterized by a sense of uselessness in an era dominated by technology, nevertheless nourishes itself on the very "demons" it criticizes.[11] Therein lies the source of its contradictions, breakdowns, and evolution. Stated differently, lyric poetry, which in its anti-utilitarian form rejects the material and artificial comforts of industrialization, must inevitably accomodate itself to its new mistress or else perish. For this reason, there developed a poetic love/hate relationship to the city, and the connections between industrial methods of production and poetic methods of composition. Industry achieved efficiency through the development of synchronization, automation, specialization of labor, and assembly lines. Poetry similarly strove for economy of expression through the techniques of simultaneity, fragmentation, vignette, montage, and telegraphic style.

Hans Magnus Enzensberg correctly observes that modern poetry "keeps abreast of prevailing methods of production, but as one keeps abreast of the enemy."[12] As a consequence, modern poetry always stood the chance of advancing to new positions and yet being uncertain how it was swept there. The greatest danger in reacting to industrialization is that such poetry will lose touch with its roots, and become its own worst enemy. Consider, in this regard, the early twentieth century's most radical poetics—Futurism. With its celebration of modern life, machinery, the great metropolis, velocity and war, Futurism (especially Italian Futurism) influenced not only the European avant-garde movement, but also Brazilian poets and writers attempting to renovate and update their own national art and culture.

II. THE EMERGENCE OF THE MODERNIST MOVEMENT

A. *The Inheritance—External and Internal Influences*

By 1920, São Paulo began to face the imbalances and contradictions inherent in the process of industrialization that the Europeans had experienced decades before. The rapid growth of industry was grafted onto an agrarian society controlled by an oligarchy of large landowners. The growth of the middle class in an urban population within a colonial tradition strongly based on patriarchal models caused a profound imbalance between the new economic system and the dominant social and psychological structures of the time. In the words of Richard Morse:

> Brazil was forced to import the techniques of industrial capitalism from societies which, along with these techniques, developed organizations and mental habits of their own. However, attitudes and forms of social structure cannot be imported from outside and incorporated into the existing structures as if they were machines or railway tracks.[13]

Change was also reflected in the spoken language, which responded to the influx of diverse groups including Europeans and Brazilian migrants from the countryside. This new, careless, dynamic, and functional language spoken by the middle and lower classes became the liveliest expression of the new emergent forces in Brazilian society. If long before these social transformations the discrepancies between written and spoken language were evident, the cleavage certainly grew more extreme with the passage of time. Official organizations in Brazil, from the press to the Academy of Letters, preserved, defended, and transmitted the dominant patriarchal mentality in the more conservative, precise, static, and ornamental forms of written expression which increasingly were at variance with the dynamic spoken language.

Confronted with changes in both social reality and language, and reinforced by contact with the European avant-garde, the Modernists wanted to update Brazilian letters. In particular, they wanted to "rid literature of its class values and make it into a form of expression common to all."[14] Incorporating this new urban speech into the form of erudite written expression was of fundamental importance to the Modernists.

Their central goal was to embrace the culture of industrialism. In his *Manifesto da Poesia Pau-Brasil (Manifesto of Brazil-Wood Poetics*, published in 1924) Oswald de Andrade called for a forthright commitment to technological civilization. It was time, he said, to "set the imperial clock of national literature ahead,"[15] to repudiate both the past and the academic tradition in order to attune Brazilian literature to twentieth century realities.

On the levels both of perception and of expression, however, the Modernists' hunger to embrace the modern was hampered by strong ties to the past. Comparing the first responses of European poets to urban-industrial growth with those of the Brazilians, we see an inversion of the dominant literary tendencies and movements. To nineteenth century Europeans, the tension was between the *thematic negation* of industrial civilization and the gradual incorporation of the resources and techniques it offered. To Brazilians writing several decades later, the tension was between the celebration of modern life and, often, the problems of relating their forms of *expression* to that modernity. Thus many poets who were active in formulating the Modernist program were unable to implement the new esthetics in their works.[16]

B. *Hallucinated City: The Birth of Brazilian Modernism*

Within this framework of contradiction and conflict, the first poetic rendering of industrial São Paulo appeared in 1922. This was Mário de Andrade's *Hallucinated City*.[17] His collection of poems was not only the first expression of the city's new configurations, but also the first book of Modernist construction published in Brazil. As such, it reflects the thematic and stylistic conflicts between Mário's Modernist stance and his own background.

In *Hallucinated City*, he approached the urban theme from a modern perspective but tempered it with humanism.[18] The city is often portrayed as a woman ("São Paulo, oh my beloved. . . ."[19] "Lady Macbeth made of fine mist;"[20] "Woman who is my stepmother and sister!"[21]). The city is internalized and then externalized in a manner causing analogical and metaphorical intersections between the "poetic I" (subjective world) and the city (objective world). "My soul hunchbacked like the Avenue St. John . . ."[22], "harlequinate city"[23], and "harlequinate interior"[24] are some of the best examples of this. Yet behind the harlequinate costume, Mário evinces the same love/hate relationship to the city previously mentioned. His criticism of the evils of civilization is extensive: "Horrid cities! . . . No wings whatsoever, no poetry whatsoever! No joy / whatsoever"[25]; "Are jails necessary / to preserve civilization?"[26], "Futility, civilization . . . ."[27]

Mário de Andrade's humanist perspective is more in keeping with his Catholic upbringing than with any Futuristic exaltation of machinery, velocity, and violence. The same might be said about his relationship to the past. In the poet's *"Extremely Interesting Preface"*—which is the first systematic theoretical elaboration of Modernist poetics—statements such as these appear:

> And forgive me for being so behind the times regarding
> present date artistic movements. I am old-fashioned, I
> confess.[28] I am not a futurist (after Marinetti). I have said
> so before and I repeat it. I have points of contact with
> futurism.[29]

> My vindication? Freedom. I use it; I do not abuse it. I know
> how to bridle it from my philosophical and religious truths
> . . . .[30]

Thus, if his reading of European avant-garde theories was framed by
what he called his philosophical and religious truths, perhaps his
reading of the industrial-urban growth of São Paulo was likewise
framed. This interpretation would explain his oscillations between
acceptance of modern civilization and nostalgic negation of it.

The so-called "pope of modernism" considered the Futurist pro-
posals, especially the urban theme and the celebration of machinery,
as but one of many paths to modern art. The "eternal themes" (such
as the universe, homeland, and love) were still "open to adoption
because of their modernity."[31] To Mário de Andrade, taking on the
modern required one to assume the "expression of modernity"—not
merely to write about modern themes. Consider his fundamental
statement about the artificality of modern themes:

> In my opinion, to write modern art never meant to repre-
> sent modern life through its externals: automobiles,
> movies, asphalt. If these words frequent my book, it is not
> because I think that I write "modern" (*sic*) with them; but
> since my book is modern, these things have their reason for
> being in it.[32]

The *Extremely Interesting Preface* goes on to give a fuller exposition
of these poetic and aesthetic theories. In reading the poems and that
preface, however, one cannot but note the discrepancies between
Mário's advanced theories (which were marked by psychological
analysis) and the actual achievements of his first Modernist verses.
Contrary to his statement of the artificiality of modern themes, he
attained greater success in writing about the modern theme of the
great city than in creating a modern expression. This proposition is
shown by looking at the poetic process and style in the poet's work.

C. *The Stylistic Evolution of Modernity*

To Mário de Andrade, poetry is pulled between *lyricism* which
springs from the subconscious and hence is psychological in nature,

and *art*, which is the conscious task of purification. The *Extremely Interesting Preface* outlines their symbiotic relationship in terms of the theories of harmonic and polyphonic verse.[33] Polyphonic verse is equivalent to the simultaneity of the Futurists and of the Cubists in painting. It is an attempt to present the same phenomenon from various angles at the same time. The technique thus disrupts the linear conception of art and breaks away from figurative representations and the logical-discursive structure which predominated in the melodic verse of the Parnassian poets.[34]

Mário saw that simultaneity originated from "the present life as well as from the observation of our inner self."[35] Thus the laws proclaimed by the aesthetics of the new poetry are part of the lyric motion, which is constantly changing.[36] In short, multiplicity is not restricted only to aspects of the real world (in his case São Paulo) but also includes aspects of the inner world, of the poet's lyric "I."

Such transformations are represented through the use of technical resources such as harmonic and polyphonic verse, free rhyme, free verse, and what Mário called "the victory of the dictionary"[37] (equivalent to Marinetti's "liberated words"). The use of cliche words like "harlequinate" is also very important in this sense. As in the painting by the Cubist Dellaunay, Mário de Andrade used clowns in *Hallucinated City* to suggest duality and multiplicity:

> And they say that clowns are happy!
> I never rattle the little bells in my harlequinate interior![38]

For example, the connotative versatility of harlequin appears in "Inspiration," the first poem in *Hallucinated City*. Note that the language refers equally to the multiple aspects of the objective world and of the internal world:

> São Paulo! tumult of my life . . .
> My loves are flowers made from the original . . .
> Harlequinate! . . . Diamond tights . . . gray and gold . . .
> Light and mist . . . Oven and warm winter . . .[39]

The ideas of multiplicity, fragmentation, and simultaneity contained in the word, however, are not enough, by themselves, to achieve the "modern" process of composition. The exploration of harmonic and polyphonic verse in the poem is limited to very slight breaks from the linear and logical. The excessive use of both suspension points (to interrupt the thought contained in the sentence) and exclamation marks illustrates the impossibility of carrying out simultaneity at the level of language. Such punctuation marks function as crutches to

indicate breaks in the linear structure of the discourse. Again, however, they alone are not enough to provide the discourse with either
modernity or equilibrium. The working out of these themes becomes
clearer by examining certain other poems in the collection.

In *Hallucinated City*, the poet's oscillations between the new and
the old are represented by images of past and present, the primitive
and the civilized, by the tension between an objective world of "nude
bronze statues eternally coursing, in fixed disdain for velocities
. . ."[40] and the subjective world of "I am a Tupi Indian strumming a
lute!"[41]

The first three lines of the poem "The Animal Tamer", which is
one of the most successful compositions in the book, indicate how he
has updated the techniques of simultaneity, polyphony, and the exploration of visual images.

> Around the Avenue. Trolley 3.
> Asphalts. Vast, high fountains of dust
> beneath the harlequinate of the sky gold-pink-green . . .[42]

Then, from the second stanza onward, the poet introduces himself.
He becomes an actor in the urban scene of progress, technology, and
commercial transactions, while simultaneously indicating his ambivalence to present and past, primitive and civilized, tradition and modernity. Yet the fact that his eyes are part of the poem affirms the
definite need to take on the present, a need that is strongly associated
with the image at the stanza's end of an "immigrant's son . . . blondly
taming a motor car."[43]

> Mário pay a penny.
> There are five on the bench: one white,
> one night, one gold,
> one consumptive grew and Mário . . .
> Solicitudes! Solicitudes!
> But . . . behold, oh my eyes longing after yesterdays
> that enchanted spectacle of the Avenue!
> Revive, oh ancestrally *paulista* gauchos!
> and oh horses of blood-red rage!
>
> Oranges, oranges, oranges!
> Avocados, cambucás and tangerines!
> *Guardate!* At the applause of the whizzing clown.

> heroic heir of that lordly race of pioneers,
> an immigrant's son elegantly passes by,
> blondly taming a motor car![44]

The immigrant is the symbol of industrialization denied by the coffee aristocracy. To accept him, either as one who already achieved status as in the poem mentioned above, or as one who is still struggling like that "Little seamstress from São Paulo / italo-franco-brasilico-saxon"[45] who appears in the poem "You," is to accept and assume the technological society and progress of São Paulo. That society's destruction of the natural and primitive, however, receives an emotional and nostalgic criticism in the poem "Anhangabaú:"

> These my parks of the Anhangabaú or of Paris,
> where are your waters, where the sorrows of your toads?
> "My father was a king!"
> "He was." "He was not." "He was." "He was not."
> Where are your banana trees?
> Where is your river grizzled by the mists
> telling tales to the forest imps? . . .
>
> My beloved and worthless palimpsest!
> Chronicle in faulty Latin
> overlying an eclogue which may not be from Virgil! . . .[46]

The poem "Landscape 4" is an even more violent criticism of the modern, in particular of the economic and political aspects of a coffee crisis due to the confrontation of industrial and agricultural interests:

> At the intersection the English cry of the São Paulo Railway
> But the windstorms of disillusion! the drop in coffee
> prices! . . .
> . . . .
> Oh! This supreme pride in existing São Paulo-wise!!![47]

This interest in the political culminates in Mário's satire of "Ode to a Bourgeois Gentlemen" and, in particular, in "The Flock" which criticizes the Brazilian Congress and portrays a process of deformation in which the deputies gradually turn into goats:

> I insult the bourgeois. The money-grabbing bourgeois
> the bourgeois-bourgeois!

The well-made digestion of São Paulo!
The man-belly! The man-buttocks!
The man who being French, Brazilian, Italian,
is always a cautious little take-your-time![48]

Oh! my hallucinations!
But the deputies, high-hats,
little by little changed into goats!
Their horns grow, their chin whiskers sprout . . .
And I saw that the high-hats of my beloved state,
with the wooden triangles at their necks,
in the green hopes, beneath the golden tassles of the after-
      noon,
were beginning to graze
next to the palace of his honor the governor . . .
Oh! my hallucinations![49]

Despite his limitations, Mário de Andrade successfully presented
a new and challenging reading of São Paulo in the 1920's and broke
with the academic and conservative tradition of Brazilian literature.
As Mário da Silva Brito, the leading historian of the Modernist movement in Brazil, has said:

> The book sings São Paulo with its picturesque scenes, its
> vices, vanities, and the mixed blood of its population. It
> satirizes the bourgeoisie and the politicians, gives witness to
> the presence of the workers in factories, and takes note of
> it in verses that wind traditionalism and the aristocracy.[50]

In sum, *Hallucinated City* can be considered an emotional and critical
answer to the multiplicity and ambiguities of a society undergoing
industrialization. The title itself suggests the poet's relationship to the
experience. "Hallucinated" refers to the tumult of the city, to the
poet's perplexity, if not astonishment, at the face of the metropolis,
this new "Pauličéia." But although *Hallucinated City* was an initial
response to this multiplicity, the contradictions of a Brazilian reality
composed of underdeveloped areas and urban industrial centers
were left to be confronted by those who followed Mário de Andrade's
search for new modes of expression and of representation.

III. THE MATURATION OF MODERNISM: THEMATIC
AND STYLISTIC REFINEMENTS

> *There is a history of literature that projects itself upon*
> *the city of São Paulo; and there is a history of the city*
> *of São Paulo which projects itself upon literature.*[51]
> Antônio Cândido

The next step in the Modernist movement was the phase of nationalism launched by Oswald de Andrade in 1924 with the publication of his *Manifesto da Poesia Pau-Brazil*.[52] This phase can be traced to two roots. The first was the contribution of Mário de Andrade in *Hallucinated City*: the criticism of political and social structures of city and country, the introduction of popular creations into erudite speech, and the use of urban dialogues (in the form of personification of the city, cries of street vendors, and elements of folklore). The second basis of the nationalist phase of Modernism was stimulated by the European avant-garde movements, especially Cubism, which was exploring primitive art and culture. Such an exploration found favorable conditions in Brazil since it met with Brazilian reality. Antônio Cândido observes that:

> [I]n Brazil, primitive cultures merge into everyday life or are still live reminiscences of the recent past. The terrible darings of a Picasso, a Brancusi, a Max Jacob, a Tristan Tzara, were really more related to our cultural heritage than to theirs.[53]

Prior to the discovery of this cultural heritage, Futurism's celebration of modern life had met with obstacles in Brazil due to the contradictions of industrialism installed in a patriarchal society.

It was Oswald de Andrade who proposed and carried out the welding of primitivism and industrialization:

> The base of our society is double the forest and the school. The dualist credulous race and geometry, algebra, and chemistry, come right after the baby bottle and cambric tea (Chá de erva de doce). A mixture of "sleep baby or the bogey man will come and get you" and mathematical equations.

. . . .

Elevators, cubes of skyscrapers, and the wise solar laziness.
Prayer. Carnival, Intimate energy. The "sabiá" bird. The
hospitality which is somewhat sensuous, amorous. Nostal-
gia for the witch-doctors and the fields of military avia-
tion.[54]

What is most remarkable is that the primitivist tendency inside
nationalism should have been proposed and developed in São Paulo.
The manifestos and practice of Oswald de Andrade, the researches of
Mário de Andrade, and even the proudly nationalistic "Ver-
deamarelismo" (flag waving) were all products of Paulistas.[55]

The poems of *Brazil Wood*[56] were not directly inspired by the
urban theme or by technology, but rather by a rediscovery of Brazil in
all its aspects (historical, geographic, and social). They also represented the most radical use of language and construction up to that date.
As Oswald de Andrade explained in his *Manifesto*:

[Stylistically we must make] efforts against naturalistic de-
tail by synthesis; against romantic morbidity by geometric
equilibrium and technological *finishing*; against imitation
by *invention* and *surprise*.[57]

According to the Concrete poets, who started writing in the
1950's, it was Oswald de Andrade who was the pioneer of a new
syntax and of the constructive radicalization of Brazilian literary
language.[58] The Brazilian Concrete poet and critic Haroldo de Campos called Andrade's poems industrial type, minute poetry, and cap-
sular poetry because

Oswald resorted to a primitive sensibility . . . and to a
concrete poetics . . . to adapt Brazilian literature to the
new need of communication engendered by technological
civilization.[59]

Concrete Poetry was launched in São Paulo as a radical reconsid-
eration of the combative spirit of Oswald de Andrade, who struggled
for a "poetry of exportation" in the "provincial Brazil immersed in the
syrupy parnassian limbo, the Brazil of Coelho Neto and Bilac," as
noted by Haroldo de Campos.[60] In Concrete Poetry we find the most
drastic process of aesthetic radicalization in the last twenty-five years.
It has been exported, reached international recognition as one of the
most important tendencies of contemporary poetry, and shown that a

truly Brazilian art and culture could spring from the nation's urban, industrial, and—by definition—cosmopolitan experience.

IV. CONCLUSION

Although developments in poetry do not follow a logical progression, the response of Brazilian Modernist poets to urbanization has many parallels to that of European poets. The work of Mário de Andrade clearly fits the model of poetic ambivalence towards the urban environment characterized by Baudelaire and the early Romantics. Oswald de Andrade saw within the dichotomy of urban and rural life the seeds of a nationalistic conscience, which he developed through his advocacy of a culture common to all Brazilians: an integration of the primitivism of Brazil's hinterland into the intellectual life of São Paulo. This transformation is in a similar vein to the potentiality of the masses vaguely forseen by Baudelaire, Whitman, and Blake. To the Brazilian poets, however, this potentiality of urban life was created not by looking toward the city itself but by the city's respect for its rural heritage. After Oswald de Andrade's work harmonized the previous thematic and stylistic dissonances of modern Brazilian poetry, his successors were able to concentrate fully on developing a modern style. The result, as found in the Concrete poets, is the complete appropriation of the techniques of industrial production into the poetic process.

NOTES

1. *Le Salon de 1859*, OEURVES 771 (Paris: Gallimard, 1956).
2. DÉCIO PIGNATARI, CONTRA COMUNICAÇÃO 93 (São Paulo: Editora Perspectiva, 1971).
3. *See* HAROLD BLOOM, ed., ROMANTICISM AND CONSCIOUSNESS 9 (NY: Norton & Co., 1970).
4. RAYMOND WILLIAMS, THE COUNTRY AND THE CITY 149 (NY: Oxford U. Press, 1973). *See also* DOUGLAS BUSH, SCIENCE AND ENGLISH POETRY 84 (NY: Oxford U. Press, 1950), and E.J. HOBSBAWM, THE AGE OF REVOLUTION 1789–1848, at 263 (Cleveland, NY: The World Publishing Co., 1962).
5. *Id.*
6. HUGO FRIEDRICH, THE STRUCTURE OF MODERN POETRY FROM THE MID-NINETEENTH TO THE MID-TWENTIETH CENTURY 19 (Evanston, Ill.: Northwestern U. Press, trans. Joachim Neugroschel, 1974).
7. WALTER BENJAMIN, ILLUMINATIONS 167 (NY: Harcourt, Brace & World, ed. Hannah Arendt, 1968).
8. *Id.*
9. FRIEDRICH, *supra* note 6, at 25.

10. Still in the nineteenth century, Mallarmé published his poem-constellation *Un Coup Des Dés* (1897), incorporating the visual structure of newspapers into the structure of the poetic text, although he despised journalists because they were "trained by the mob to give everything its vulgar character." FRIEDRICH, *supra* note 6, at 84.

11. Friedrich explains this process by saying that "this poetry is marked by the era to which it opposes its extreme freedom. The coolness of its craftsmanship, its hardness of heart, and other features as well, are immediately derived from the *Zeitgeist*. Poetry attempts the 'synthetic poem' in which primal images—stars, seas, winds—mix with technological entities and scientific jargon." *Id*. at 129.

12. HANS MAGNUS ENZENSBERGER, THE CONSCIOUSNESS INDUSTRY 57 (NY: The Seabury Press, 1974).

13. RICHARD MORSE, FROM COMMUNITY TO METROPOLIS 224-25 (NY: Farrar, Straus & Giroux, Octagon Books, 1974).

14. ANTONIO CÂNDIDO, LITERATURA E SOCIEDADE 144 (São Paulo: Companhia Ed. Nacional, 1965).

15. OSWALD DE ANDRADE, DO PAU-BRASIL À ANTROPOFAGIA E ÀS UTOPIAS 9 (Rio de Janeiro: Civilização Brasileira for the Instituto Nacional do Livro, 1972).

16. Worthy of mention are Menotti del Picchia, Guilherme de Almeida, Ribeiro Couto, Tácito de Almeida, and Plínio Salgado, all of whom were participants in the "Week of Modern Art" which took place in 1922 as a public demonstration against traditional art and mentality dominant in Brazil at that time.

17. MÁRIO DE ANDRADE, HALLUCINATED CITY PAULICÉIA DES-VAIRADA (Nashville: Vanderbilt U. Press, trans. Jack E. Tomlins, 1968), translated from PAULICÉIA DESVAIRADA (São Paulo: Livraria Martins Ed., 1922) [hereinafter cited as HALLUCINATED CITY].

18. This shows that Mário de Andrade's modernity is a different concept than the "modernolatria" of the Italian Futurist Marinetti.

19. HALLUCINATED CITY *supra* note 17, at 41.

20. *Id*. at 63.

21. *Id*.

22. *Id*. at 41.

23. *Id*. at 29.

24. *Id*. at 41.

25. *Id*. at 25.

26. *Id*. at 35.

27. *Id*. at 43.

28. *Id*. at 5.

29. *Id*. at 7.

30. *Id*. at 11.

31. *See* Mário de Andrade, *Extremely Interesting Preface*, *Id*. at 16.

32. *Id*.

33. Jack Tomlins summarizes these theories in his introduction to HAL-LUCINATED CITY: "Melodic verse is old-fashioned, nineteenth century declarative statement, containing a complete thought: São Paulo is a stage for Russian ballets. Harmonic verse is the combination of distinct words which bear no immediate relationship to one another and, therefore, do not form a logical series: Pack of dogs . . . Stock Market . . . Gambling . . . . Polyphonic verse is the combination not of words, as above, but rather of distinct phrases to achieve the same effect as harmonic verse: The gears palsy . . . The mist snows . . . ." *Id*. at xiv-xv.

34. *See also* Mário de Andrade, *A Escrava que não é Isaura*, OBRA IMADURA 195 (São Paulo: Livraria Martins Ed., 1960).

35. *Id*. at 265.

36. *Id*. at 225.

37. HALLUCINATED CITY *supra* note 17, at 11. *See also* OBRA IMATURA *supra* note 34, at 234-42.

38. HALLUCINATED CITY *supra* note 17, at 41.

39. HALLUCINATED CITY *supra* note 17, at 21.

40. *Id.* at 49.

41. *Id.* at 23.

42. *Id.* at 49.

43. *Id.* at 47.

44. *Id.*

45. *Id.* at 63.

46. *Id.* at 49.

47. *Id.* at 75.

48. *Ode to the Bourgeois Gentleman, Id.* at 37.

49. *The Flock, Id.* at 31.

50. Brito, *A revolução modernista*, 4 A LITERATURA NO BRASIL 431 at 458 (Rio de Janeiro: Ed. Sul Americana for the Instituiçao Larragoiti, ed. Afranio Coutinho, 1959).

51. Antonio Cândido, *A literatura na evolução de uma comunidade*, LITERATURA E SOCIEDADE 167.

52. OSWALD DE ANDRADE, *supra* note 15.

53. ANTONIO CÂNDIDO, *supra* note 14, at 145.

54. OSWALD DE ANDRADE, *supra* note 15, at 9.

55. This phrase is symbolic of Brazilian patriotism: the dominant colors in the Brazilian flag are green and yellow.

56. OSWALD DE ANDRADE, POESIAS REUNIDAS 57 (São Paulo: Difusão Européia do Livro, 1966).

57. OSWALD DE ANDRADE, *supra* note 15, at 8.

58. Campos, *Uma poetica da radicalidade*, intro. to OSWALD DE ANDRADE, *supra* note 56 at 7-54. *See also* Campos, *Miramar na mira* and *Serafim: um grande não livro*, intro. to OSWALD DE ANDRADE, MEMORIAS SENTIMENTAIS E SERAFIM PONTE GRANDE xiii-xlviii and 99-127 (Rio de Janeiro: Ed. Civilizaçáo Brasileira, 1971).

59. Campos, *Uma poética da radicalidade, supra* note 58, at 45.

60. Campos, *A poesia concreta e a realidade nacional*, 4 TENDÊNCIA 83 at 84 (Belo Horizonte: U. de Minas Gerais, 1962).

Contemporary Interpretations of Manchester in the 1830's and 1840's[†]

*VALDO PONS**

I. INTRODUCTION

THIS ARTICLE attempts to demonstrate that contemporary writings on Manchester in the 1830's and 1840's constitute excellent materials for a deeper sociological analysis of the city than we have yet received. It shows that some of the well-known writings of the period are extremely valuable evidence of different visions and conceptions of Manchester society, and that their differing interpretations usually stemmed from different assumptions about the city and the wider society, rather than from disagreements about the "facts" of early Manchester. The "facts" were stark enough, and generally not in dispute. However, as Marcus observes, writers on Manchester at this period were "never 'neutral' in any sense of that term;" their accounts were "always highly charged with meanings of all kinds and significances that extend in every direction."[1] We must therefore uncover these "meanings" if we are to move towards a thorough analysis of the early industrial city.

The first section of this paper attempts to evoke the newness, enormity, and dynamism of the city, drawing attention to the mixtures of admiration, awe, and apprehension with which it was greeted by many observers. The next section examines a small selection of well-known writings of the period, evaluating each to see what it can tell us about the city if we are willing to embrace the vantage point of the author. Finally, a brief comparison is made of the principal conceptions of urban society that emerge from the writings reviewed,

† This paper stems from research conducted under the auspices of the Greater Manchester Urban Study Programme (1969–72) financed by the Social Science Research Council (Britain). The author gratefully acknowledges his indebtedness to the S.S.R.C.
* Professor of Sociology, The University of Hull.

and a comment is made on them in light of what became of Manchester in the second half of the nineteenth century. Only a few contemporary observers are considered so as to allow for specificity in a field where there already exists a wealth of historical reconstruction and received wisdom. However, while few in number, the writings chosen express a wide range of interpretations.

To aid the analysis, we may postulate a number of possible views of the city in early industrial society:

(1) We may view the new city as a product of technological, economic, and social forces inherent in industrial capitalism. We may assume that it will continue to change, and that its internal ecological and social divisions will not endure. Our primary concern should therefore be with such change as will release "potential man" in a classless society rather than with the present plight of "suffering man."

(2) We may accept the city as it is, but insist that relief be found for "suffering man" through reformist legislation and administrative action.

(3) We may accept the new city on the assumption that the plight of "suffering man" stems essentially from circumstances of transition and cultural innovation, and that the extremes of poverty and squalor will in due course be arrested through "natural" development.

(4) We may view the evils of the city as a direct threat to the middle classes, and insist on charity and philanthropy for that reason or in the name of God.

(5) We may sing a bourgeois eulogy of the city in the belief that anything so powerful and dynamic should not be challenged: the Destiny of Man must simply be left to unfold.

(6) We may reaffirm our loyalties to traditional society, and assume either that superior and stronger fundamental values will ultimately reassert themselves, or that the whole process of industrial urbanism is an unfortunate but inevitable historical development.

The above conceptions provide us with an initial framework for analyzing writings on Manchester in the 1830's and 1840's. The task is, however, not as simple as the framework may suggest. First, several of the conceptions are commonly found intertwined in the views of a single author, or of several authors sharing an otherwise seemingly common stance. Second, some of the conceptions do not in logic necessarily exclude each other. Third, there are several different levels or orders of social reality involved, and these must be identified and distinguished. Despite these difficulties, however, postulating conceptions such as those listed above can contribute to a fresh reading of well-known writings.

II. THE NOVELTY AND ENORMITY OF THE INDUSTRIAL CITY

The rapid growth and change of Manchester—in population, in commercial importance, and in character and social structure—is well documented, and cannot be reviewed in this article. However, a few aspects of the rise of Manchester must be recalled if we are to evaluate the chosen writings in their correct context.

It is impossible to give the beginnings of Manchester's boom a precise date, but there is much evidence that far-reaching change had struck an otherwise ordinary market town well before the 1770's. Writing in 1795, Aikin recorded that the growth of Manchester had been remarkable even in the period 1730 to 1770, but he drew particular attention to "the prodigious extension . . . of the Manchester manufactures"[2] which had been taking place since then. In the late eighteenth century and early nineteenth century, the city became, in the retrospective view of Marshall and other historians, a new "unique element in English society, a factory town," and from this it was soon transformed into "the foremost industrial city of the nineteenth century."[3]

The rate of development and innovation astounded all commentators of the period. The population grew rapidly from some 30,000 in the 1770's to well over 70,000 in 1801 when the first official census was taken, and to about 130,000 in 1821, and 243,000 in 1841. The increase in population in the 1820's and 1830's was the result more of immigration than of the excess of births over deaths.[4] In 1816, it was estimated that "not one half of the adult inhabitants, perhaps not more than one third, are natives of Manchester."[5] Even in 1851, only 28 per cent of the adults were Manchester-born, while almost a fifth were natives of Ireland.[6]

The changes in the nature of social relations and institutions in the community as a result of this growth were inevitably extensive and profound. "Before 1780 Manchester society had developed slowly under the impact of the commercial revolution. A small number of gentlemen and wealthy merchants, assisted by clergymen, lawyers, and physicians dominated the town."[7] But this changed rapidly over the next few decades as new men of wealth appeared. By the 1830's and 1840's, a new social and political order was gaining ascendancy in the region. This order soon acquired the denomination of the Man-

chester School and had national and international significance. In its
local manifestation, with which we are concerned, it was an order in
which the factory owners, bankers, merchants, and wealthy shopkeepers were dominant. At the same time, "[t]he old professional
classes and the new ones—newspaper editors, teachers, commercial
clerks, overseers, and engineers—propagated the views of the business men and administered their enterprises."[8]

To this profile, we must add a comment on the rapid growth of
smaller towns surrounding Manchester. In 1842, Love was able to
claim with obvious wonderment that "[w]ithin a radius of twelve miles
from the Manchester Exchange, there is a population little short of
one million, the greater portion of which is engaged, directly or
indirectly, in manufactures."[9] As early as 1795, Aikin had referred to
Manchester as the heart of a vast system of manufacturing. By the
1830's and 1840's, this was even more so. In 1844, the point was made
graphically by Faucher in an oft-quoted passage.

> Nothing is more curious than the industrial topography of
> Lancashire. Manchester, like a diligent spider, is placed in
> the centre of the web, and sends forth roads and railways
> towards its auxiliaries, formerly villages, but now towns,
> which serve as outposts to the grand centre of industry.[10]

The changes which were taking place in the center of Manchester,
and in the town's physical pattern and ecological structure, were
striking.

> During most of the eighteenth century the greater part of
> the inhabitants had lived within a quarter of a mile of the
> medieval centre of the town, . . . but in the second half of
> the century leading inhabitants began to complain of the
> congestion of the streets and courts leading into the Mar-
> ketplace. The centre of the town began to move in the last
> decade of the century when the merchants, in order to
> secure more open locations, turned some of the residences
> of the wealthy on the periphery of the old town into ware-
> houses.[11]

This was one of the earliest responses of the town to what Marshall
sees as "the needs of expanding business and the pressures of population." These needs were soon to change the very shape and form of
Manchester and to make it conform to "the requirements of the

industrial entrepreneurs." The requirements he lists were "sites for the factories, habitations for their 'hands,' and facilities for the concentration of business activities." As the "mills and factories were erected along the rivers and canals," the new population of operatives "burst through the limits of the old town and settled in slums around the factories."

One of the most detailed descriptions of the way in which the center was set in the midst of the whole is provided by Engels.

> Manchester contains, at its heart a rather extended commercial district, perhaps half a mile long and about as broad, and consisting almost wholly of offices and warehouses. Nearly the whole district is abandoned by dwellers, and is lonely and deserted at night; only watchmen and policemen traverse its narrow lanes with their dark lanterns.[12]

Around this commercial area, Engels then explains, there were "unmixed working people's quarters, stretching like a girdle, averaging a mile and a half in breadth," and beyond these in turn were the areas inhabited by the middle and upper class population which had leap-frogged over the girdle of working-class houses. Writing twelve years earlier, Kay[13] had already emphasized one of the main points made by Engels. After referring to the central divisions of the city as being occupied mainly by warehouses and shops, Kay wrote that there were "a few streets of dwellings of the more wealthy inhabitants," but that "Manchester, properly so called, is chiefly inhabited by shopkeepers and the labouring classes." Even "the superior servants [of the] opulent merchants" tended to "inhabit the suburban townships" rather than immediate peripheries of the center.[14] Faucher vividly confirmed the contrast drawn by Engels between the city center during the daytime and at night, and he dwelt explicitly on some of its implications.

> [A]t the very moment when the engines are stopped, and the counting houses closed, everything which was the thought—the authority—the impulsive force—the moral order of this immense industrial combination, flies from the town, and disappears in an instant. The rich man spreads his couch amidst the beauties of the surrounding country, and abandons the town to the operatives, publicans, mendicants, thieves, and prostitutes, merely taking

the precaution to leave behind him a police force, whose duty it is to preserve some little of material order in this pellmell of society.[15]

Faucher concluded that Manchester was not a place of beauty or of leisure, and he seemed to doubt that it ever could be.

Within this city, there were glaring disparities between the rich and the poor in every conceivable respect. Yet the bourgeoisie remained seemingly oblivious and insensitive to the social conditions of the workers. According to Engels, the daily journeys to town of the wealthier residents from the suburbs were effected along routes which concealed the circumstances of the operatives from their eyes.[16] "There they live," Cooke Taylor wrote, in independent corroboration, "hidden from the view of the higher ranks by piles of stores, mills, warehouses, and manufacturing establishments, less known to their wealthy neighbours, . . . than [to] the inhabitants of New Zealand or Kamtschatka."[17]

The way in which Manchester was transformed and restructured in the 50-year period prior to the 1830's and 1840's is evidence of some of the most powerful forces of change ever experienced in urban history. How was it possible for the whole structure of a well-established town to change in this way? Contemporary attempts to answer this general question were often confused, but all concurred on the novelty, power, and dynamism of what they saw. Thus Kay had no doubt that "a stranger visiting Manchester regards with wonder the ingenuity and comprehensive capacity" of the city. He considered that "the sudden creation of the mighty system of commercial organization" based on Manchester attested to "the power and dignity of man."[18] Cooke Taylor, writing of his first visit to Lancashire in the 1830's, recalls that the "forest of chimneys pouring forth volumes of steam and smoke, forming an inky canopy which seemed to embrace and involve the entire place," made him feel that he was "in the presence of those two mighty and mysterious agencies, fire and water . . . ."[19] Tocqueville perceived Manchester as a "foul drain [from which] the greatest stream of human industry flows out to fertilize the whole world," a "filthy sewer [from which] pure gold flows." He saw it as the place where "humanity attains its most complete development and its most brutish."[20] Even Engels, the bitterest of all observers, wrote that "the history of South Lancashire contains some of the greatest marvels of modern times,"[21] while Faucher viewed the town "as an agglomeration the most extraordinary, the most interesting, and in some respects, the most monstrous, which the progress of society has presented."[22]

The general tone of all such accounts leaves us in no doubt of their authors' very strong responses to the new phenomenon which they were attempting to describe and comprehend.

III. SELECTED WRITINGS OF THE 1830's AND 1840's

A. *Friedrich Engels*

Our first conception of Manchester—as a product of technological, economic, and social forces, but a product that was bound to continue changing radically—is represented by Engels. His analysis is the most coherent and comprehensive of any that we have. It is therefore easier to delineate, and it bears other advantages which derive from the nature of his personal experiences in the city. Engels first came to Manchester when he was only 22 years of age, but in about 18 months of deep involvement, he came to know it in an almost intuitive way. In many respects his description is comparable to that of a modern participant observer. He claimed to know Manchester as intimately as his own native town, and more intimately than most of its residents. His account is very detailed, yet also fresh because his observations are those of an outsider. In addition, his is the only analysis we have of early industrial Manchester which can be compared with ecological studies of twentieth-century cities. Unlike most of these, however, Engels's account is presented to us as an integral part of a broader conception of the new industrial society as a whole.

To appreciate Engels's account, we must consider his overall conceptual framework. In essence he saw the Industrial Revolution as transforming society through a series of interlocking processes. The first of these was triggered by mechanical inventions. The factories in which the machines were concentrated as a result of technological imperatives could only be erected through large and increasing investments of capital; furthermore, the more profitable the enterprises were, the larger they became. From this, all else followed. There developed a concentration of wealth, followed by the concentration of large populations around the factories. "The rapid extension of manufacture demanded hands, wages rose, and troops of workmen migrated from the agricultural districts of the towns."[23]

Concentration, polarization, and urbanization were thus interrelated processes. Great cities became the stage on which, and through which, the drama was enacted. One net effect was, as Hobs-bawm forcefully interprets Engels, that "capitalism pitchforks the new proletariat, often composed of immigrants from pre-industrial back-grounds, into a social hell in which they are ground down, underpaid, coerced, not only by the impersonal forces of competition but by the bourgeoisie as a class, which regards them as objects not as men, as 'labour' or 'hands' and not as human beings."[24] The ultimate outcome of the new ways of harnessing the "forces of Nature" was that

> [T]he social conflict, the war of each against all, is here openly declared . . . people regard each other only as useful objects; each exploits the other, and the end of it all is, that the stronger treads the weaker under foot, and that the powerful few, the capitalists, seize everything for them-selves, while to the weak many, the poor, scarcely a bare existence remains.[25]

The key to Engels's specifically urban analysis lies in his assess-ment of the relation between the social and residential situations of the bourgeoisie and the working classes. The various observations made by Engels together yield a particular explanation of the urban structure of Manchester in the 1840's.

The first major point is that the segregation of the classes was thoroughly institutionalized, and was reflected in the very physical structure of the town; the second is that the bourgeoisie was insensi-tive to, and in large measure unaware of, the circumstances of the poor; the third is that retailers, responsive to the requirements of their businesses and to differential land values, took up a significant position in the new urban pattern; and the fourth is that the whole structure was unplanned but systematic. We may also recall how Engels explained that segregation and separation were not simply between the bourgeoisie and the workers, but between gradations of them, particularly in the case of the bourgeoisie.

Engels is amazed at how "the whole crazy fabric still hangs to-gether." This "crazy fabric" could not, however, be expected to re-main unchanged. Engels estimated that the bourgeoisie "dwelt on a soil that is honeycombed, and may any day collapse . . . ."[26] Then, inevitably, the social and ecological divisions of the fractured city would either disintegrate or just wither away. It is in this sense that Engels was centrally concerned with "potential man." He clearly also had compassion for "suffering man," but he considered the social and economic structure of the city to be so crazy that there was no point to philanthropy or to meliorative measures. The dignity of man could only be re-established in a completely changed social order, albeit one based on industry and commerce.

Part of Engels's purpose was to explain why piecemeal reform could never improve the conditions of the working classes. However, his sweeping prediction of imminent revolution was proved wrong by history. Some of the reasons for this can be found in the writings of his contemporaries. This is not to suggest that his contemporaries "understood" Manchester any better. But, with the benefit of hindsight, we can see that Engels failed to give sufficient weight to certain "facts," and that the attitudes, opinions, and beliefs of his contemporaries were among these "facts."

B. *J. P. Kay*

Unlike Engels, none of the writers whom I take as more concerned with "suffering man" than "potential man" attempted a systematic analysis of the city as a whole. Instead, each focused on partial aspects of the city or particular problems facing the society. Most of them believed that the city would endure in the form in which they found it, but some believed passionately that certain particular aspects of the new urban-industrial scene could, and should, be changed without disrupting the entire social and economic order. I first consider Kay, who, in his essay of 1832, took the general view that the poverty and misery of the vast majority of the city's dwellers was a "disease" which could, and would, be "cured."[27]

Kay was a physician, 28 years of age, practising at a dispensary for the poor. He came from a prosperous middle-class family in Rochdale with banking connections, but he had studied medicine at Edinburgh University before returning to practise in Manchester for five years before he wrote his essay. His professional work brought him into direct contact with the poor, and in 1831-32 he was appointed secretary to the Manchester Board of Health, established to combat the threat of cholera. Some 15 to 20 pages of his essay give us factual statements drawn from the reports of inspectors charged by the Board of Health to investigate sanitary and housing conditions in the town, but our main interest lies in his general conception of the nature of the society in which he lived.

Kay believed that what he called the "loathsome haunts of poverty and vice" could be removed from Manchester, and that the self-interest of the bourgeoisie and the amelioration of poverty and squalor went hand in hand. But this was a difficult position for him to defend. He recognized that "we have arrived at a great moral and political crisis," that this was "a restless era", and that some (un-specified) "intellectual errors" and "moral deviations" of the past have brought society to "the gates of suffering."[28] Yet he argued that "[t]he evils here unreservedly expressed, so far from being the necessary consequences of the manufacturing system, have a remote and acci-dental origin, and might, by *judicious mangement*, be entirely re-moved."[29] He believed in society's evolutionary capacity "to reform and renovate its fabric."[30] His writing carries strong overtones of an organic view of society: the evils he sees are difficult to cure because "every part of the system appears necessary to the preservation of the whole."[31]

When Kay becomes more specific, he produces a long list of factors which he sees as directly affecting the conditions of workers. Ignorance, drunkenness, lack of moral dignity, dissipation, and im-providence are among the root causes. Despite numerous admissions of the extremity of the material conditions of the poor, Kay still sees their low "character" and "morals" as basic causes of their plight. "It is melancholy to perceive how many of the evils suffered by the poor flow from their own ignorance and moral errors."[32] Yet he accuses others of prejudice, and offers us a sympathetic explanation of how wretched conditions of life render continual intoxication excusable.[33]

Kay was torn between the humanitarianism of an enlightened physician and middle-class moralism. While he is compassionate in some passages, in others he is carried away by moral indignation as, for example, when he writes about the Irish, whom he regarded as a menace to the other workers. "Debased alike by ignorance and pauperism, they have discovered, with the savage, what is the minimum means of life, upon which existence may be prolonged." He considered that the habits of the Irish were "contagious" and were largely responsible for the demoralization of the rest of the workers.[34]

There is constant ambivalence in Kay's mind over the entire question of urban-industrial life. He regards Manchester as the prod-uct of a commerce which "surrounds man with innumerable inven-tions" and has "a constant tendency to multiply, without limit, the comforts of existence . . . ."[35] Yet he considered large sections of Manchester's population to be "a squalid and debilitated race, who inherit from their parents disease, sometimes deformity, often vice, and always beggary," and he detects in the town a "natural progress of barbarous habits."[36]

The way in which Kay reconciles these, and other, seeming contradictions, is by attributing the conditions he reports to unfortunate circumstances: the old order had been disrupted too rapidly, and "the disruption of natural ties had created a wide gulf between the higher and lower orders of the community, across which, the scowl of hatred banishes the smile and love of charity . . . ."[37] But he constantly repeats his basic view that "the evils affecting the working classes, so far from being the necessary results of the commercial system, furnish evidence of a disease . . . ."[38]

Kay prescribed a wide range of different remedies, which are unambiguous evidence that he considered far-reaching change imperative. His prescription took multiple forms,[39] but his fundamental assumption was as clearly that reform was possible. His concern for "suffering man" is evident throughout his essay, but so is his conviction that society must be preserved in its existing form. Despite an attempt to appear noncontentious and apolitical, his essay shows that he was a Liberal and an ardent Free Trader.[40]

For a full appreciation of Kay's work, we need to examine the way in which he presented it to the public. In an Introductory Letter to the essay, he drew distinctions between the aristocrats, merchants, and manufacturers of the country, and exonerated each group in turn. He first wrote apologetically on behalf of the aristocrats, pointing out that few "of their order resided in or near the large industrial towns," and that their visits were too few and too transient to allow them to gain "any correct knowledge of the moral and physical conditions of the poor." He is equally at pains to explain why the merchants were not more responsible to the conditions of the masses: "The pure merchant is seldom in immediate contact with the people," and "no association exists between him and them." When he finally turns to the manufacturers, he again starts by enlisting sympathy for them. They were, he claims, "staggering under the burdens of an enormous taxation and a restricted commerce," and they had to contend with "organized associations of the working classes," with "large funds" subscribed against them, and with various other "most flagrant excesses."[41]

Recalling Kay's own social position, it is not surprising that his views about the lack of response by aristocrats, merchants, and manufacturers are stated apologetically and under the cover of pleas of the self-interest of the bourgeoisie.[42] Many of the qualifications in his text were probably also intended to make his most forthright passages acceptable. Despite his obviously genuine concern for "suffering man," he was unable or unwilling to abandon the social stance and political doctrines of his class.

C. *W. Cooke Taylor*

Cooke Taylor's book of 1842 differs from Kay's in several important respects. Yet there is an underlying similarity in their conceptions of Manchester. Like Kay, Cooke Taylor was basically ambivalent about the city: he expressed compassion for the poor but identified with the bourgeoisie. Unlike Kay, however, he had little faith in reform, believing instead that the plight of "suffering man" would in due course be alleviated partly through what he conceived of as "self-correcting tendencies" in the process of industrialization, and partly through the ultimate compassion and common sense of the middle classes.

To appreciate the full significance of Cooke Taylor's book we must, however, examine it as a whole. First, it is an account of the manufacturing districts of Lancashire, and especially of "the Factory System," rather than an essay on Manchester itself. Second, despite Cooke Taylor's protestation that "a life spent in retirement, and devoted to literature" had left him "free from prejudices of party," it is evident from the text that he was highly partisan. His claim that his "sole anxiety was to tell the truth, the whole truth, and nothing but the truth,"[43] rings hollow in the light of his open sympathy in the book with the principles of free trade. (The book was actually sponsored by the Anti-Corn Law League, though this was not public knowledge at the time of publication.) Third, Cooke Taylor was not a Mancunian. Born in Ireland, he spent most of his life in London as a man of letters, and he only visited Lancashire as an interested political observer. Finally, Cooke Taylor takes a much broader historical perspective than Kay. In this respect his writing can in some ways be more meaningfully compared with that of Engels.

Like Engels, Cooke Taylor recognizes and stresses that industrial *society* is a new phenomenon. He writes that the "factory system is a modern creation" and that the inventions which led to its existence had passed "so rapidly through their age of infancy that they had taken their position in the world and firmly established themselves before there was time to prepare for their reception."[44] But he draws very different implications from this than Engels does. He is confident that the evils associated with factories will somehow be alleviated once society comes to terms with industrialism. Cooke Taylor's supreme confidence in the inevitability of a happy outcome was scarcely typical of the times, and his reasoning is in places difficult to credit. For example, while he recognized the demographic and cultural realities of industrial towns, he claimed that large-scale urbanization was an accident of history. He saw no *essential* reason why industrialism should lead to large towns or to the squalor and poverty associated with them. He was fascinated by the country mills he visited, and thought that one of the factory system's self-correcting tendencies would be the dispersal of population away from large towns.[45] His reasons for believing this are not clear. He simply asserted that it was "a misfortune of the factory system that it took its sudden start at a moment when the entire energies of the British legislature were preoccupied with the emergence of the French Revolution . . . [so that] large towns crept unnoticed into existence . . . ."[46] This argument is very curious, for it implies that Cooke Taylor thought that, at any ordinary period, the growth of towns would have been, and should have been, controlled by legislation. Yet in all other respects he consistently argued for the minimum of legislative control.

Another striking difference between Cooke Taylor and Engels was that Engels saw Manchester as a classic example of the industrial town, while Cooke Taylor saw it as an aberrant example. "Contrary to general belief," he wrote, "experience has shown me that Manchester does not afford a fair specimen of the factory population in any of the conditions of its existence . . . ."[47] He thus took greater interest in the surrounding towns where "the influence of factories could be seen undisturbed by the perturbations of an immigrant and fluctuating population," and unperturbed also by a series of other "special evils" which he thought afflicted Manchester as a result of the rapidity of its growth.[48] Associated with this difference between Engels and Cooke Taylor was the latter's belief that the confusion and suffering which resulted from the factory system would disappear after the difficult task of readjustment was completed. He argued that one "result from the large amount of capital invested in factories is the creation of a perceived identity of interest between the employer and the employed."[49] Yet he stressed quite as strongly as other writers that the great divide between rich and poor, and especially their separation "into districts in which relative poverty and wealth form the demarcation of the frontiers," was an "evil" of "fearful magnitude."[50] And he commented critically and forthrightly on the social exclusion of the workers by the bourgeoisie.

> I love the men of Manchester, but I will not flatter them and I tell them that they have done much to alienate from them the affection of the working classes. I would say to them, You have public places of recreation, Zoological and

Botanical Gardens, but have you rendered them accessible
to the operative? Have you not, on the contrary, availed
yourself of the most flimsy excuses to shut every door of
recreation against him? Does the working man believe your
excuses? Ask him, and he will laugh in your face.[51]

Cooke Taylor's general assessments stemmed from a similar political stance to that of Kay, but he refrained from making any recom-
mendations for the alleviation of the plight of "suffering man." He
did, however, appeal strongly to manufacturers for common sense.
Thus, for example, he unabashedly stressed that "workers are capital"
and should be well treated for that reason alone.

[T]hose engaged in factories are not mere labourers: they
are strictly and truly *educated* labourers, whose training has
cost something. The proprietor cannot treat them like neg-
roes . . .; if he permits any waste of human life, he
consents to a waste of his own capital: no small portion of it
is invested in the lives of his workmen . . . .[52]

To an even greater extent than Kay, his pleas on behalf of "suffering man" are linked to the self-interest of the bourgeoisie. The
ambivalence is similar though the observations and arguments often
differ. Whereas Kay could not overlook the immediate pressing day-
to-day problems which confronted him as a local doctor, and was thus
compelled to advocate a series of practical reforms, Cooke Taylor
largely ignored the slums, affected a neutral stance, and indulged in a
great deal of general moralism and quasi-historical reflection.

D. *Richard Parkinson*

I now turn to a short pamphlet written by Richard Parkinson in
1841.[53] Parkinson's writing on Manchester was more detached than
that of either Kay or Cooke Taylor, and also more keenly analytical.
Parkinson was directly involved in Manchester life as a local clergyman, but also distanced from it by virtue of his deep religious interpretation of the state of man. He wrote forthrightly, but he refrained from identifying himself closely with either the bourgeoisie or
the workers.

Parkinson came from a yeoman family in North Lancashire, but
was educated at Cambridge University. He wrote profusely on a
diversity of scholarly subjects, though his writing on Manchester was

guided by an overriding concern to analyze aspects of local life for practical and philanthropic purposes.

His writing attracted a good deal of attention. He was quoted by both Engels and Cooke Taylor, and is often referred to by modern historians. The paragraph from his pamphlet that has attracted most attention is that in which he, like others, stressed the distance between the rich and poor in Manchester—the gap, for his purposes, between the "givers" and "receivers."

> [T]here is no town in the world where the distance between the rich and poor is so great, or the barrier between them so difficult to be crossed . . . . The separation between the different classes, and the consequent ignorance of each others' habits and condition, are far more complete in this place than in any country of the older nations of Europe, or the agricultural portions of our own kingdom . . . . I mention this not as a matter of blame, I state it simply as a *fact*.[54]

This passage is, however, misleading when taken out of context. A full reading of Parkinson shows that he was not simply repeating the observations of many others on the gulf between the rich and the poor. He was primarily concerned to show that "the great impediment in the way of any judicious and effectual relief of the poor" was ignorance, and his central theme is that urban society in Manchester *as a whole* was fragmented. He anticipated twentieth-century views on the eclipse of community among the urban middle classes, attributing "ignorance of each other" among the rich to three circumstances: their geographic dispersal in the new suburbs, their division into different "branches of trade," and their differences of religion and politics, which split them into sects and divided them into parties.[55] Hence there was a lack of communication about their problems even among the bourgeoisie. It was, he wrote, only in the face of crises and calamities that "religious opinions, party prejudices, and commercial rivalries are scattered to the winds," but to little avail, because there "*then* appears, in a form which . . . would be ludicrous were it not melancholy, our utter ignorance of each other, and of the actual condition of the poor."[56] But, very significantly, he stressed that the poor also lived under peculiar difficulties of considerable ignorance of each other.

> They have neither a common origin, nor a common object
> . . . [other than] that of obtaining, it may be at each other's
> expense, a mean and precarious subsistence; they have no
> tie of communion and fellowship with each other, beyond
> the accidental circumstances of locality, or a participation
> in the same trials and privations. Hence they too are often
> mutually deceiving and deceived.[57]

The great gap between rich and poor is thus only one aspect of
Parkinson's analysis. The absence of mutual intercourse *in general* is a
major factor in his assessment of Manchester society. Like Cooke
Taylor and others, he attributed this to the recency and rapidity of
the development of the city: "most other towns have been young
before they became old . . . ." But Manchester had no infancy.

> We have not *grown*, but accumulated; we are not stratified,
> but a conglomerate. We are but, as it were, a *debris* which
> the vast whirlpool of human affairs has deposited here in
> one of its eddies, associated but not united, contiguous but
> not connected.[58]

Rather like Engels, Parkinson is left wondering how Manchester
coheres, for he notes that irregularities and anomalies, which would
not be tolerated elsewhere, are in Manchester regarded as natural.
But, unlike Engels, he wrote for practical and philanthropic purposes, clearly concerned with relieving the plight of "suffering man."

E. *The Eulogists: Robert Lamb, J. P. Culverwell, and J. S. Gregson*

From writers whose visions and conceptions of Manchester were,
in one way or another, formed through deep human concern, I turn
to those who may be seen as "bourgeois eulogists" of the city. It is,
however, not a clean break. Among the eulogists were some who did
express concern about what was happening in Manchester even if
their main emphases were not humanitarian. This is well illustrated
by Robert Lamb, who was a local clergyman of similar social orgins to
Parkinson. Unlike Parkinson, however, Lamb wrote on Manchester
mainly for a middle-class magazine readership.[59]

In an article published in 1848, Lamb opens with the common
reference to the division of Manchester into rich and poor, and he
refers to clergymen as "one order of men . . . who have the privilege
of being acquainted with both."[60] He then describes some of the
squalor of Manchester, refers to the conditions of insecurity of work

and residence of the operatives, and their "besetting sin" of drink. He even pleads with his middle-class readers for understanding of the plight of the poor, but his tone is patronizing and arrogant, and he criticizes the "mistake of almost all the writers on our manufacturing population," whom he sees as *too* sympathetic to the poor. Thus he attacks Cooke Taylor for whom, he claims, "every suffering operative is indiscriminately an object of admiration" and "every foul-mouthed Chartist is invested with the dignity of a noble-minded patriot struggling for the freedom of his country."[61] He makes no constructive suggestions for the alleviation of Manchester's problems. On the contrary, he simply urges his readers to gird themselves "for the struggle against the powers of darkness . . . ."[62] But he responds with adulation to other aspects of the Manchester scene. Thus he reacts ecstatically to the beauty of machinery and to the organizational marvels of large mills. He concedes that "the engine 'Manchester' now and then runs off the rails," but he claims that "it is soon right again, and away it goes."[63]

The most significant difference between Lamb and writers like Kay and Cooke Taylor is that Lamb does not betray any ambivalence towards the city and its problems. Despite expressions of concern, he is unequivocal in his attitude to Manchester. He admires it, and he openly and unambiguously aligns himself with the bourgeoisie and their values.

There were, however, other local writers who wrote about Manchester with even fiercer pride. An excellent example of this group is J. P. Culverwell, a minor and brash writer. The son of a Manchester manufacturer, he was educated locally and then joined his father's firm. He was apparently not successful. He retired from business when still in his thirties, and left Manchester for good. Before leaving the city, he was an active member of the Manchester Athenaeum and the local Young Men's Anti-Monopoly Association.

Culverwell reasoned that the new social order in Manchester could not be the result of chance, and must therefore have a "mission" and a "new Destiny, ill-understood, yet instinctively believed by all."[64] Like Cooke Taylor, he admitted that "ages of transition are always painful in human progress," but he had no doubt that the new society would "prepare the way for a higher sphere of social and moral development."[65] Manchester had, he claimed, already "done miracles": it had "found Lancashire in a morass" but was now "the high Capitol [*sic*] of the world's industry."[66] He defended Manchester against all and every criticism. Thus, for example, he claimed that Manchester would not remain smoky, for owners of factories would soon "be compelled to cause [their furnances] to consume their own smoke."[67] He regarded life in Manchester as far superior to life in the country. If it were not so, why did the immigrants not return to the countryside?

In direct conflict with Kay and others, he flatly denied that there was any physical degeneration in the manufacturing districts. In response to an article in the *Manchester Guardian* in August, 1843, which argued that the height of the people was declining, and that recruiting officers were having difficulty in finding men suitable for the army, Culverwell wrote:

> Does this difficulty arise from a deterioration, or from an improvement of the race? Is it that the men are not big enough, or that they are too big to stoop to the degradation of selling their liberty, and becoming instruments of slaughter for eighteen pence a day?[68]

Culverwell regarded Manchester as the essence of progress. The only threats to the city which he saw lay in the growth of charitable institutions, and in the increase of "indiscriminate relief" given to the poor.

> Let no one cavil at these remarks, and say that they are dictated by an uncharitable feeling towards the poor . . . it is our duty to lessen the amount of suffering by withdrawing the premium which now exists upon idleness and improvidence.[69]

Culverwell emerges as a petty near-fanatic in his concern that Manchester should be allowed to develop unfettered by outside interference. His enthusiasm for the city was euphoric; his philosophy was crudely expressed, but quite clear.

A fair number of local professional and business men on occasion attempted to write about Manchester, partly, it seems, for profit, but perhaps also out of a simple desire to express themselves and their points of view on the town and their own milieu. One of these, a bookseller, J. S. Gregson, published a book written partly in doggerel verse and partly in prose, in which he dwelt on a variety of ill-assorted topics: the contrast between the new and the old in Manchester, the atmosphere of business in contrast to that of leisure at the race course, the Manchester subscription library, and the like. Gregson praised Manchester:

Speed on, my pen; and flow, thou gentle verse,
Whilst I the wonders of this town rehearse.[70]

But he is nonetheless critical of Manchester society and its ethos:

> The "lust of gold" . . . is too much the prevailing sin of
> Manchester . . . . A thorough Manchester Man sees more
> beauty in rows of red brick than he would in groves and
> "alleys green": he hears more music in the everlasting
> notion of the loom than he would in the songs of the lark
> or the nightingale.[71]

Gregson's writing leads us directly to the sixth conception listed in
the introduction to this paper. As Vicinus has shown, Manchester of
this period produced a significant working-class literature which
sought refuge either in an idealized past or in the world of literary
imagination.[72] There was here a frequent mixture of dismay and
admiration of urban-industrial society, and sometimes a nearly total
rejection of it. Taken as a whole, the working-class voices of the
industrial town stand in very sharp contrast to certain middle-class
responses, such as Lamb's to machine and factory as objects of adulation, or Culverwell's to the city as a progressive force. That praise and
appreciation of urban-industrialism is absent among working-class
writers may not surprise us. It is the seemingly almost total absence of
any strong articulated response to the city as such which is puzzling.[73]

IV. EVALUATION AND CONCLUSION

To begin an evaluation of the reports reviewed in this article, I
take up a comment made by Briggs in *Victorian Cities*. He writes that
"Manchester had its depth in the 1840s as well as its riches and
poverty . . . . It was by no means as raw as some of its shocked
visitors thought . . . . These sociologists who talk of the 'anonymity'
of the city should look again at the close personal relationships,
through friendship and marriage, without which a city like Manchester could never have developed either its own culture or its links with
the outside world."[74]

I take one aspect of Briggs's comment for granted: all cities
develop "establishments" and elites whose members are closely related in various ways. But this does not necessarily invalidate the
"sociological thesis" of urban anonymity. We have seen that Parkinson
(whom Briggs himself quotes) considered social fragmentation and
division as salient features of Manchester society. No sociologist has
ever suggested that top elites suffer from anonymity. The more

important aspect of Briggs's comment is, however, that it reminds us forcefully that there are different levels and orders of social reality. The "shocked visitors" and the local writers often dwelt on quite different aspects of Manchester life. We must therefore highlight the difference between the aims of a general history like that provided by Briggs and the type of analysis attempted in this article. The subject of Briggs's analysis was Manchester as a world city with great economic and political influence. This paper focuses instead on the internal structure of the city, and it should not surprise us that our analysis of Manchester is very different from that of Briggs.

The basic problem that arises in analyzing Manchester of the period on the basis of internal reports is precisely that locally-involved writers held such varied views. Even the few writers considered in this paper present us with a wide variety of visions and conceptions of the city. This is no doubt partly because we always find variation in urban life, but largely too because Manchester was a vibrant, complex, changing city *which different people perceived in different ways*. Yet I take it that *all* contemporary authors either represented or reflected "reality." In most respects the works reviewed cannot be directly compared; but we can move towards a snythesis of them, especially if we work with classifications which lead us to ask meaningful questions about the basic conceptions represented in each.

Returning now to our original working views of the city, Engels clearly has the strongest claim for showing any interest in "potential man." Some might argue that such an interest could also be attributed to Cooke Taylor, in that he believed that the future ideal situation would be one in which industry found its way into the countryside and might there become closely integrated with rural life. But this is stretching the conception of concern with "potential man" beyond usefulness.[75]

The essence of the attitudes expressed by most of those who were in varying degrees concerned with "suffering man" is not that the working classes had, or could strive for, a golden future of opportunity, but that their extreme suffering could and would be relieved. W. R. Greg, one of the Manchester manufacturers' most lucid spokesmen, gave us a clear and explicit statement of this view.

> We must carefully distinguish between poverty and destitution . . . . Poverty we do not consider an evil: destitution is one of the greatest evils. The former, it is probable, must always be the lot of the chief body of people in all populous countries: the latter need be the lot of a few

. . . . In a healthy condition of society, the earnings of the
labouring classes will be sufficient to support them in de-
cency and comfort . . . .[76]

It is this belief which essentially divides those concerned with
"potential man" from those with compassion for "suffering man."
Apart from Engels, Faucher was the only writer mentioned in this
paper who, seeing Manchester as "two towns in one," posed the
radical question: "is not that an unnatural state of society . . ." for "in
one portion, there is space, fresh air, and provision for health; and in
the other, everything which poisons and abridges existence . . . ."[77]
None of the local writers reviewed could bring himself to share
Faucher's views, let alone that of Engels.

Kay was the most insistent advocate of reform, and he was immediately challenged from a revolutionary stance.

The doctor is no friend to the oppressed operative . . .
[His] unreserved exposition of the astounding evils which,
in his enquiries, he found besetting the working classes are
truly creditable; but his attempts to apologize for them by
senseless sophistry, and to preserve the whole system, is no
less deserving of our most hearty reprobation.[78]

Such an objection was not, however, in keeping with any dominant views of the time; and it would appear to have received little
response. The objection to Kay's stance was based on his "organicism"
and his belief that "every part of the system was necessary to the
preservation of the whole." The system which Kay—and his critics—
had in mind was, however, essentially the factory or industrial system.
Kay did not see the *city* as a system, and he thought that improvements in the lot of the workers could be achieved through
"judicious management": by a series of administrative, urban, and
educational reforms. This theme was further developed by several of
his middle-class reviewers, and at least one stated Kay's position much
more concisely and categorically than he did.

The depression of health among the manufacturing population results more from municipal, social, domestic, and
moral evils, than from the nature of their employment.[79]

The factory system as such was healthy enough; it was the "fabric
of society" surrounding it that was "diseased." Extraordinary as it may
seem, Kay could not admit any direct connection between the indus-

trial system as such and the conditions he exposed in the slums of Manchester.

Cooke Taylor, also, was naive about the relation between industrialization and urbanization. His position is, in the final analysis, that there were some good employers and some bad ones. He blamed the bad ones, and criticized them for being blind to their own interests. Beyond that, he was prepared to leave it to the "self-correcting tendencies" of the factory system to improve the conditions of the workers. He clung to the belief that the worst features of their plight in the 1830's and 1840's were due to the disorganization of transition. Cooke Taylor's writing was, however, used by reformers, and was often linked with the work of others who advocated reform.

Parkinson's analysis is difficult to classify. In a sense, he was closer to Engels than to any of the reformers. Though he did not quite see Manchester as the scene of Engels's war of "each against all," he did stress the deep-rooted conflicts *between* rich and poor, as well as *among* both rich and poor. His reading of the situation was less affected—if at all—by identification with the bourgeoisie than were the interpretations of writers like Kay and Cooke Taylor.

The writers who sang a bourgeois eulogy of the city are most clearly represented in this paper by Lamb and Culverwell. But they were not alone. Kay's pride in Manchester was unshakeable despite his concerns and fears. Strong or weak traces of the Cobdenite spirit—a belief in the values of modernity, efficiency, vitality, and expansion—pervaded all local Manchester literature, expect for the few who specifically rejected its materialistic ethos, and even they were often of two minds, as is well illustrated by J. S. Gregson.

In the 1850's and 1860's, Manchester's municipal policies and reforms developed a momentum which soon caused some of the literature of the 1830's and early 1840's to seem outdated. In 1868, the middle classes of Manchester were sufficiently strong to start building a Town Hall which cost over a million pounds and took nine years to complete. In 1873, Kay (by then Sir James Kay-Shuttleworth and nearly 70 years old) was writing with greater confidence, but in the same vein as before.

> The North of England is a great laboratory, in which research is in progress for the solution of social problems . . . . The difference between revolutions made in three days and reforms spread over thirty years is like the contrast between the explosion of a mine and the slow growth of a great tree.[80]

In 1894, W. A. Shaw, a university professor of history and the son of a Manchester manufacturer, wrote a three-volume account of the city, which he presented to the world as "the life-story of Manchester, the leading modern mercantile municipality, one that has led the way in, and epitomized in her history, the commercial revolution which has cleft the history of our planet atwain with so deep a chasm of separation, that even now we cannot measure or bridge it."[81]

It may be noted that, despite the confusions and ambivalences in Kay's early book of 1832, the prescriptions he there advocated were of the kind applied in the second half of the century. That does not, of course, prove that the "analysis" he gave us was right; it implies no more than that his views were of the kind which the middle classes were prepared to embrace. It has often been argued that Engels was proved "wrong" by history because he overestimated the growing class awareness of the workers. Whatever the merits of that argument, I suggest that one of the most important points which Engels grossly underestimated was the strength and conviction with which the bourgeoisie held the values expressed both by out-and-out boosters and eulogists and by more restrained preachers and reformers. Like Parkinson, he recognized the "crazy fabric" and the fragmentation of Manchester, and he gave us a most convincing analysis of how and why it was so. But we must conclude that he did not fully appreciate the strengths of other rival visions and conceptions of the city.

NOTES

1. STEVEN MARCUS, ENGELS, MANCHESTER, AND THE WORKING CLASS 56 (London: Weidenfeld and Nicolson, 1974).

2. JOHN AIKIN, A DESCRIPTION OF THE COUNTRY FROM THIRTY TO FORTY MILES ROUND MANCHESTER 176 (NY: Augustus M. Kelley, new ed., 1968).

3. LEON S. MARSHALL, THE DEVELOPMENT OF PUBLIC OPINION IN MANCHESTER, 1780–1820, 14 (Syracuse: Syracuse U. Press, 1946).

4. Cannan, *The Growth of Manchester and Liverpool, 1801–1891*, 4 THE ECON. JOURNAL 111 at 113 (1894).

5. JOSEPH ASTON, A PICTURE OF MANCHESTER 25 (Manchester: J. Aston, Printer, 1816; reprinted by Morton, Didsbury, Manchester, 1969).

6. Marshall, *The Emergence of the First Industrial City: Manchester, 1750–1850*, in CAROLINE F. WARE, ed., THE CULTURAL APPROACH TO HISTORY 146 (NY: Columbia U. Press for the American Historical Association).

7. *Id.* at 146.

8. *Id.* at 145.

9. BENJAMIN LOVE, THE HAND-BOOK OF MANCHESTER 95 (Manchester: Love & Barton, 1842).

10. M. LEON FAUCHER, MANCHESTER IN 1844, 15 (London: Frank Cass, trans., ann., Member of the Manchester Athenaeum, 1969).

11. Marshall, *supra* note 6, at 143.

12. FRIEDRICH ENGELS, THE CONDITION OF THE WORKING CLASS IN ENGLAND 79 (London: Panther Books, 1969).

13. JAMES P. KAY, THE MORAL AND PHYSICAL CONDITION OF THE WORKING CLASSES EMPLOYED IN THE COTTON MANUFACTURE IN MANCHESTER 79-80 (London: Frank Cass & Co., 2d ed., 1832).

14. *Id.* at 20.

15. FAUCHER, *supra* note 10, at 26-27.

16. ENGELS, *supra* note 12, at 78-79.

17. W. COOKE TAYLOR, NOTES OF A TOUR IN THE MANUFACTURING DISTRICTS OF LANCASHIRE 13-14 (London: Frank Cass & Co., 1st ed., 1842; 3d ed., with intro. by W.H. Chaloner, 1968).

18. KAY, *supra* note 13, at 76-77.

19. COOKE TAYLOR, *supra* note 17, at 1-2.

20. ALEXIS DE TOCQUEVILLE, JOURNEYS TO ENGLAND AND IRELAND, 1835, 107-108 (London: Faber & Faber, ed., J. P. Mayer, trans., G. Lawrence & K. P. Mayer, 1958).

21. ENGELS, *supra* note 12, at 43.

22. FAUCHER, *supra* note 10, at 16.

23. ENGELS, *supra* note 12, at 50.

24. Hobsbawm, *Introduction*, in ENGELS, *supra* note 12, at 12.

25. ENGELS, *supra* note 12, at 58.

26. *Id.* at 52.

27. KAY, *supra* note 13. References to Manchester as a "diseased society" are found throughout the text.

28. *Id.* at 13.

29. *Id.*

30. *Id.* at 14.

31. *Id.* at 44. This and related parts of Kay's analysis drew an angry response from *The Union Pilot* (a weekly socialist newspaper of short duration) in its issues of April 14 & 21, 1832.

32. *Id.* at 5-6.

33. *Id.* at 26.

34. *Id.* at 21. Writing of the Irish in even stronger condemnatory tones was common at this period. *See, e.g.*, R. COBDEN, under the pen name "A Manchester Manufacturer," ENGLAND, IRELAND, AMERICA (London: P. Brown, 1835). Cobden referred to the influence of the Irish as "a moral cancer" that was spreading "throughout the entire mass of our labouring population," *Id.* at 18.

35. KAY, *supra* note 13, at 78-79.

36. *Id.* at 4, 81.

37. *Id.* at 49.

38. *Id.* at 79.

39. Kay's proposed remedies are scattered throughout his writing. They include the encouragement of manufacturers to take "an interest in the workers," but also to "constantly admonish them;" the urging of clergymen to take more interest in social problems and of the authorities to increase the number of police; wide-ranging legislation to regulate and control planning and house-building, and also to compel landlords to keep their properties in good repair; the spread of "substantial education" instead of simply teaching children to read and write.

40. It is relevant to note that later in life Kay devoted much of his time to philanthropic and educational work and to problems of trade unions and of industrial and social policy.

41. KAY, *supra* note 13, at 8-11.

42. It is also not surprising that *The Union Pilot*, April 14, 1832, wrote of Kay's publication "that whoever gives this work a patient perusal, will, we think, arrive at the conclusion that the chief incentive of the author . . . was to obtain by it a passport to the favour and patronage of master manufacturers."

43. COOKE TAYLOR, *supra* note 17, at v-vi.

44. *Id.* at 4.

45. *Id.* at 140.
46. *Id.* at 3.
47. *Id.* at 12-13.
48. *Id.* at 13.
49. *Id.* at 120.
50. *Id.* at 164.
51. *Id.* at 164-65.
52. *Id.* at 114.
53. RICHARD PARKINSON, THE PRESENT CONDITION OF THE LABOURING POOR IN MANCHESTER (London: Simpkin, Marshall, & Co., 1841). The pamphlet was addressed to the Churchwardens and Sidesmen of Manchester.
54. *Id.* at 12-13.
55. *Id.* at 7-8.
56. *Id.* at 14.
57. *Id.* at 11-12.
58. *Id.* at 11.
59. Lamb was a regular contributor to *Fraser's Magazine*, either under the pen name of "A Manchester Man" or anonymously.
60. Lamb, *The Manufacturing Poor*, anon. in 37 FRASER'S MAGAZINE 1 (No. 217, 1848).
61. *Id.* at 12.
62. *Id.* at 3-4.
63. Lamb, *Manchester*, under the pen name of "A Manchester Man," 47 FRASER'S MAGAZINE 626 (No. 282, 1853).
64. *Preface* in FAUCHER, *supra* note 10, at vi-vii. Culverwell was the translator and annotator of Leon Faucher's writings published in English as *Manchester in 1844*. To Faucher's text of some 35,000 words, Culverwell added over 16,000 of his own in the form of a preface and of copious footnotes in which he frequently took issue with Faucher's less favourable interpretations of Manchester.
65. *Id.* at viii.
66. FAUCHER, *supra* note 10, at f.n. 34.
67. *Id.*, at f.n. 30.
68. *Id.* at f.n. 35.
69. *Id.* at f.n. 26.
70. J.S. GREGSON, GIMCRACKIANA, OR FUGITIVE PIECES ON MANCHESTER MEN AND MANNERS OF TEN YEARS AGO, under the pen name of Geoffrey Gimcrack, 10 (Manchester: W. H. Jones, 1833).
71. *Id.* at 158-59.
72. Vicinus, *Literary Voices of an Industrial Town, Manchester, 1810–1870*, in H. J. DYOS & M. WOLFF, eds., 2 THE VICTORIAN CITY 739 (London: Routledge & Kegan Paul, 1973).
73. Further research may well resolve this puzzle, for there has so far been little study of various expressions of popular culture of the period. Yet we do know that many of the songs sung by workers in Manchester pubs were recorded. *See* DAVID AYERST, GUARDIAN: BIOGRAPHY OF A NEWSPAPER 47 (London: Collins, 1971).
74. ASA BRIGGS, VICTORIAN CITIES 110 (London: Pelican Books, 1968). In support of his 'depth' view of Manchester, Briggs might well have added a great deal more local evidence, such as the fact that, as early as 1837, the Manchester Athenaeum had over 1,200 members.
75. Robert Owen would be a much truer contender. *See* ROBERT OWEN, A NEW VIEW OF SOCIETY (London: Macmillan, new ed., 1972).
76. Greg, *Outbreak in the Manufacturing Districts*, 38 WESTMINSTER REVIEW 385 at 398 (No. 11, 1842).
77. FAUCHER, *supra* note 10, at 69–70. It is interesting to note that Culverwell, in his translation of Faucher, attempts to divert our attention from this passage by

writing of a new "scavenging-machine cart" which had, he claimed, cleaned up Manchester in recent years, making it "decidedly the cleanest large town in the kingdom." *Id.* at 69, f.n. 31.

78. THE UNION PILOT (April 14, 1832).

79. Anonymous, *Condition of the Working Classes, and the Factory Bill*, 36 WESTMINSTER REVIEW 396 (April, 1833).

80. SIR JAMES P. KAY-SHUTTLEWORTH, THOUGHTS AND SUGGESTIONS ON CERTAIN SOCIAL PROBLEMS vi (London: Longmans, Green, & Co., 1873).

81. W. A. SHAW, 1 MANCHESTER, OLD AND NEW vi (London: Cassell & Co., 1894).

Agrarian Organization and Urban Development[†]

BRYAN ROBERTS*

I. INTRODUCTION

MANCHESTER'S GROWTH at the end of the eighteenth century and the beginning of the nineteenth century signalled a new stage in urbanization. In previous centuries, the urban population had been small in proportion to the rural population and had been relatively unchanging.[1] The nineteenth century witnessed an ever-increasing concentration of the world's population in towns and cities. The basis for this new stage in urbanization was a factory industralization whose productivity accelerated the division of labor on a national and international scale and created economic opportunities in the towns far in excess of those available in agriculture. This pattern of urbanization is now transforming the underdeveloped world, including the notable example of São Paulo.

Conventional analysis has stressed that in the classic English case, the rural economy was thoroughly commercialized prior to urban-industrial development. By comparison, in underdeveloped countries like Brazil, the backwardness of the rural regions and its inhabitants is said to serve as an obstacle to economic or political development. This paper will compare the role of agrarian structure in the development of Manchester and São Paulo, concentrating on migration and the formation of an industrial labor force. The aim is to demonstrate the dangers in using the "classic" case of Manchester as a benchmark

---

* Reader in Sociology, University of Manchester.

† This paper is part of a research project in comparative urbanization financed by the British Social Science Research Council. I am grateful to Ms. Caroline Bedale for providing me with data on the Manchester case and for helpful discussions. I am also grateful to the Ford Foundation for a travel grant that made possible my attendance at the Stanford Conference in April, 1977. Finally, the comments of Alex Field were extremely useful in aiding me in this revision of the original conference paper.

against which to evaluate subsequent cases of urban-industrial growth.

The Manchester experience is unique in many respects. São Paulo is neither repeating the sequence of Manchester's growth nor is it simply a developing country version of that growth. Both cities were produced by the same underlying force: the development of industrial capitalism. Yet, each city experienced this change at different stages of economic development and within a different international context. Both cities have had similar importance in the consolidation and expansion of capitalism within their respective countries. Through the factory system and the massing together of a work-force totally dependent on wage labor, both cities contributed directly and indirectly to radical economic, social and political changes. The purpose of comparing Manchester and São Paulo is thus not to produce any single model of urban-industrial development. The interest of the comparison is that it shows that there are various paths to economic development under capitalism, and that political and social factors are as important in determining that development as are purely economic factors.

A framework for exploring the significance of the agrarian context for the development of industrial capitalism is provided by Marx's emphasis on the supply of labor.[2] The crucial factor in the development of industrial capitalism is the creation of a permanent industrial labor force which has little or no alternative to selling its labor to obtain the necessities of life. This process of primitive accumulation occurs with the weakening and eventual destruction of a relatively self-sufficient agrarian economy based on rural artisans and small peasant farmers. The destruction of this economy is achieved either through direct political mechanisms such as taxation and land enclosure, or through the action of market forces in concentrating and commercializing production. A labor supply is thereby created which the capitalist can use and organize as he sees fit, enabling him to conduct production without the necessity of relying on relatively independent producers who could control both the quantity and the quality of output. Labor thus becomes a commodity to be bought and sold like any other. This process has the additional consequence of generalizing people's dependence on the market and creating opportunities for the sale of industrial goods.

Primitive accumulation is not a natural process. It depends in varying degrees on political action and compulsion. For example, even market forces are bolstered by a legal apparatus to enforce contractual obligations. The degree of overt political intervention needed to create and maintain a supply of free labor is a crucial variable in shaping government institutions and urban development, affecting class formation and economic organization.

This is the analytic framework within which the following discussion will be placed. The focus on labor will provide a basis for comparison between two cities whose organization and historical position differ in so many particulars.

The process of urbanization in Manchester will be traced through two phases. First, the agrarian structure of Lancashire prior to the Industrial Revolution will be detailed. It will become evident in the course of this section that the changes which occurred in Lancashire prior to the nineteenth century resulted in an agrarian structure which was almost completely commercialized on the eve of the urban Industrial Revolution. Second, the paper will focus on the process of urbanization which occurred in and around Manchester in the nineteenth century. In describing that process, emphasis will be placed on the interrelated topics of demographic change, migration and the creation of an urban labor force. The description of Manchester's urbanization will be traced through the late nineteenth century, when the rapid changes which had characterized the area began to slow. Finally, the section will highlight the implications of the process of urbanization on Manchester's class structure and its political system.

After analysis of the development of urbanization in Manchester, the paper will then focus on the São Paulo case. After outlining the agrarian structure which provided the background for the urbanization of São Paulo, the focal point will be the role of the coffee boom in the subsequent development of Brazil. Unlike the Manchester example, the rural areas of Brazil were still in the throes of change when the process of urbanization began. Second, the paper will describe the urbanization of São Paulo in its early years. Third, the legacies of the city's early urbanization with respect to class and political structure will be discussed. It will become apparent that the different economic bases in Manchester and São Paulo resulted in markedly different political and social characteristics in the two cities. Finally, the paper will discuss the growth of São Paulo in later years, focusing on the dynamics of the change, its limits, and its impact on the development of Brazil as a whole.

II. THE MANCHESTER EXPERIENCE

A. *Background: Agrarian Structure of Lancashire Prior to The Industrial Revolution*

This section will outline the nature of the changes which occurred in rural Lancashire in the years prior to the nineteenth century. The central distinguishing aspect of the Manchester case is that the agrarian structure which resulted from these changes was one which was almost completely commercialized prior to the time of urban-industrial development. "[I]n no economy was the countryside so closely integrated into the commercial circuit; nowhere were the local pockets of self-sufficiency so broken down"[3] as in Lancashire on the eve of the Industrial Revolution.

1. *Aspects of agrarian development.*

Several aspects of Lancashire's agrarian development provide evidence of its increasingly commercialized nature. First, the agriculture had been modified so that, by the end of the eighteenth century, farming had become predominantly capitalist. A system of land tenure evolved under which the vast majority of land was owned by a few large landowners.[4] These landowners directly exploited only a small proportion of their land and leased the rest to farmers in small to medium-sized parcels. During the course of the eighteenth century, the leasing system changed from one of relatively long-term leasing to one of short-term leases.[5]

Since Lancashire did not have an extensive field-crop agriculture, the country was not affected to any great extent by the legal movement to enclose open fields. Most farm land in Lancashire was pasture, with 21 percent of farm land given over to corn and green crops.[6] Lancashire still depended on other counties and foreign imports for about three-fourths of its consumption of corn crops.[7] The possibility of capturing such market opportunities stimulated local farmers and landowners to reclaim extensive tracts of marsh and waste land. By 1948, reclamation of the mossland of South-West Lancashire had turned this area into a major arable farming region.[8]

This pattern of agricultural tenure and development was followed by the expansion of wage labor in the agricultural sector by the end of the eighteenth century. Analysis of the position of rural laborers at this time reveals several ways in which this trend manifested itself.[9] The practice of retaining live-in farm servants became less common, in part because of the expense of feeding such workers. Lancashire farmers came to rely on a large reserve of casual labor which was drawn mainly from the locality. Few farm laborers had access to significant amounts of land to farm for themselves, and the chances of attaining social mobility through the letting of land were less than elsewhere in England. Family employment appears to have been the rule among laborers: wives and children did agricultural work at harvest or other times, or found industrial or service work.

Hence, while land ownership became increasingly centralized in the hands of a few, the group of agricultural wage laborers was growing. This picture should not, however, be overdrawn: the degree of agricultural concentration in Lancashire never attained the dimensions of such counties as Norfolk or Wiltshire. Even by 1851, when the commercial transformation of agriculture was almost complete, there were still approximately 16,000 farmers in Lancashire as compared with 24,000 agricultural laborers.[10] Nonetheless, the pressures towards an increasing commercialization of farm production were strong in Lancashire and, by the 1860's, the county had become an important center of dairy farming. It was one of the few counties in which employment in agriculture was expanding in the years from 1851 to 1861.[11]

The second facet of Lancashire's agrarian structure which demonstrates the degree of commercialization was the development of rural industry prior to the urban-industrial growth of the nineteenth century. Lancashire was considered to be backward in its agriculture as compared with other counties, and contemporaries laid the blame on industry.[12] By the end of the eighteenth century, Lancashire had one of the highest proportions of people employed in industrial occupations of any county in England. This industry was primarily based on domestic hand-loom weaving. Although by the early eighteenth century weaving shops had been established in the towns of the county, most of the industry was carried out in cottages in the rural districts.[13]

A survey of various regions of Lancashire illustrates the extent of rural industrialization. In those areas of South and Central Lancashire that were to provide most of the migrant population to Manchester and its industrial towns, domestic industry had become the predominant form of employment with agriculture as an increasingly supplementary occupation. The process of industrialization also had a long history in Saddleworth, an important center of the woolen industry. Of the 70 local residents entered in the register of baptisms in 1722, 50 are scheduled under the general trade description of clothier.[14] A local informant estimated that there were 10,000 weavers in the three miles around Tyldesley.[15] Another contemporary obser-

ver described the 40 mile area around Manchester as one of the
greatest industrial regions of the day, estimating that by 1774 about
30,000 people about Manchester were engaged in the cotton industry.[16] By the end of the eighteenth century, the sixteen square miles of
the Oldham chapelry held a population of 16,000 and, of the working
population, approximately 50 percent were weavers.[17]

This pattern of rural industralization was characterized by a trend
towards an increase in wage labor and a decrease in worker independence. A similar development was noted above in connection with
agricultural changes in Lancashire. Textile production became increasingly centralized in the eighteenth century: a higher proportion
of cottage weavers rented their looms from merchants and fewer of
them carried out all the operations of their trade from purchase of
the wool or cotton to the marketing of the finished product.[18] The
few acres of land that a cottage weaver retained supplemented his
subsistence but were insufficient to make him independent. In sum,
in both agriculture and industry, the agrarian structure was marked
by increasing centralization and commercialization and a concomitant
expansion of the wage labor force.

2. *Causes of economic centralization.*

Rural industralization was the product of several forces. It was, in
part, based on the demands of the national and export markets for
the goods produced in Lancashire. By the early eighteenth century,
the increasing specialization of Lancashire in the production and
commercialization of textiles had made the area one of the major
industrial regions of Europe. The textile trade was organized out of
Manchester with sub-regional centers such as Bolton becoming prominent by the mid-eighteenth century.[19] Merchant houses in London
and other major English cities participated in the trade. Similarly,
foreign merchants were attracted to Lancashire. Thus, textiles became an important source of local capital. Many of the most prominent nineteenth century factory owners, such as the Lees of Oldham
and the Ashworths of the Bolton area, originated from families who
had made their money from employing domestic weavers.

In addition, technological innovations assisted the development
of rural industralization. For example, invention of the warping-mill
in the 1740's was an important factor in encouraging this economic
centralization since merchants were able to distribute warps ready-
prepared for insertion into the looms. Previously, the weavers had
been required to prepare the warp themselves by peg-warping.[20]

The processes of economic centralization in agriculture and industry occurred mainly as a result of the gradual development of market forces. The rising standard of living was a stimulus to such centralization. Eighteenth century England was a prosperous country in which wealth was relatively evenly distributed; even laborers had money to spend on items other than food.[21]

3. *Consequences of economic centralization.*

Contemporaries were aware of many of the consequences of economic centralization, one of which was the gradual disappearance of what had once been the backbone of England: the yeoman.[22] While the yeoman did not necessarily own his land, he was a man of substance and economic security. The significance of yeoman status was its relative independence, enabling a man and his family to negotiate their own terms with landowners or merchants.

In the industrial areas of rural Lancashire, the yeoman would combine farming and weaving. He would also often own the looms and spinning equipment used in the latter enterprise. The household of the yeoman farmer was organized around both manufacturing and farming: the women carried on the spinning and butter-making while the men tended the looms and cultivated the fields. The architecture and lay-out of the houses of these farmer-weavers were specially designed for the dual occupation.[23]

An additional consequence of this economic centralization was an increase in work opportunities in Lancashire which, in turn, was reflected in the demographic changes of the eighteenth century. This was a period of long-term population growth. Between 1700 and 1750, population increased by 9 percent in England and Wales, whereas population increased by 83 percent in Lancashire and 23 percent in Cheshire. From 1750 to 1801, Lancashire increased by 134 percent and Cheshire by 51 percent as compared with a 41 percent increase for England and Wales.[24]

The precise source of this growth is difficult to determine. Increases in population in Lancashire may have been attributable to migration. Observers remarked on the drift of population into the North-West from the seventeenth century onwards. Such migrants were attracted by the growing opportunities in trade and industry.[25] It is also possible that the employment structure of eighteenth century Lancashire encouraged a higher birth rate than elsewhere. The combination of agricultural and industrial occupations may have encouraged earlier marriage, while child labor in weaving and spinning made large families an asset rather than a burden.

On balance, centralization was achieved with surprisingly little disruption. There is little evidence that enclosure of agricultural land displaced many rural inhabitants. The impact of enclosure was undoubtedly to promote wage labor both by increasing employment opportunities and by removing one possible element of the rural family's subsistance, namely, the use of common land. Similarly, centralization in industry was not based simply on the expropriation of independent artisans. Many handloom weavers were set up in their trade by town merchants.[26]

In sum, these demographic and economic processes antedated, in part, the rapid population and industrial growth of the Manchester area at the turn of the nineteenth century. The agrarian structure had become commercialized both in its agricultural and industrial development; wage labor was becoming a predominant way of life; and population growth had already commenced. It is against this background that we can assess the process of urban-industralization which occurred in Manchester.

B. *The Urban Phenomenon: Manchester In the Nineteenth Century*

1. *Description of the process of urbanization.*

Population concentration and migration. The process of urbanization in Manchester and other industrial towns of Lancashire was marked by several distinctive features. Foremost among the characteristics of urbanization in the nineteenth century was the concentration of population in and around Manchester. In 1788, Manchester and Salford had perhaps 50,000 inhabitants; by 1851, probably over 400,000 people lived in the contiguous built-up area of Manchester, Salford and Chorlton.[27]

The concentration of population in and around Manchester resulted from several interconnected forces: the technological innovations in spinning and, to a lesser extent, weaving, made it profitable to concentrate workers in factories; the use of steam power made it unnecessary to disperse factories in river valleys; and the improvements in transport, particularly canal transport, facilitated industrial agglomeration. These developments stimulated the growth of Manchester as well as that of neighboring townships such as Stockport, Oldham and Ashton-under-Lyne. By the early twentieth century, the separate towns had become one contiguous built-up area of well over a million people.[28]

A detailed analysis of the migration patterns which fed Manchester's growth is essential to an understanding of the dynamics of this population concentration. There were essentially three types of movement: (a) short-distance migration from rural areas into the towns, (b) inter-town migration, and (c) migration from Ireland. Before turning to discussion of these movements, it is necessary to point out that, for purposes of this analysis, Manchester and the industrial townships that circle it will be treated as one urban area. However, we should keep in mind some of the factors differentiating this area. In the early nineteenth century, Manchester developed as an industrial town with steam-powered mills built along the banks of its canals. By mid-century, it was also becoming a commercial, transport, and administrative center. Towns such as Oldham, on the other hand, continued to be primarily textile centers. The development of a different economic structure in the mill towns from what evolved in Manchester resulted in certain differences in the patterns of migration between the mill towns and Manchester. Manchester provided more opportunities for white-collar and professional employment. It also provided more opportunity for casual and unskilled labor, especially in construction. The Manchester population was consequently a somewhat more cosmopolitan one than that of Oldham and the other textile towns. It was able to attract more Irish, more Southern English, and more foreigners.[29]

The migration that contributed to Manchester's growth was predominantly that of the first type cited above, namely, short-distance migration from the rural areas into the towns. Most migrants to Manchester and its neighboring towns probably came from the surrounding industrialized rural areas.[30] Research into the household schedules of the 1851, 1861, and 1871 censuses of Oldham has confirmed this characterization.[31] It would appear that only a small minority of all adult migrants from the rural areas had previously been agricultural workers. It was probably the younger inexperienced farm workers who migrated permanently.[32] They would often move to other agricultural situations or to work in mines and quarries. The predominant impression one gets—and, given the lack of census data on previous occupations of migrants, it can only be an impression—is that most adult migrants to the Manchester urban areas had prior experience in industrial work. In support of this proposition, statistics from Preston, a town located near to the agricultural areas of Lancashire, indicate that only 13 percent of its migrants came from villages in which more than 50 percent of the over-20 male population was recorded as being engaged in agriculture in 1831.[33]

The distinctive feature of the Manchester pattern of migration is that it was based on industrial concentration. Initially, work had been available in the rural regions. The earliest factories were driven by water-power and thus were often located in fairly remote river valleys.[34] Factories such as those of the Greggs at Styal near Manchester, or of the Ashworths near Bolton, found it difficult to recruit sufficient labor in their early years. They later succeeded in attracting a stable workforce by building houses or using the Poor Law to obtain a supply of young apprentices from rural districts. By the early years of the nineteenth century, the supply of labor had increased sufficiently through the movement of population from the country districts near the towns. These country factories put out work to the surrounding countryside and were themselves used for outwork by the town factories.[35] The experiences of writer Ammon Wrigley are illustrative of this pattern of labor.[36]

By the mid-nineteenth century, however, this system was beginning to collapse. In the parishes near Oldham, the wool industry was in crisis, and many country factories were forced to close down. As textile production increasingly concentrated in the urban areas, those who had relied on craftwork or domestic out-work in the rural areas as their means of subsistence sought work in or near the towns. The 1851 household schedules of Oldham show a substantial migration of families from these rural parishes to Oldham.

This migration was essentially short-distance in nature. In the absence of any substantial migration of Lancashire agricultural workers (as opposed to workers with industrial backgrounds) to work in Manchester and its surrounding towns, it is not surprising to find that there was little long-distance migration of agricultural labor. On various occasions, Manchester area manufacturers attempted to promote such migration, but they had little success in doing so. It is unlikely that many more than 2,000 families ever moved to Lancashire from the Southern counties on any of the various schemes to assist migration.[37] The length of the journey and the risks involved in moving far from home and changing their type of work deterred even the low-paid agricultural laborers of the far South.

In addition to the movement from countryside to city, people also moved from town to town in search of job opportunities. Such inter-town migration appears to have been one of the largest components of migration movement in those years.[38] The available biographies of workers who chose to remain as craft workers show a high degree of geographical mobility in the first half of the nineteenth century.[39] For example, John Critchley Prince, the reedmaker poet, spent much of his life moving from one textile township to another.[40] For him, as for many others, Manchester was an important focal point since it provided the greatest range of opportunities. Therefore, after work failed in one of the neighboring towns, he would return to Manchester before journeying on again.

The third wave of migration was from Ireland. The Irish example provided an exception to the observation that migration in Lancashire was predominantly short-distance. These migrants left their native land because there were few opportunities for supplementary work in rural Ireland either in agriculture or in industry. Subdivision of tenancies and inefficient farming meant that employment opportunities in agriculture were few, and a high rate of natural population increase put pressure on inadequate land resources. Irish cities also failed to offer opportunities for employment. The high points of the Irish migration to Manchester and the area occurred in the 1850's and 1860's, when the potato famine finally destroyed the precarious fabric of the Irish rural economy.[41] Most of the Irish immigrants who came to Manchester settled in the towns, since the countryside already had an ample supply of native labor. By 1836, a fifth of Manchester's population was estimated to be of Irish origin.[42]

These three patterns of migration complete the description of population movement in the period of urban industrialization. Despite the great degree of intra-county mobility and the Irish influx, the absolute growth of the population in the Manchester area and of its labor supply was only moderately fast when viewed in comparison with urbanization in some other cities. The "rapid" growth of Manchester's population from 1801 to 1851 consisted of an average annual increase of 2.1 percent, while that of the neighboring township of Oldham was 2.4 percent per annum. The sharpest increases in population occurred in the early decades of the century, with the highest rate of increase being 3.2 percent a year between 1801 and 1811. The normal rates of increase were, however, just above 2 percent.[43] Even during the period of most rapid growth, then, the towns of the Manchester area faced nothing like the population explosions of Latin American cities in which yearly rates of increase of 5 percent or more are not uncommon.[44]

It is likely that a considerable proportion of the increase of the population of Manchester and the surrounding area was due to the natural increase of its own population rather than the influence of migration patterns.[45] Comparison of Manchester's population increases with the natural increases of population in England and Wales, as well as evidence of the unchanging character of Manchester's population, support this hypothesis. Manchester's 2 percent per annum population growth is not substantially greater than the 1 to 1

1/2 percent annual increase in England and Wales which has been attributed to natural increases.[46] In 1851, over 40 percent of the populations of Liverpool and Manchester were born within the city limits.[47] A survey taken in Oldham shows that 53.7 percent of all heads of households and 38.5 percent of lodgers and relatives were born in Oldham.

The urban labor supply. Although the migration into Manchester was not excessive, there was an ample labor supply for urban industry by mid-century. This labor was relatively cheap for several reasons. First, there were few alternative employment possibilities.[48] There were no significant patterns of return migration to the villages of Lancashire and Cheshire during times of industrial crisis or during old age to counter-balance the migration from country to town. The dominance of commercial farming meant it would have been difficult to absorb returning migrants either by intensifying cultivation on small family farms or through diversification of the rural economy. Such practices have frequently been reported for Latin America.[49] There seems to have been a steady decline in the vitality of the social life of the Lancashire countryside in the nineteenth century. Contemporaries recorded the decline of village customs and village schools were closed as a result of depopulation.[50] The mainly rural areas of Lancashire showed only a 1.3 percent per annum increase between 1801 and 1851, as compared with the 2.8 percent annual increase of the industrial regions. After 1851, almost all rural townships were losing population.[51]

Second, labor was cheap and abundant in the Manchester area because of the changes in industrial organization that were creating a permanent industrial labor force for factory production.

Social changes. The demographic and labor changes which accompanied urbanization did not necessarily imply any sharp disruptions for society. Social events often remained the same. Village practices, such as wakes to celebrate the harvest, were readily transferred to the neighboring towns. In addition, kinship and friendship ties remained important: they often were the basis for finding housing and employment in nineteenth century towns. Such was the case in Preston,[52] and such relationships were likely to be equally strong in Manchester.

Further evidence that the changes were not cataclysmic is the fact that Lancashire did not at first divide sharply between towns dominated by factory employment and a countryside with a declining domestic industry. Instead, craft and factory production coexisted within the towns. There were approximately 300 handloom weavers in Oldham in 1841,[53] and many more survived in the damp cellars of the other textile towns.[54] Craft and workshop production was important in other branches of manufacture as well. In 1851, 1,357 males over the age of twenty were employed as hatters, tailors or shoemakers in Oldham.[55] The equivalent number for Manchester was 5,000.

The various components of Manchester's growth suggest, moreover, that there was considerable continuity in the work experience of its growing population. Most factory workers in the Manchester area appear either to have been born in the industrial towns or have spent much of their childhood there. Even the Irish were no exception to this pattern. The Oldham household schedules of the 1871 census suggest that while Irish fathers tended to be employed in unskilled work, including farm labor, or as artisans such as tailors or cordwainers, their children generally were employed in the mills.[56]

Market base of urbanization. An important distinguishing feature of Manchester's growth has thus far been left implicit in this analysis: the type of market on which the city's industrial production was based. This market was characterized by several features. It was broad in nature. In the eighteenth century and earlier, Manchester was important chiefly as a market town for the agricultural and industrial areas of North Cheshire and South-West Lancashire. This relationship weakened in the nineteenth century as the city's production became increasingly more oriented toward the national and international market. Industrial employment in Manchester was in relation to a much wider ecological base than has normally been existent for cities that have industrialized subsequently. Manchester's factories were able to absorb, with fluctuations, all available labor because they produced for a rapidly expanding external market. It was this base that permitted an expansion of manufacturing employment to the point where well over 60 percent of the economically active male population in the mill towns was engaged in manufacture.[57]

2. *The waning of urbanization: Late nineteenth century.*

By the mid- to late-nineteenth century, the process of urbanization was waning in comparison with the rapid change and growth period immediately prior thereto. The growth of most of the area's towns was slowing down. In the second half of the nineteenth century, migration to Manchester and its neighboring towns, including inter-town migration, diminished considerably. The last great wave of Irish migration was over by the 1860's, and the Irish born became a decreasing percentage of Manchester's population. The Irish constituted only 3.6 percent of the population in the 1901 Census, in contrast with 16.6 percent in the 1851 Census.[58] Natural increase accounted for almost all the growth of the Manchester area by the end of the century.[59] In the 1901 Census, 77.5 percent of males resident in Lancashire had been born in that county.

There are clear signs that intra-town residential mobility was also substantially reduced from the 1880's onwards. Research into intra-town mobility in Oldham at the end of the nineteenth century and beginning of the twentieth century supports this observation.[60] Thereafter, families were increasingly likely to stay in the same house and on the same street from one decade to the next. This phenomenon of residential stabilization in the Manchester area is of interest because it implies that when the available industrial reserve of skilled and casual workers was absorbed by the expansion of factory production in the second half of the nineteenth century, there were no further supplies to take their place.[61] The Irish were the last readily available supply of labor but, as has been seen, migration from Ireland became quite insignificant. British industry had a relatively low rate of technological innovation at the end of the nineteenth century, but could maintain production in part because of the security of the imperial markets for basic products in textiles and in the machine industries. Under conditions of demographic stability and technological stagnation, there was little stimulus to change in the industrial or social organization of the Manchester towns. As a result, clearly demarcated working-class areas developed which, by the beginning of the twentieth century, were composed of relatively stable populations. Families persisted in such areas for generations.

3. Implications of the development of urbanization.

The picture of Manchester's urban industrialization in the nineteenth century has thus been drawn. Several implications of this development are worthy of note. *First*, it is possible to hypothesize as to the effect such urbanization had on the formation of Lancashire's class structure. In connection with the residential stabilization of the working class which occurred in the latter part of the nineteenth century, one might conclude that this stabilization was one factor in establishing the cohesiveness of the working class in the Manchester area. The cohesiveness was manifested both in terms of a common class consciousness and culture as well as a similarity in socio-political outlook. For example, the solidarity of that class was evident in its attempt to protect employment by resisting technological innovation.[62]

The period also witnessed the polarization of two groups: landowners and industrialists. Industrialization was possible in Lancashire partly because technology was simple and did not require large expenditures of capital, and partly because the extensive network of country banks provided a ready means of short-term credit.[63] Manchester's industry was primarily comprised of family firms set up by entrepreneurs on the basis of relatively small amounts of savings or loans from family and friends.[64] The early industrialists were often of local origin and had been engaged previously in the textile trade; they had few family or financial ties with the large landed proprietors of the region.

By and large, agriculture and industry developed separately. In part, this separation was merely the result of indifference: neither party needed the assistance of the other. Landowners showed little interest in industrial production and, though they held the most important political offices, even less interest in developing administrative strategies to deal with urban-industrial concentration. There was, indeed, little impetus for landowners and industrialists to coordinate strategies. Little direct legal coercion or administrative action was needed either to consolidate farms or to provide labor for industry.

In addition to simple indifference, there were circumstances which made for an active divergence of interests between industrialists and landowners. The commercialization of agricultural production prior to the Industrial Revolution meant that the growing populations in the towns were faced with high food prices. Prices were especially high in the early decades of the nineteenth century, falling once again in the 1820's and 1830's.[65] There were several reasons for these high prices, namely, the early inefficiency of English agriculture, its protection from foreign competition, the land monopolies of the large landowners, and the lack of informal markets where town inhabitants could purchase surplus harvests from subsistence farmers.

The political issue of the Corn Laws[66] provided a focal point for disagreement among industrialists and landowners. Manchester industrialists such as Henry Ashworth, John Platt and Samuel Greg were prominent in the anti-Corn Law movement.[67] These manufacturers wanted to end the "protection" of English agriculture, encourage free trade, and lower the cost of foodstuffs at home. Henry Ashworth considered the common enemy of the manufacturer and his workers to be the aristocratic English landowners who lived off their rents and maintained their dependents in a semi-servile state. He and other industrialists considered the way of life and the economic behavior of these landowners to be economically inefficient. The Corn Laws, by preventing external competition, protected this inefficiency.

In turn, the landowners viewed the growing wealth and power of the industrialists with distaste and suspicion. They also feared the social disruption that the changes in England's economic and social organization implied. The Corn Laws were seen to provide a degree of security for agriculture after the crises of the early nineteenth century which had produced considerable rural poverty and offered no easily available alternative source of income.[68] The supporters of the Corn Laws drew a picture of a factory England in which masses of unhealthy, brutalized workers posed a threat to the established order. Some writers were deeply concerned that England's military strength would severely decline if recruitment were to become based on an urban, factory population.[69]

For most of the nineteenth century, the terms of public debate and the political conflict of interest were such as to oppose the industrial and agricultural classes. The large landowners saw their political control threatened by the rise of the cities, and some of their spokesmen sought to reveal the inhumanity and despotism of the factory owners. Out of this debate came a plethora of inquiries and statistics which were used by both sides to prove their points. Shaftesbury, a large landowner, commissioned studies into conditions of urban and factory life. Likewise, the Ashworths eagerly collaborated in studies demonstrating the plight of the agricultural laborer.[70]

Despite the continuing conflict between the two interests throughout the nineteenth century, agricultural interests in England in fact benefited substantially from the development of industry. Land prices went up near the towns, improved agriculture provided considerable returns, and many landowners were to make their fortunes from urban property development.

Second, the pattern of urban industrialization affected the evolution of Lancashire's political structure. One of the most significant aspects of this industrialization was that its scope was out of step with the development of local political and administrative institutions. Manchester shocked contemporaries because severe problems of political control and order faced the dominant classes in a city in which jurisdictions were fragmented and the police force was weakly developed.[71]

This chaotic political structure illustrates the special circumstances of Manchester's development. The evolution of industrial capitalism did not require the concerted effort of the dominant classes. Britain's lead in industrialization meant, in fact, that industrialists had more interest in diminishing government intervention. It was to their advantage to keep the state out of their affairs rather than develop alliances with other classes—landowners, shopkeepers, urban landlords—as the basis for a coherent project of urban administration and development.

It was on the basis of the haphazard political structure of Manchester that Shirley emphasized the contrast between this chaos and the relative orderliness of São Paulo's growth.[72] It is perhaps this facet of Manchester's growth which differs most drastically from the experience of São Paulo in the twentieth century.

III. THE SÃO PAULO CASE[73]

A. *Description of the Process of Urbanization*

1. *The agrarian background and the coffee boom.*

In striking contrast to Manchester, São Paulo's urban industrialization began at a time when the transformation of its agrarian structure was still in progress. The agrarian changes commenced in the region of São Paulo and subsequently spread throughout Brazil. Not even in the region of São Paulo has this transformation ceased. The *colono* system[74] has only recently been replaced by casual labor forces from nearby towns and villages. Livestock ranching and small-scale commercial farming oriented to the urban market are becoming predominant in the region, but sharecroppers and pockets of peasant cultivation still remain.[75] In other parts of Brazil which constitute both a market and a labor reserve for São Paulo industry, there are indications that peasant production is in fact expanding. This is notably true in the northeastern portions of the country.[76]

The São Paulo experience is not simply an example of the uneven development of underdeveloped countries. Most of the developed world also began to urbanize and industrialize when their agrarian structures were still in the throes of transformation. For example, until the twentieth century, frontier settlement provided a counterattraction to industrial work in the United States and workers continued to commute from peasant villages to locations of industry in much of Europe. This suggests that the Manchester experience was exceptional rather than the pattern of change to come.[77]

The discussion of São Paulo must therefore focus on the concurrent and inter-connected developments of agrarian and urban growth. The early growth of the city of São Paulo was based on the expansion of the coffee economy in the last half of the nineteenth century. São Paulo's coffee expansion was facilitated by the availability of abundant and suitable virgin land that yielded good crops and required little investment. It was also made possible by an abundant supply of cheap labor imported primarily from Italy. This free labor supply, like that of Manchester, was created by processes of primitive accumulation: but these processes occurred abroad in Italy instead of at home. The Italian small farm economy was undermined by the importation of cheap grain from the Americas and, together with substantial demographic increases, created a surplus population in the Italian countryside. São Paulo was sparsely populated before the coffee expansion, and the first plantations were worked by slave labor. The available supplies of black slaves were insufficient for the needs of the plantations.[78] Also, whether through expediency or conviction, the coffee planters claimed that native labor was not suited to their purposes. Thus, they instituted a scheme to bring in massive supplies of free labor from Europe. More than one and a half million immigrants were brought to Brazil between 1880 and 1920. The majority of these went to work on the coffee plantations of São Paulo. Both the state government and the planters were explicit in their intention of bringing in sufficiently large quantities of immigrants so that labor would be cheap. Planters consciously recruited the following categories of immigrants: entire families rather than individuals, agricultural workers, and the poor. Such people were thought to be less likely to return home, buy land, or find other work.[79]

Conditions of life on the plantations were bad. By 1914, the real level of wages was considerably lower than they had been at the beginning of the immigration. There was substantial turnover in the plantation labor force as the discontented left, but the number of immigrants more than compensated for this mobility. This cheap labor increased the rate of capital accumulation in agriculture.

2. *Urbanization: The early years.*

It was on the basis of the coffee boom that the city of São Paulo grew as a center for handling commerce and administration. The city's population grew from 31,000 in 1872 to 580,000 in 1920[80] in the wake of the boom. However, despite its rapid growth from 1870 onwards, São Paulo remained merely an urban adjunct to a predominantly rural society for many years. Until 1890, the city's population constituted only four percent of the state's population. São Paulo was mainly a commercial and administrative center with little industry at the turn of the twentieth century. Thus, in 1893, manufacturing industries employed only 7 percent of the city's population as compared with the 43 percent so employed in Rio de Janeiro.[81] Whereas 26 percent of São Paulo's economically active population was employed in domestic service in 1893, the comparable figure for Manchester was 5 percent in 1851.[82]

This slow urban industrial growth characterized the early period of São Paulo's development. The city grew as a service center for an agricultural economy which exported its product and recruited its labor from abroad. The slow industrial development is not surprising given this dependence on an external market for sales and an external supply of labor. The standard of living of the immigrants, and thus their purchasing power, was low. The spread of rural development was uneven without creating a stable, large-scale demand for industrial products. There was thus no compelling impetus to urban growth.[83]

3. *The legacies of São Paulo's early urbanization.*

Two of the most important legacies of this period of immigration and development contrast sharply with the case of Manchester's period of urbanization: (1) the development of an efficient state apparatus; and (2) a class structure marked by an alliance between industrialists and landowners and a lack of solidarity within the working class.

The planters were commercially oriented and eager to sponsor developments in infrastructure and administration that would further their interests. The need to sponsor and organize immigration and the problem of controlling immigrants working under appalling conditions gave the planters an interest in strong government. The state government of São Paulo was dominated politically by the planters and speedily developed the police and administrative apparatus to enforce their will.

There was to be no severe conflict of interest between the industrial bourgeoisie and the landowners. Indeed, the infrastructure demanded by coffee expansion was to facilitate industrialization. Roads and railways were built to transport coffee. By the end of the nineteenth century electricity was installed in São Paulo.[84] The large São Paulo police force effectively guaranteed law and order in town and countryside and suppressed labor disputes. The planters also invested in, and owned, industry; many of the textile mills were started by coffee planters.[85] In addition, immigrant industrialists married into planter families.

Unlike the divisive issue of the Corn Laws in England, there was little conflict of interest over tariff policy in São Paulo. Though the planters might have been expected to favor free trade and the "efficiency" of importing manufactures from those countries that produced them most cheaply, they generally supported a tariff protection that favored local industry. Much of early São Paulo industry made use of products that could be produced by local agriculture such as cotton. Also, the tariff provided one of the few sources of revenue for the central government. The planters preferred the revenue to be raised through tariff than through direct taxation of land or profits.[86]

In comparison with the Manchester situation, both agriculture and industry were expanding under conditions in which neither would necessarily lose by the other's increasing importance. The situation was conducive to the creation of class alliances in São Paulo. Until the 1930's, both planters and industrialists had a common interest in developing the power of their own state relative to that of the other states of Brazil. After the 1930's, both classes still had compatible interests within Vargas's[87] new centralized state. The planters received support for coffee prices from the federal government. The industrialists eventually obtained government help: they received assistance in terms of control of labor and gained access to an increasingly integrated national market.[88] In contrast, industrialists and landowners of Manchester vied for power in a society in which success for one party inevitably eroded the political base of the other.

The organization of Paulista agriculture, even its archaic features, actually benefited the industrial interest. In contrast to the Manchester situation, peasant production and the surplus from *colono* production helped provide cheap foodstuffs for the urban population, the profits of coffee a major source of industrial finance, and the prosperity of coffee attracted foreign investment in infrastructure and in industry. These considerations demonstrate that a rising industrial bourgeoisie will not necessarily come into conflict with a traditionally dominant landowning class. The expansion of capitalism in underdeveloped countries can be accomplished by the alliance of landowners and industrialists.[89] Their interests are not incompatible where both sectors must rely on intensively exploiting labor in the face of a general scarcity of capital.

A further point of contrast is evident between the cases of Manchester and São Paulo. The characteristics of industrial labor were sharply different in the two cities. The resulting class consciousness of São Paulo accordingly was at variance with that discussed above in connection with the development of Manchester.

São Paulo has witnessed a constant flow of migration which has not yet stopped. The first wave of migrants was from Italy. In 1900, 92 percent of the industrial workers in the state of São Paulo were foreign; 81 percent were Italian.[90] The cohesiveness of these workers was weakened by regional antagonisms and by an individualism fostered by geographical and social mobility. Many of the migrants moved elsewhere in Brazil, back to Italy, or on to Argentina and the United States. Those who stayed often accumulated enough capital to set up small businesses.[91] The consequences of this mobility were similar to those reported in the United States:[92] it undermined both class consciousness and class organization.[93]

After international migration lost its importance in the 1920's, it was replaced by a series of internal migrations which provided an adequate source of industrial labor. Migration from the state of São Paulo and from neighboring states such as Minas and Gerais began the flow of internal migration. This was subsequently followed by migration from the poorer and more distant state of North-East Brazil.[94] This migration was not simply a one-way movement from rural areas into the city; it included substantial "return" migration both to areas of new colonization and to regions of origin.[95] It also included the movement of casual farm workers who lived in urban areas and supplemented their agricultural wages by employment in the urban informal economy.[96]

This extensive pattern of migration was the result of various factors. The improvement of communications systems stimulated movement. The increasing integration of the national market also caused substantial migration. As industrial production became concentrated in São Paulo, its products began to displace those of artisan or factory production in other regions. Finally, the increasing commercialization of farming throughout the country was an additional factor in destabilizing the rural areas, thereby creating the forces making for migration.

4. *São Paulo's growth in later years.*

São Paulo was thus thrust into a new stage of development. Whereas initially its growth had been based on an external market and labor supply, the city's subsequent growth was sustained by the creation and gradual extension of an internal market for its manufactures and by internal migration. However, even the increase in industrial production was insufficient to provide employment opportunities to meet the needs of the rapidly expanding city population. Much of the labor force was absorbed into the service sector instead of the industrial. Such service activities in commerce, transport and personal services in turn directly and indirectly facilitated the expansion of the industrial sector since the availability of cheap services reduced the pressure on industrial wages. Many of the services essential to industrial expansion, *e.g.*, distribution, were provided through the intensification of labor, thus saving scarce capital for industry.

From the 1950's, São Paulo's industry became increasingly capital-intensive. Manufacturing employment increased almost as fast as employment in the services from 1960 to 1970. The dynamic of industrial expansion was thus demonstrated.[97]

The processes of development created additional bases of differentiation among the working class. Whereas skilled jobs in industry required lengthy training and thus an abundant labor supply was not a significant factor in lowering wages, posts which were semi- and unskilled made use of the ample reserve of casual labor in the city. Ecological differences between the old industrial center of São Paulo with its more "traditional" working class and their peripheral industrial towns with their labor forces of more recent migrants provided additional reasons for the growing heterogeneity and lack of cohesiveness of São Paulo's working class.[98]

São Paulo's subsequent industrial growth was constrained by the industrial dominance of the advanced economies of the world. Manchester was the first city of the Industrial Revolution which helped to create the pattern of inter-dependency that subsequently characterized the world economy. For example, English capital was attracted by the profits to be gained by exporting coffee to the European market and by selling manufactures in Brazil. England thus helped to open up the interior of São Paulo. The consequence of this foreign involvement in São Paulo has been to limit the industrial development of São Paulo.[99]

A limited internal market has also stunted São Paulo's industrial growth. In addition, some branches of production remained based on imported advanced technology while other branches continued to rely on labor-intensive techniques.[100] As a result, the city's industrial development has been slower and more uneven than the development in Manchester.

Despite these contrasts, however, São Paulo is a fast-growing modern industrial city which has helped transform Brazil from an agricultural exporting economy. Its industry now exports part of its product and has a larger share of the gross domestic product than does agriculture. Subordination to the advanced economies has not prevented a significant degree of structural change in the Brazilian economy.

IV. CONCLUSION

The patterns of development in Manchester and São Paulo stand in sharp contrast to each other. Manchester first grew on the basis of the prior commercialization of its agrarian structure and the increasing prosperity of the English domestic market. Its subsequent growth in the nineteenth century was affected by the role of external markets. Ireland, the Americas, Africa and Asia sustained Manchester by providing a market for its manufactures, and Ireland also supplied the city with a migrant workforce. São Paulo grew as a service center for an agricultural economy which not only exported its product, but also recruited its labor from abroad. Its agrarian structure was still in the process of change when urbanization began. The city's subsequent growth was sustained by the creation and gradual extension of an internal market for its manufactures and by the increase of internal migrations.

It is, therefore, not accidental that the development of the two cities should follow paths that are almost the reverse of each other. This paper has focused particularly on the differences in political and class structure that resulted from the divergent processes of urbanization. Manchester's political structure was "chaotic" and weak; São Paulo's was "orderly" and highly centralized. Manchester's working class was a cohesive unit with an identifiable class consciousness; São Paulo's working class has remained heterogeneous and divided. The period of urbanization saw Manchester's industrialist and landowner classes polarize; São Paulo's equivalent classes allied politically in furtherance of common interests.

Comparison of the patterns of development raises the issue of how complete the transition to industrial capitalism must be in order for development to occur. The transition was almost complete in Manchester by the end of the nineteenth century. The majority of the area's working population was employed in fairly large factories and few remnants of artisan forms of production were discernible. Yet, the Manchester case is exceptional: factory production was able to absorb the surplus population because of an extensive external market and a relatively low rate of technological innovation. The completeness of the transition in fact may have had negative consequences for the continuing expansion of industrial production in Manchester. Without the stimulus of abundant reserves of labor and faced by an increasingly stabilized population,[101] industrialists had little incentive to introduce technological innovation.

The transition to industrial capitalism in São Paulo has been less complete and more complex than that of nineteenth century Manchester. However, this incompleteness has been an important factor in contributing to São Paulo's industrial growth. The reserves of labor that are maintained by migration and high population growth permit considerable flexibility in industrial organization. Examples of such flexibility can be seen in the use of casual labor and the way in which modern industry has developed complementary relationships with workshops which "put out" portions of its overall production. Such flexibility reduces the risks for industrial capital since it is possible to expand production without committing capital or permanently expanding the workforce.

The existence of alternative "flexible" economic arrangements has resulted in the coexistence of two distinct trends in São Paulo: a modern, capital-intensive sector of the urban economy and an "informal" labor-intensive sector. This situation explains the persistence of apparently marginal forms of employment as well as underemployment.[102] Complex patterns of stratification are created among the urban workforce by these economic arrangements; such patterns often become associated with differences of ethnicity, race, or rural-urban origin. These differentiations weaken the solidarity of the working class, thereby reducing both pressure on wages and the force of demands for improvements in urban infrastructure and social services.

Unlike the situation in São Paulo, the Manchester industrialists were faced with a working class which possessed a strong sense of solidarity. As a result, the industrialists had little leeway in reducing costs of production to meet international competition since such attempts were met by the resistence of the working class. Their Brazilian counterparts were better able to reduce their costs in the absence of a well-formed working class.

The São Paulo model of industrial expansion has been dependent upon a state willing and able to keep wages down and to ignore demands to improve living standards of the working class. In this respect, the Manchester/São Paulo comparison shows the importance of the political structure in shaping capitalist development. Principles of individualism and laisse-faire dominated the attitudes of the Manchester industrialists, because their capital could best be accumulated through such 'natural' processes as the relatively spontaneous migration of free labor and an open world market for their products. Despite sporadic recourse to the army to suppress labor disputes in the early nineteenth century, Manchester industrialists remained suspicious of central government and its attempts to foster or influence industrial development. In contrast, despite defeat of their attempts to attain local autonomy in 1932, the São Paulo industrialists soon adapted to the new circumstances and used strong federal government as a basis of rapid industrial expansion.

NOTES

1. Lampard, *Historical Aspects of Urbanization,* PHILIP M. HAUSER & LEO F. SCHNORE, eds., THE STUDY OF URBANIZATION 519-54 (NY: John Wiley, 1965).

2. KARL MARX, 1 CAPITAL 713-64 (NY: International Publishers, 1975).

3. DAVID S. LANDES, THE UNBOUND PROMETHEUS 50 (Cambridge: Cambridge U. Press, 1950).

4. This conclusion is based on analysis of the general surveys conducted in Lancashire at the turn of the 19th century. *See, e.g.,* JOHN HOLT, 6 GREAT BRITAIN AGRICULTURAL REPORTS 1793–1796 (Newton Abbott, Devon: David & Charles Reprints, 1969); WILLIAM MARSHALL, 1 THE REVIEW AND ABSTRACT OF THE COUNTY REPORTS TO THE BOARD OF AGRICULTURE (Newton Abbott, Devon: David & Charles Reprints, 1969).

5. HOLT, *supra* note 4, at 14, 26.

6. *Rural Conditions,* 79 FRASER'S MAGAZINE 79 (1869), reprinted in C.J. WRIGLEY, ed., THE WORKING CLASSES IN THE VICTORIAN AGE: RURAL CONDITIONS (Westmead, England: Gregg International Publishers, 1973).

7. HOLT, *supra* note 4.

8. "Enclosure" is a legal device employed to restrict access to arable lands. By contrast, "reclamation" is simply the process of bringing hitherto unusable land into production.

9. Marshall, *The Lancashire Rural Laborer in the Early Nineteenth Century,* 71 TRANSACTIONS OF THE LANCASHIRE AND CHESHIRE ANTIQUARIAN SOCIETY 90–128 (Manchester: H. Rawson & Co., 1961).

10. CENSUS OF GREAT BRITAIN, 1851-2 POPULATION TABLES, II, 638–39 (London: Eyre and Spottiswoode for Her Majesty's Stationery Office, 1854).

11. *On the Relative Demand for Labour in the Agricultural and Manufacturing Districts,* C.J. WRIGLEY, ed., 4 THE WORKING CLASSES IN THE VICTORIAN AGE: RURAL CONDITIONS 404 (Westmead, England: Gregg International Publishers, 1973).

12. Holt cites, among others, a Lincolnshire farmer as saying: "Never enquire about the cultivation of land, or its produce, within ten or twelve miles of Manchester: the people know nothing about it. Speak of spinning-jennies, and mules, and carding machines, they will talk for days with you." HOLT, *supra* note 4, at 211.

13. SIDNEY S. CHAPMAN, THE LANCASHIRE COTTON INDUSTRY 2–17 (Manchester: Manchester U. Press, 1904).

14. AMMON WRIGLEY, SONGS OF A MOORLAND PARISH 111 (Saddleworth: Moore & Edwards, 1912).

15. HOLT, *supra* note 4, at 216.

16. CHAPMAN, *supra* note 13, at 3.

17. JOHN FOSTER, CLASS STRUGGLE AND THE INDUSTRIAL REVOLU-TION 12, 33 (London: Widenfeld & Nicolson, 1974).

18. H.D. FONG, TRIUMPH OF FACTORY SYSTEM IN ENGLAND 5 (Tientsin, China: Chihli Press, 1930); CHAPMAN, *supra* note 13, at 2–17.

19. S.D. CHAPMAN, THE COTTON INDUSTRY IN THE INDUSTRIAL REVOLUTION 13 (London: Macmillan, 1972).

20. FONG, *supra* note 18, at 47.

21. LANDES, *supra* note 3, at 47–48.

22. *Condition of the English Peasantry*, 1 QUARTERLY REVIEW 240–84 (1829), reprinted in WRIGLEY, *supra* note 6, at —.

23. AMMON WRIGLEY, *supra* note 14, at 12.

24. R. Lawton, *Population Trends in Lancashire and Cheshire from* 1801, CXIV TRANSACTIONS OF THE HISTORICAL SOCIETY OF LANCASHIRE AND CHESHIRE 191 (Manchester: The Historical Society of Lancashire & Cheshire, 1962).

25. RHODES BOYSEN, THE ASHWORTH COTTON ENTERPRISE 64 (Oxford: Clarendon Press, 1970).

26. LANDES, *supra* note 3, at 44, n.1.

27. CENSUS OF GREAT BRITAIN, 1851—2 POPULATION TABLES I, Northwestern Division, at 4 (London: Eyre and Spottiswoode for Her Majesty's Stationary Office, 1854).

28. CENSUS OF ENGLAND AND WALES, 1901: COUNTY OF LANCASTER, Table 9 (London: Her Majesty's Stationery Office, 1902).

29. CENSUS OF GREAT BRITAIN, 1851—2 POPULATION TABLES II, *supra* note 10, at 636–47, 662.

30. MICHAEL ANDERSON, FAMILY STRUCTURE IN NINETEENTH CENTURY LANCASHIRE 34–41 (Cambridge: Cambridge U. Press, 1971); ARTHUR REDFORD, LABOUR MIGRATION IN ENGLAND 1800-1850 at 94-96 (Manchester: Manchester U. Press, 1964).

31. The information contained in this and all subsequent textual references to the "household schedules" of the government census offices has been microfilmed and is available in the Oldham Public Library. The author is currently sampling streets of households to determine the origins of Oldham's population in these census years.

32. Marshall, *supra* note 9, at 93–94.

33. ANDERSON, *supra* note 30, at 38.

34. Marshall, *Colonisation as a Factor in the Planting of Towns in North-West England*, H.J. DYOS, ed., THE STUDY OF URBAN HISTORY 215–30 (London: Edward Arnold, 1968).

35. WRIGLEY, *supra* note 14, at 122.

36. Wrigley was born to a family of cottage weavers in a moorland parish and went with his parents at the age of fourteen to find work in a valley near Oldham. *See,* AMMON WRIGLEY, OLD SADDLEWORTH DAYS (Oldham: W.E. Clegg, 1920).

37. BOYSON, *supra* note 25, at 190.

38. ANDERSON, *supra* note 30, at 36.

39. *See, e.g.,* WRIGLEY, *supra* note 14; BEN BRIERLY, HOME MEMORIES AND RECOLLECTIONS OF A LIFE (Manchester, Heywood, 1886).

40. R.A. DOUGLAS LITHGOW, LIFE OF JOHN CRITCHLEY PRINCE (Manchester: Abel Heywood & Son, 1880).

41. K.H. CONNELL, THE POPULATION OF IRELAND, 1750–1845 at 182–83 (Oxford: Clarendon Press, 1950).

42. ARTHUR REDFORD & INA S. RUSSELL, 2 THE HISTORY OF LOCAL GOVERNMENT IN MANCHESTER 105 (London, Toronto & NY: Longmans, Green & Co., 1940).

43.   INTERCENSAL RATES OF POPULATION GROWTH
        IN OLDHAM AND MANCHESTER (1851 CENSUS)

| | INTERCENSAL PERIOD | | | | |
CITY	*1801–11*	*1811–21*	*1821–31*	*1831–41*	*1841–51*
Manchester	13.5%	34.8%	32.1%	17.0%	18.7%
Oldham	36.9%	29.2%	29.5%	18.6%	19.8%

Source: CENSUS OF GREAT BRITAIN, 1851—2 POPULATION TABLES I, Northwestern Division, *supra* note 27, Table 34.

44. MANUEL CASTELL, THE URBAN QUESTION 54, table 13 (London: Edward Arnold, 1977).

45. LAWTON, *supra* note 24, at 201–11.

46. *Id.* at 193.

47. CENSUS OF GREAT BRITAIN, 1851— 1 & 2 POPULATION TABLES I–II (London: Her Majesty's Stationery Office, 1852 (Tome I), 1854 (Tome II)).

48. *See*, H.J. HABAKKUK, AMERICAN AND BRITISH TECHNOLOGY IN THE NINETEENTH CENTURY: THE SEARCH FOR LABOUR-SAVING DEVICES 136–37 (Cambridge, England: Cambridge U. Press, 1962).

49. Roberts, *The Provincial Urban System and the Process of Dependency*, ALEJANDRO PORTES & HARLEY L. BROWNING, eds., CURRENT PERSPECTIVES IN LATIN AMERICAN URBAN RESEARCH 120–25 (Austin: U. of Texas Press, 1976).

50. WRIGLEY, *supra* note 14, at 99.

51. Lawton, *supra* note 24, at 197.

52. ANDERSON, *supra* note 30, at 154–57.

53. JOHN FOSTER, CLASS STRUGGLE AND THE INDUSTRIAL REVOLUTION: EARLY INDUSTRIAL CAPITALISM IN THREE ENGLISH TOWNS 294 n.8 (London: Weidenfeld and Nicolson, 1974).

54. FONG, *supra* note 18, at 46–47.

55. CENSUS OF GREAT BRITAIN, 1851, *supra* note 10, at 636–47.

56. *Id.*

57. *Id.*

58. CENSUS OF ENGLAND AND WALES, 1901, *supra* note 28, at 184; CENSUS OF GREAT BRITAIN, 1851, *supra* note 10, at 662.

59. Lawton, *supra* note 24, at 206, 211.

60. This research is based on the yearly local tax records of the Oldham municipal council. These records document the names of owners and occupants of dwellings from the end of the nineteenth century.

61. Hobsbawm, *La marginalidad social en la historia de la industrializacion Europea*, 5 REVISTA LATINOMERICANA DE SOCIOLOGIA 237–48 (July 1969).

62. LANDES, *supra* note 3, at 316–20; HABAKKUK, *supra* note 48, at 155-56.

63. LANDES, *supra* note 3, at 74–75; L.S. PRESSNELL, COUNTRY BANKING IN THE INDUSTRIAL REVOLUTION (Oxford: Clarendon Press, 1956).

64. BOYSON, *supra* note 25; CHAPMAN, *supra* note 13.

65. MARSHALL, *supra* note 4.

66. The Corn Laws of 1815 protected English production of cereal crops against foreign imports by a system of import duties. They gave rise to a vigorous movement for repeal, as the Anti-Corn Law League allied industrialists, workers, and Radicals against the landed interest. The laws were repealed in 1846.

67. BOYSON, *supra* note 25, at 215.

68. ERIC HOBSBAWM, INDUSTRY AND EMPIRE 99–100 (Harmondsworth, Middlesex: Penguin Books, 1969).

69. *Our Rural Population and the War*, 78 BLACKWOOD'S EDINBURGH MAGAZINE 734 at 735 (—: —, 1855), reprinted in 4 THE WORKING CLASS IN THE

VICTORIAN AGE (Westmead, England: Gregg Int'l Publishers, comp. C.J. Wrigley, 1973).

70. BOYSON, *supra* note 25, at 84–87.

71. *See* Shirley, *Legal Institutions and Early Industrial Growth*, this volume at 157.

72. *Id*. at 157.

73. The discussion of São Paulo will rely on selected accounts of the city's early growth and industrialization, and will focus on those features of São Paulo's development that contrast most with the Manchester case. WARREN DEAN, THE INDUSTRIALIZATION OF SÃO PAULO, 1880–1945 (Austin & London: ILAS/U. of Texas Press, 1969); Hall, *Emigrazione italiana a 1880 e 1920*, 25 QUADENI STORICI 138-59 (Italy: —, 1974); Hall, *Approaches to Immigration History*, RICHARD GRAHAM & PETER SMITH, eds., NEW APPROACHES TO LATIN AMERICAN HISTORY 175–93 (Austin: U. of Texas Press, 1974); Hall, *Immigration and the Early São Paulo Working Class*, RICHARD KONETZKE & HERMANN KELLENBENZ, eds., BAND 12, JAHRBUCK FÜR GESCHICHTE LATEIN-AMERIKAS, SONDERDRUCK 393–407 (Cologne & Vienna: Bohlau Verlag, 1975). In addition, the discussion shall emphasize the diversity of political and economic institutions that accompany and produce economic modernization. Lopes, *Capitalism in the Periphery: Agrarian Conditions and the Development of the Working Classes in São Paulo* (Unpublished paper presented at Stanford Conference, April 1977).

74. The *colono* system evolved out of the conditions of coffee cultivation in the late nineteenth century. The need for an abundant supply of labor for the coffee plantations led planters to experiment with cheap ways of finding subsistence for this labor. As finally instituted, the *colono* system provided laborers with wages to care for a set number of trees as well as a plot of land on which to grow subsistence crops.

75. Lopes, *Développement capitaliste et structure agraire au Brésil*, 19 SOCIOLOGIE DU TRAVAIL 59–71 (Paris: Assn. for the Development of Sociology of Work, 1977); Goodman & Redclift, *The 'Bóias-Frias': Rural Proletarianization and Urban Marginality in Brazil*, 1 INTERNATIONAL JOURNAL OF URBAN AND REGIONAL RESEARCH 348–64 (London: Edward Arnold, 1976).

76. *Id.*, at 69–70.

77. BRIAN J.L. BERRY, THE HUMAN CONSEQUENCES OF URBANISATION: DIVERGENT PATHS IN THE URBAN EXPERIENCE OF THE TWENTIETH CENTURY 143–44 (London: Macmillan Press, 1973); HABAKKUK, *supra* note 48, at 36.

78. Hall, *Approaches to Immigration History*, *supra* note 73.

79. Hall, *Emigrazione Italiana a San Paulo Tra 1880 e 1920*, *supra* note 73, at 139–41.

80. DEAN, *supra* note 73, at 4.

81. BORIS FAUSTO, TRABALHO URBANO E CONFLITO SOCIAL, 1880–1920 at 30–31 (São Paulo & Rio de Janeiro: Difel, 1976).

82. The 1851 Census in Manchester indicates that 55 percent of the city's adult males worked in craft and manufacturing production, 29 percent worked in service jobs, and 7 percent were employed in construction. CENSUS OF GREAT BRITAIN, 1851, *supra* note 10, at 636–47. While there are difficulties inherent in comparing census categories from the nineteenth century with contemporary statistics in São Paulo, it appears that the percentage of service employment in Latin American cities is considerably higher than the comparable figures for nineteenth century Manchester.

83. Katzman, *São Paulo and its Hinterland: Evolving Relationships and the Rise of an Industrial Power*, this volume at 107.

84. DEAN, *supra* note 73, at 8.

85. *Id*. at 37–38.

86. *Id*. at 71.

87. Getúlio Dornelles Vargas (President of Brazil, 1930–45, 1950–54).

88. Love, *Autonomia e interdependência: São Paulo e a federação brasileira, 1889–1937*, BORIS FAUSTO, ed., O BRASIL REPUBLICANO TOMO III 67 (São Paulo: Difel, 1975).

89. Laclau, *Feudalism and Capitalism in Latin America*, 67 NEW LEFT REVIEW 19 at 36, 37 (England: Balding & Mansell, —).

90. Hall, *Immigration and the Early São Paulo Working Class, supra* note 73, at 394.

91. *Id.* at 399.

92. *See,* STEPHAN THERNSTROM & PETER R. KNIGHTS, MEN IN MOTION: SOME DATA AND SPECULATION ABOUT URBAN POPULATION MOBILITY IN NINETEENTH-CENTURY AMERICA 36–37 (Los Angeles: Institute of Government and Public Affairs at U. of California, 1970).

93. Hall, *Approaches to Immigration History, supra* note 73, at 192.

94. Graham, *Divergent and Convergent Regional Economic Growth and Internal Migration in Brazil—1940–1960*, 18 ECONOMIC DEVELOPMENT AND CULTURAL CHANGE 362–82 (Chicago: U. of Chicago Press, 1970).

95. Lopes, *supra* note 75.

96. Goodman & Redclift, *supra* note 75, at 348–63.

97. Kirsch, *Employment and the Utilization of Human Resources in Latin America*, 18 ECON. BULL. FOR LATIN AMERICA 46 at 70 (NY: United Nations, 1973).

98. Lopes, *supra* note 73.

99. *See,* RICHARD GRAHAM, BRITAIN AND THE ONSET OF MODERNIZATION IN BRAZIL (Cambridge: Cambridge U. Press, 1973).

100. Singer, *Urbanization and Development: The Case of São Paulo*, JORGE E. HARDOY, ed., URBANIZATION IN LATIN AMERICA 435–56 (Garden City, NY: Anchor Books, 1975).

101. This stabilized population has been described as an "almost hereditary class of cotton-mill operatives." M.T. COPELAND, THE COTTON MANUFACTURING INDUSTRY OF THE UNITED STATES 72–73 (Cambridge, Mass.: Harvard U. Press, 1912). *See also,* Chapman & Abbott, *The Tendency of Children to Enter Their Fathers' Trades*, LXXVI JOURNAL OF THE ROYAL STATISTICAL SOCIETY 1912–1913, 599–604 (London: Royal Statistical Society, 1913).

102. *See,* LÚCIO KOWARICK, CAPITALISMO E MARGINALIDADE NA AMERICA LATINA (Rio de Janeiro: Paz e Terra, 1975).

São Paulo and its Hinterland: Evolving Relationships and the Rise of an Industrial Power

*MARTIN T. KATZMAN**

I. INTRODUCTION

A. *Interdependence Between City and Hinterland: Theories*

A CITY AND ITS HINTERLAND interact through several channels, whose relative importance vary over time and space. In a natural resource frontier, the growth of exports from the hinterland influences the development of non-resource activities, which are generally but not invariably urban, such as commerce and manufacturing. Economists have formed several theories to describe the impact of the hinterland on the city: The *staple* theory best describes the sectorial linkages between resource and non-resource activities;[1] the *central place* theory focuses on the spatial effects of development in the non-resource sector.[2] Balancing these theories, which analyze the impact of the hinterland on the city, are two which focus upon the impact of urban development on the extension and modernization of the frontier, *i.e.*, the theory of *rents* and the *industrial-urban* hypothesis.[3]

This article examines the changing interaction between city and hinterland in the São Paulo region of Brazil over the past 100 years, the degree to which staple exports have stimulated industrial urbanization, and the degree to which industrial urbanization in turn has stimulated frontier expansion and rural modernization. The pre-1930 and post-1930 eras will be analyzed separately, since the general pattern of city–hinterland interaction differed markedly during those two periods. For example, from 1860 to 1929, coffee exports were the engine of growth in the São Paulo region and the industrial structure remained largely traditional. After 1940, however, the industrial sector became the engine of growth, undergoing substantial structural change and modernization. Thus, the year 1930 is taken as a conven-

* Professor and Head, Program in Political Economy, University of Texas at Dallas. The author benefited considerably from discussions with Brian Berry, Joseph Love, and Paul Mandell, and from comments on an earlier draft by Nathaniel Leff.

ient dividing line within a period of marked social and economic change.

B. *Highlights of the São Paulo Experience*

The metropolis of São Paulo arose as a marketing and distribution center for its coffee producing hinterland in the latter half of the nineteenth century. Until well into the twentieth century, however, São Paulo exerted little independent influence on the economy of its surrounding hinterland. On the contrary, São Paulo's own development remained largely dependent on events taking place in the rural economy. The industrialization of the metropolis proceeded only as a result of the accumulation of capital, the development of transportation facilities, and the increases in market demand and in labor supply associated with the expansion of the coffee frontier. Particularly after the 1940's, however, the industrial urbanization of São Paulo began to exert a significant impact on the hinterland. As a result, the hinterland itself became somewhat less dependent upon international market forces. In the course of this century and a quarter of development, the food supply hinterland has expanded from the Paulista Plateau in the 1870's, reaching the Minas Triangle, southern Goiás, and northern Parana by the 1940's.

C. *São Paulo's Distinctiveness*

There are several remarkable aspects of the evolving city-hinterland interaction in São Paulo. First, São Paulo emerged as a direct result of the development of the export region. Yet, industrial urban centers do not inevitably arise out of export regions. For example, in Brazil itself, exports of sugar and cotton from the Northeast throughout the eighteenth and nineteenth century, and from Amazonia in the brief period between 1870 and 1910, led to the florescence of mercantile cities but little industrialization. Indeed, the literature on tropical export economies suggests that export-led industrialization is exceptional.[4] However, the literature on temperate regions argues that rural exports are a sufficient or even necessary condition for industrialization. This distinction between temperate and tropical economies seems applicable even in the United States, where wheat exports encouraged local industrialization but where cotton exports did not.[5] Rather than encouraging southern manufacturing, cotton facilitated industrialization in New England. São Paulo, then, provides a comparatively rare case of industrialization emerging from a tropical resource frontier.[6]

Second, the São Paulo experience contrasts with conventional theories of urban system growth which suggest that a city with a head start in industrialization (due to the exports of its hinterland or some other reason) maintains its primacy over time through the ability of its industries to achieve scale economies and a superior division of labor.[7] Many developing countries perceive themselves to be plagued by a primary city which inexorably grows and extracts capital and the most productive workers from all other cities.[8] Therefore, the Brazilian experience, with São Paulo overtaking and surpassing Rio de Janeiro as the primary industrial center of the nation, is somewhat unique.

Third, as a recently developing city, São Paulo has had available to it a backlog of technologies developed in the United States and Europe. While a preponderance of capital goods in Brazil have always been produced domestically,[9] modern industrialization has been based largely upon technologies transferred from countries with strikingly different factor proportions and factor prices. Much technology transfer has been embodied in direct foreign investment. Although some adaptation of technologies to reflect local factor proportions has taken place in other nations, less adaptation of technique—to the abundance of unskilled labor—is apparent in São Paulo today.[10] While the predominance of inappropriate capital-intensive technologies is a common facet of "modern" manufacturing in many developing countries, the lack of adaptation to local conditions in São Paulo may be attributed to educational policies rooted in the staple export era.

D. *Comparisons with North American Export Regions*

With few exceptions, economic historians have tended to limit their comparison of the São Paulo coffee frontier to other Brazilian staple regions which have not industrialized, particularly the Northeastern sugar coast, the gold mines of Minas Gerais, or the Amazonian rubber frontier.[11] In this context, industrialization, which appears impossible in most tropical resource frontiers, seems almost inevitable in São Paulo.

To place the coffee region of São Paulo in broader perspective, it is therefore useful to compare it with the American Southeast and Midwest during their export-propelled periods. By 1840, the cotton export economy of the South was well in place and the grain frontier of the Midwest was expanding geographically, as exports to the American Northwest and Europe accelerated. By the last quarter of the nineteenth century, the Southeast was still a cotton export economy, while the Midwest was undergoing substantial industrial urbanization. By the turn of the century, the cotton region commenced resource-linked industrialization (textile manufacturing), while the grain belt had developed a diversified and extensive industrial base.

When placed in an international context, the industrialization of São Paulo during the coffee export era can therefore be seen as minuscule. The fact that the metropolis of São Paulo is now one of the largest industrial agglomerations in the world suggests that the rate of change in recent decades, then, is all the more remarkable.

II. THE GROWTH OF SÃO PAULO
AS AN EXPORT FRONTIER

Until well into the nineteenth century, the São Paulo region was largely uninhabited and populated only by a few adventurers seeking the quick extraction of wealth (such as the seventeenth century *bandeirantes*[12]). These adventurers found little to induce massive settlement, and São Paulo remained incapable of producing and transporting commodities that could compete in world markets.

São Paulo's modern phase of development began with the production of coffee, especially after 1860. During the earlier part of the nineteenth century, the West Indies, Ceylon, and Java dominated world coffee production. However, Brazil's share of world production rose gradually throughout the century—from 20 percent in the 1820's to 52 percent in the 1850's, and finally to 75 percent after the turn of the century.[13]

A. *The Supply of Land and Capital*

The redistribution of world coffee production in favor of Brazil occurred largely as a result of supply factors. Coffee grows under rather strict climatic constraints. Consequently, there are few areas in the world where the most palatable species thrive, notably in the volcanic soils of the tropical highlands. Introduced into the Amazon basin in the early eighteenth century, coffee production spread to the lowlands around Rio de Janeiro around 1770, to the narrow Paraíba Valley between Rio and the Paulista capital by the 1850's, and then to the highlands northwest of the capital after the 1860's. Acreage continued to expand in a westward direction well after the 1930's, when the world coffee market collapsed.[14]

In the early phases of the coffee export economy, surplus labor and land in the environs of Rio de Janeiro were sufficient to meet demand. However, expansion of coffee production into the Paraíba Valley and especially into the Plateau required additional capital and labor. Given the increasing international mobility of capital, there was no difficulty in attracting the required capital which was highly sensitive to differentials in profitability. As in many other parts of Latin America, the British financed much of the marketing infrastructure in the province of São Paulo[15]—the ports, railroads, and urban amenities.[16]

B. *The Supply of Labor and European Immigration*

The shortage of labor posed a more significant problem. Prior to the cessation of the Atlantic slave trade in 1850, labor was imported to the coffee frontier directly from Africa. As frontier expansion continued, there was a substantial reallocation of slaves from less productive activities within the coffee region and its environs. Similarly, after 1850 there was some redistribution of slaves from the decadent sugar regions to the coffee frontier.[17]

Indigenous labor was less mobile. In 1872, as coffee began its rapid expansion on the Paulista Plateau, fully 90 percent of the Brazilian-born population living in São Paulo were born in the state, while an additional seven percent were from neighboring Minas and Rio de Janeiro.[18] Consequently, when abolition appeared imminent in the 1880's, Brazilian coffee planters were deeply concerned about the need to find alternative sources of labor. Few Europeans immigrated to Brazil because it was a slave holding country. Moreover, prior to abolition, those Europeans who were induced to settle in the country were either reduced to slave-like conditions on the coffee plantations, or were relegated to inaccessible and infertile colonies.

Abolition dramatically altered the situation. Whatever one's view of the causes of abolition, its consequences were unmistakable.[19] Almost immediately, there was an influx of southern European immigrants, primarily Italians, to the coffee plantations of São Paulo.[20] The new immigrants were more literate, more skilled, and, by virtue of their age and sex composition, more likely to participate in the labor force than the Brazilian norm.[21] In São Paulo state, immigration had a tremendous quantitative impact on the labor supply. From 1872 to 1890, the state's population grew by 0.5 million, of whom 0.1 million were migrants, two-thirds being foreigners. During the period between 1890 and 1900, the population grew by 0.9 million, of whom half were migrants, two-thirds being foreigners. By the turn of the century, foreigners comprised over 65 percent of the rural work force. In the later period, 1900-20, foreign immigration comprised virtually all the net migration to São Paulo. As a result, by 1920, 18 percent of the population was foreign born. It was not until after

1920 that internal migration became a significant factor in the population growth of the state. While almost half the net migration to São Paulo was internal in the period 1920;40, nearly four-fifths was internal in the 1940's.[22]

The qualitative impact of immigration on the São Paulo labor supply was also highly significant. The average southern European immigrant had more education than the average Brazilian native. Thus, in 1920, 44 percent of the foreign-born population in São Paulo state were literate in contrast to 27 percent of the native-born population. In the metropolis, the foreign/native differences were minimal but the levels higher (61 percent versus 57 percent). Along with Rio Grande do Sul and Santa Catarina, Brazilian states which also received substantial Italian and German immigration, São Paulo has had among the highest levels of literacy since the 1890's.[23]

The immigrants exploited their comparative educational advantage and assumed a leading role in the onset of industrialization. By 1920, the majority of the industrial labor force in São Paulo was foreign born, as were 60 percent of the owners. About half of the firms existing in São Paulo by 1960 were founded by immigrants; the bulk of the rest were founded by the children or grandchildren of immigrants.[24]

III. EXPORT-GENERATED INDUSTRIAL GROWTH IN SÃO PAULO

A. *The Staple Theory*

The influx of capital and labor made possible the development of the São Paulo region into an export economy. It did not ensure that São Paulo would subsequently undergo transformation into an industrial society. Even a thriving export economy may not make the transition to industrialization, as the staple theory illustrates. According to the staple theory, the rate of growth of an empty region depends initially upon its ability to produce a staple for world markets at a competitive price and upon the growth of demand for that staple. Export expansion in a resource frontier at the outset attracts labor and capital from other parts of the world, as new lands on the frontier are opened for exploitation. Subsequently, however, the export economy may undergo structural change into an industrial urban society, or it may instead merely continue its extensive growth in the export sector. The particular course taken by an export economy will depend upon the strength of the linkages between the export sector and the remainder of the regional economy, which may be defined in terms of the "export-base multiplier" concept. Mathematically, the export-base multiplier is the ratio of total income generated (directly and indirectly) by exports to income directly generated by exports. The *regional multiplier* has as its numerator only the total income generated directly within the export region itself, while the numerator of the *national multiplier* also includes income indirectly generated by other regions of the nation.

B. *Multiplier Mechanisms*

The export base exerts a multiplier effect on regional and national economic activity through four major channels: forward linkages, backward linkages, consumer-demand linkages, and public revenues and expenditures. Forward-linked activities involve the processing and handling of the export product, such as drying and bagging of coffee beans. In an income accounting sense, forward-linked activities add directly to the value of exports. Backward-linked activities include the provision of implements and tools, transportation facilities, and supporting services (insurance, finance, government) that make exporting possible. Such activities can have consequences that spill over to other non-staple activities. For example, the shops that repair railroad equipment may soon learn to make machine tools. Consumer demand activities are those which are generated by income earned in the export sector and spent on consumer goods produced within the region, in particular perishable foodstuffs, bulky dry goods, and personal services. Finally, public revenues and expenditures are derived by the government of the exporting country directly from taxes on staple production and sales, or indirectly from duties on imports paid for by staple exports.

C. *Quantifying the Multiplier for São Paulo*

Measurement of the multiplier requires tracing out the income flows originating in the coffee sector. Although there are no empirical data to directly measure the São Paulo multiplier, there are fragmentary indicators that the multiplier was not very large. First, in the early 1920's, after nearly a century of expansion of coffee production, all exports comprised 18 percent of gross national income; coffee exports accounted for about 10 percent of national income.[25] The share of coffee exports in São Paulo income, which is the most relevant base, must have been closer to 30 percent.[26] By contrast, in the antebellum United States, North notes that "direct income from the cotton trade was probably no more than six percent of any plausible estimate of national income . . . ."[27] Accordingly, cotton appears to have accounted for no more than 18 percent of regional income in the South. At the height of the coffee era, then, when multiplier effects had sufficient time to develop fully, the ratio of total income/ coffee income was about three to one in São Paulo state. As noted, the comparable ratio in the ante-bellum South, whose industrial forward linkages clearly occurred in New England, was about five to one. These ratios, of course, exaggerate the multiplier effects of exports, since not all regional income was derived, directly or indirectly, from the staple.

Second, the share of the São Paulo labor force that was non-agricultural was only 37 percent in 1920, the first year for which reliable data are available. While the United States as a whole reached this level by 1840, the Midwestern grain belt surpassed it by 1870, and the southeastern states approached it by 1900. In other words, 50 years of the coffee frontier expansion in São Paulo resulted in a level of industrialization equivalent to the least industrial region of the United States.[28]

Third, the urban population of São Paulo remained relatively small throughout the export-propelled phase of development. Only four percent of the state population lived in the capital in 1870 and 1890. Residence in the capital rose to 11 percent in 1900, where it remained for approximately 20 years. While there are no hard data on total urban populations before 1940, the urban population in the state was probably less than 20 percent prior to 1920. In contrast, the American Midwest surpassed this level of urbanization by 1870; the Southeast, by 1900.[29]

There are three plausible explanations why the multiplier effects of coffee exports were relatively small in the case of São Paulo: First, the inherent characteristics of the staple were not conducive to local marketing and processing; second, the size of the local market was too small to encourage import substitution; and third, the terms of trade were especially favorable to production of staples and unfavorable to production of other goods and services.

1. *Inherent characteristics of the staple: forward linkages*

Presumably, the need for local processing of a staple would be conducive to the development of an entrepreneurial class. Rothstein suggests that the reason the American wheat region developed a larger indigenous commercial and industrial class than the cotton region is that wheat necessitated greater processing and handling than did cotton. Thus industrial urbanization would not have been likely to occur in a coffee-producing region, since most of the coffee processing occurred on the farm (pulping, fermenting, drying, thrashing) or in the consuming areas (roasting). However, if this is correct, one would expect that regions growing sugar cane should be relatively more industrial because cane is processed immediately on site. A cursory examination of sugar-producing regions, such as the Caribbean and Northeastern littoral, does little to suggest that forward-linked processing results in self-sustaining industrial development.[30]

2. *Size of the local market and income distribution*

Import substitution occurs when the price of the imported goods, including transportation, exceeds the price of a domestically produced substitute. Since most manufactures are produced under economies of scale, and since the developed areas have a large industrial sector, imports initially undercut local production in the emerging region. The same transportation improvements which encourage export expansion often hinder import substitution by lowering the price of imports. The domestic market can expand with the rise of population, rise of per capita income, and the naturalization of immigrants in terms of their taste and disposition of earnings.

Factors affecting income distribution in Brazil may have been partially responsible for the small multiplier. To the extent that income is distributed narrowly and the wealthy are luxury importers who are disdainful of local crafts, potential domestic manufacturers have difficulty attaining the threshold market size necessary for import substitution. Market size is also lessened by income leakages to foreign laborers, who tend to repatriate a large proportion of their earnings. Many early Italian immigrants of São Paulo made significant unrequited transfers to Italy.[31]

While income distribution factors may thus have affected the size of the São Paulo multiplier, the determinants of income distribution itself are not easy to isolate. Some scholars have suggested that the income distribution is determined by the technology of staple production or by land abundance. First, Baldwin argues that tropical crops tend to be labor-intensive and produced under increasing returns to scale, while temperate crops tend to be land-intensive and produced under constant or diminishing returns to scale.[32] Newly settled tropical regions, therefore, would have an unequal social structure and income distribution, with an illiterate mass of unskilled workers supporting a super-stratum that controls the political system. This hypothesis does not stand up well against the evidence. It is difficult to distinguish "democratic" from "hierarchical" crops by technology.[33] While wheat was associated with family farms in the Midwest, it was associated with *latifundia* and short-term tenancy in Argentina.[34] Second, Frederick Jackson Turner hypothesized that opening up and settling an empty frontier are inherently equalizing processes. While this thesis influenced several generations of historians in the early 1900's, there are too many counter-examples—from sixteenth century Eastern Europe to the Americas thereafter—to give much credence to that thesis.[35]

The experience of São Paulo, like that in Argentina, indicates that the initial patterns of land tenure, the major influence on income distribution, is determined politically.[36] How these relations evolve apparently depends somewhat upon the technology of production. While both the Paulista and Argentine landlords intended to produce a hierarchical rural structure, they had different kinds of labor demands. In the case of coffee, labor was required year round in Brazil and carelessness in the tending of trees would have been costly to the landlord. An unstable labor force for wheat production was less costly to the Argentine landlord, whose labor force needs were more seasonal and who had an alternative product in cattle. The Paulista landlord's greater necessity for a stable labor force resulted in the creation of a land tenure system more favorable to the worker. Under the *colono* system, the worker received a fixed fee per tree tended, a share of the harvest, and a piece of land for subsistence crops. While far from a freehold, the system permitted some income redistribution and capital accumulation. Cyclical crises in the coffee sector which often resulted in foreclosures contributed to the fragmentation of some estates for sale to the colonists. By the turn of the century, for example, immigrants owned 30 percent of the properties and somewhat less of the land; by 1920, 40 percent.[37]

3. *The terms of trade*

On balance, however, the most important factor accounting for the low multiplier was the relative internal price of coffee vis-a-vis manufactures, which reflected conditions unique to Brazil among nineteenth century export economies. Unlike other export economies, Brazil had a virtual monopoly over its staple around the turn of the century. Since the price elasticity of demand for coffee was low (approximately 0.3), international prices could be manipulated without significantly changing the demand for the Brazilian product.[38]

Brazil took only moderate advantage of its monopoly position in the nineteenth century. São Paulo's immigration subsidy program was financed by a surcharge on coffee exports, which was borne largely by foreign consumers (because of the inelastic demand). For local landlords, immigration subsidy was clearly a cheaper mechanism for attracting labor than the alternative of offering high wages to immigrants who would pay their own way. As a result of this policy, migrants entered the coffee sector in excess of the demand for labor. While in the short run this policy decreased the cost of coffee production, in the long run it encouraged the influx of highly skilled labor to the urban areas, where wages were higher.[39]

By 1906, however, several crises in world coffee markets had occurred, and São Paulo took the lead in creating a price-support (*valorization*) plan. The purchase of surplus coffee stocks by a state agency resulted in unprecedented world prices in the short run, which in turn stimulated greater coffee production in Brazil. These price-support schemes made investment in coffee much more attractive than in manufactures.[40] That these policies were pursued well beyond the Great Depression attests to the political strength of the coffee planters as a class. If development is equated with modern industrialization, then this class is clearly an example of an elite committed to underdevelopment.[41]

IV. THE TRANSITION TO SELF-SUSTAINING INDUSTRIAL GROWTH

A. *A Central Place Theory*

In a staple economy, most nonexport activities take place within a hierarchy of towns and cities. Where these activities are located in the hierarchy depends upon economies of scale in production relative to demand, transportation costs relative to produce or service value, and "density" of demand (quantity demanded per square kilometer). Those activities with minimal economies of scale, high transportation costs, and dense demand—such as food retailing—tend to be widely dispersed, forming the basis of the smallest (or lowest-order) towns. Those activities with substantial economies of scale, low transportation costs, and sparse demand—such as floating bonds on international markets—occur only in the largest (or highest-order) national centers. The size and density of all centers in the urban hierarchy vary directly with the per capita income and density of the rural population. Rapid growth of income in a region can result in its attaining ever higher "thresholds" of import substitution so that its own cities assume the highest-order activities, formerly undertaken only in the national metropolis.

B. *The Rise of São Paulo as Brazil's Industrial Center*

Prior to 1868, almost all of the coffee in Brazil was produced in the hinterland of Rio de Janeiro. Even coffee produced in the Paulista portion of the Paraíba Valley was shipped by rail to Rio de Janeiro for ultimate export. All the multiplier effects of coffee exports, then, accrued to the national capital, which was also the largest port, manufacturing center, and urban market. The continual shift of coffee cultivation southwesterly into the Paulista plateau might have continued to benefit Rio, just as the westward shift of wheat cultivation continued to benefit the port of New York. However, in 1868, a railroad linking Santos to Jundiaí on the plateau rerouted the flow of coffee away from Rio. Astride the railroad, at the edge of the best pass through the Great Escarpment, São Paulo was able to squelch the expansion of Rio's hinterland and to capture the *entrepôt* functions for itself. While in 1870, the hinterland of Rio produced ten times the coffee export volume of São Paulo, the two were equal by 1890. During the period, 1900-30, the coffee hinterland of São Paulo was more than twice the size of Rio's.[42]

As expected, the expansion of resource-based exports in São Paulo was accompanied by industrial urbanization. Prior to 1940, the industrial structure in Brazil, and São Paulo in particular, reflected a "traditional" pattern characteristic of low-income countries. In particular, Brazilian industry was concentrated in the textile and food processing sectors. In 1920, fully 38 percent of the value added in Brazil originated in the textile-clothing sector, with another 26 percent in food processing. By 1940, these sectors still contributed the major share of national value added. The industrial structure in São Paulo state was not much different from that in Brazil, although it was somewhat more concentrated in textiles and less in food.[43]

Frontier expansion in São Paulo state was accompanied not only by industrialization but also by rapid urban growth. The eighth largest city in the nation in 1872, São Paulo had a population of 31,000, only one-ninth that of Rio de Janeiro. By 1900, São Paulo was one-fourth as large as Rio de Janeiro. As the staple economy peaked in 1940, São Paulo grew to more than one-half the size of Rio de Janeiro. Satellite cities, notably Santos, Campinas, and Piracicaba, arose as major marketing and distribution centers. Finally, in the 1950's, São Paulo surpassed Rio as the most populous city. This was a rare event from an international perspective.

In many ways, the ascendency of São Paulo was an unlikely development. In the early 1900's, Rio appears to have had all the inherent advantages—a port, an abundant supply of financial capital accumulated from the various staple booms, and, most important, a politically powerful elite whose favors could make or break an industrialist. While Rio indeed has been a growing industrial center in this century, São Paulo appears to have offset Rio's initial advantage by the sheer force of its ever-increasing market size.[44]

C. *Political Factors in the Growth of São Paulo*

It was by no means inevitable that São Paulo would become a self-sustaining industrial center. The staple model suggests that export-propelled growth is reversible. There are ample examples of the reversibility of export-propelled growth in Brazilian history: notably the exhaustion of mines in Minas Gerais at the end of the eighteenth century, the collapse of the rubber boom in Amazonia at the beginning of this century, and repeated shocks in the world coffee markets, particularly during World War I.

If the fate of São Paulo differed from that of other staple-exporting regions in Brazil, it was not through the foresight of the coffee planter class that dominated state and national politics during the First Republic, which lasted from 1889 to 1930. Acting largely through the powerful state government, the planters pursued policies favoring the extension of coffee cultivation, with little regard to improving human resources or fomenting industrialization for its own sake. The major portion of state revenues was devoted to coffee price support schemes, immigration, and interest rate guarantees for railroad investors (which were rarely needed, since Paulista railroads were usually profitable). In the entire period of the First Republic, state expenditures on military and police forces equalled those on education and exceeded those on public health, fields in which São Paulo led Brazil.[45]

Fifty or sixty years of extensive growth nevertheless had beneficial, if unintended consequences, for future industrialization. The immigration of southern European field workers resulted in a pool of highly productive workers, albeit of moderate skills by international standards. With the influx of these immigrants, the population of the coffee region comprised a relatively large market that was well-connected by an excellent railroad system. Finally, the decision to concentrate on coffee production ultimately yielded a large supply of savings which became available for investment in nonexport activities as they became profitable.

D. *The Depression as a Force for Change*

The definitive historiography of Brazil's transition from a staple-export to a rapidly industrializing nation has yet to be written, and much controversy remains.[46] Nevertheless, it is clear that a major role was played by the Great Depression, which disrupted the world coffee market, and with it, the intellectual and political foundations of São Paulo's economy. With the collapse of coffee prices, partly a result of declining world demand and partly a result of oversupply stimulated by the price-support schemes, the economic power of the coffee planters was considerably weakened. It became increasingly difficult to maintain that coffee production was Brazil's natural vocation, as determined by the impersonal forces of international comparative advantage. Within the next few decades, "structuralism", a doctrine which favors industrialization as a solution to the chronic instability and stagnation of staple-export economies, replaced economic liberalism as Brazil's dominant economic ideology. Finally, a political revolution in 1930 weakened the prerogatives of the state governments, and hence those of the coffee planters, and brought to power men from the peripheral states, who were less likely to identify the interests of the coffee sector with those of the nation. While the new regime shunned what it viewed as "artificial" industrialization and continued to support the coffee sector by purchasing surpluses, the level of support was less than before. Tentative overtures toward industrialization for strategic purposes were initiated in the 1940's; basic industries like steel and petroleum were established between 1946 and 1954; and by 1955 the national government endorsed a wholehearted effort at import-substituting industrialization.[47]

V. CONSEQUENCES OF DEVELOPMENT

A. *Frontier Expansion and Diversification*

In the hundred years prior to the Great Depression, coffee acreage continually expanded in a westward direction. Until the 1930's, the dominant crop in all areas of São Paulo state was coffee, which absorbed about half the cropland. Intermixed with coffee were foodstuffs for the rural and urban populations, particularly corn, rice and beans.

At least since the 1930's, there has been a rapid expansion of acreage in other states of South-Central Brazil, most notably in Paraná, Goiás, and Mato Grosso. The three frontier states plus São Paulo have increased their share of the nation's arable land from 30 percent in 1940 to 34 percent in the 1950's, with a slight increase thereafter.

Interestingly, very little of this expansion has been attributable to coffee. In fact, coffee acreage in the four states has remained almost stable at 2 million hectares since the 1930's. Virtually all of the increase in acreage has been devoted to foodstuffs, cane, and cotton. Furthermore, farming districts in South-Central Brazil have become increasingly specialized as distinct belts of perishables, export crops, and nonperishable foodstuffs have emerged.[48]

The patterns of expansion and specialization of the past several decades can be understood by viewing metropolitan São Paulo as a vast market center and transportation node. The demand for agricultural products in this market has grown explosively due to rising urban population and incomes within the region, rather than due to growth in exports as was previously the case. Because of the abundance of good land in South-Central Brazil, it has been more economical to increase supply by incorporating more land than by intensifying the use of existing farm land through the use of fertilizers, machinery, or the development of better seeds. Indeed, with the exception of cotton seed research aimed at increasing the quality of the fiber, almost all the increase in supply since the 1930's has been produced through the extension of traditional methods. Frontier expansion was made possible by improvements in the marketing system, particularly in highways, that resulted in a two-thirds reduction in transportation costs from farm to local market and from local market to regional market shipments.

B. *Rural Modernization*

Industrial urbanization has had some effect on modernizing agriculture. When the coffee market collapsed in the 1930's, Brazil's capacity to import was severely curtailed. The demand for domestically manufactured textiles was thereby enhanced. Native cotton, traditionally grown in the Northeastern interior, was inferior in length, yield, and ratio of fiber to seed to the imported variety. Accordingly, potential São Paulo manufacturers then encouraged publicly supported cottonseed research that resulted in substantial improvements in the quality of domestic cotton.[49] Cotton has since become a permanent fixture in the agricultural picture of the hinterland. With the recovery of coffee and growth of domestic demand for food, cotton acreage in São Paulo and Paraná subsequently declined, as the new seed was adapted to the Northeast. Furthermore, there is some evidence that localized industrialization has encouraged the capital intensification and modernization of agriculture. The major mechanisms appear to be the greater availability of credit for capital goods and intermediate products in areas closer to the cities.[50]

C. *Labor Absorption*

In labor surplus economies, such as England after the enclosures or the American Southeast at the turn of the century, industrial urbanization plays a major role in encouraging agricultural modernization by absorbing rural workers. In contrast, São Paulo's expanding hinterland has played no small role in the increase of the rural population. In the period, 1940-70, the farm work force expanded 77 percent in São Paulo, Paraná, Goiás, and Mato Grosso. This absorption of rural labor hardly kept up with the 200 percent increase in the population and workforce of these four states, and labor absorption of both the urban and rural sectors together was insufficient to raise the wages of farm workers over the past 20 years.[51]

D. *Industrial Development, Diversification, and Interindustry Linkages*

Brazilians have long pointed with pride to São Paulo as the largest industrial center in South America. In terms of industrial employment, São Paulo is exceeded by only New York and Chicago and surpasses Los Angeles. Moveover, as measured by share of employment in manufacturing, São Paulo is a much more industrial city than the three great metropolises of the United States. Of course, in terms of the value of manufacturing output, São Paulo is inferior to many North American cities; nevertheless, it is an impressive industrial agglomeration by world standards. With three percent of Brazil's land area and 19 percent of its population, São Paulo accounts for approximately 34 percent of the nation's total manufacturing employment.

The industrial structure of São Paulo is now highly diversified. Czamanski and Ablas have identified eight groups of industries in São Paulo with important cross-flow of goods and services.[52] These "industrial complexes" are, in decreasing order of employment: automobiles, textiles, communications and electronics, paper and printing, iron and steel, two petrochemical complexes, and wood products. While most large industrial centers in the United States have more than one industrial complex, only the four largest centers are as diversified as São Paulo.

In a most interesting analysis of the input-output relationships in the São Paulo metropolis, Czamanski and Ablas distinguished the static and dynamic effects of changes in output in 122 industrial sectors. The static effects include interindustry transactions, increases in consumer spending, and increases in public services; the dynamic effects include manufacturing investment, housing, and other construction. The average multiplier (including the original change in output) in the metropolis was approximately 3.0. Quantitatively, increase in consumer spending was the most important (multiplier of 1.2), followed by interindustry transactions (.39), and manufacturing investment (.36).[53]

The lion's share of the multiplier effects occurs within the state. For example, a $100 million increase in state output of chemicals, induces $53 million additional output in supplying industries throughout Brazil. Of that impact, $42 million occurs within São Paulo. The share of induced effects "leaking" to the rest of the country ranged from less than three percent for leather and paper to more than 60 percent in resource industries, mining and wood products. The modal leakage for 20 two-digit manufacturing sectors is less than 20 percent. Leakages for the other static and dynamic multipliers (with the possible exception of food consumption) are not likely to be much larger. In effect, industrial growth in São Paulo is not likely to directly spill over to other states. The major interregional multiplier effects appear to be in increasing the demand for industrial raw materials and food, predominantly in the surrounding states.

Studies focusing on interregional, as well as interindustry, linkages suggest that an increase in output of Northeastern industry spills over to a great degree to São Paulo (more correctly the Central South). The modern industrial sector in the Northeast imports approximately 70 percent of its inputs from the Central South. About half of these imports are manufactures; the remainder are primary products, fuels, and other intermediate materials. As expected, a large share of capital goods (57 percent) are imported.[54] A multiregional input-output analysis has shown that fiscal incentives for production in the Northeast result in nearly as much additional output in the Central South as in the Northeast.[55] In other words, while industrial growth in São Paulo has little stimulative effect on peripheral regions, the converse is not true.

E. *Interstate Migration*

São Paulo has affected the peripheral hinterland primarily through adjustment mechanisms such as migration, which the city's industrialization has induced, rather than through interindustry linkages or trade. Of the population residing in São Paulo in 1940, 89 percent was born there, while only 4 percent was born in the Northeast, mostly Bahia. By 1950 these figures were 87 and 5 percent; by 1970, 82 and 8 percent. In the period from 1950 to 1970, fully half of the gross interstate migration to São Paulo was from the Northeast. These direct migration effects do not exhaust the total effect of São Paulo as a labor safety valve. Northeastern migration to the Central West, which has been increasing rapidly since the 1960's, reflects the growth of the rice frontier stimulated by São Paulo's industrial urbanization. Workers from the Minas Gerais (a state in the intermediate level of development), who have been absorbed by Paulista industry or by the rice frontier, vacate places for migrating Northeasterners. In 1940 (after the great period of foreign immigration had virtually ended), only two percent of the Northeastern-born population lived in the Central South. This figure rose to 5 percent by 1950 and fully 12 percent by 1970.[56] While all of this migration cannot be attributed directly or indirectly to industrialization of São Paulo, it is likely that population would be considerably higher in the Northeast had São Paulo stagnated, in which case per capita income would have been correspondingly lower.

VI. PROSPECTS FOR THE FUTURE OF SÃO PAULO

A. *Agricultural Development*

The future portends continued agricultural growth in the São Paulo region, although with a somewhat different spatial form. The near hinterland, particularly Mato Grosso and Goiás, still contains the best underutilized land in Brazil; this area is fertile and accessible and should continue to serve as a magnet for rural immigrants. The growth of demand for food and fiber from the metropolis will propel the growth of the hinterland, although in a less extensive manner than before because of rising fuel costs.

In a reversal of past trends, agricultural exports from the hinterland have been revived as a result of government promotion and heightened world demand. Most notable has been the rise of the soybean, which has replaced coffee in much of northern Paraná. Further export expansion is likely to favor agriculture in São Paulo's hinterland because of the soils and transportation infrastructure. The revival of staple exports is unlikely to have as dramatic an impact on the metropolis as did exports during the heyday of coffee. First, the Brazilian transportation system has become more interconnected, and therefore São Paulo is no longer the focal transportation node it was during the railroad era. The hinterland can channel its exports through several alternative ports. Second, the scale of São Paulo's industrial sector is such that primary exports no longer have the leverage on the regional economy they had in former years.

B. *Industrial Deconcentration*

The high cost of labor, land, and communications within the metropolis may serve to decelerate its industrial growth. Large-scale enterprise may find that these diseconomies of urban scale more than offset the economies—a skilled labor force, the minute diversion of labor among complementary plants, and a wide variety of supporting business services. With the spread of technical training, the expansion of the banking network, and the improved transportation system, firms can benefit from the urban scale economies in many locations within striking distance of the metropolis, such as the Paraíba Valley.[57]

C. *Conclusion*

In the last century and one quarter, metropolitan São Paulo has evolved from a minor provincial capital to the apex of Brazil's wealthiest and most dynamic region. Owing its initial growth to the expansion of the coffee frontier, the metropolis is clearly the engine of growth in a hinterland that now encompasses nearly all of South-Central Brazil.

The old saying "São Paulo cannot stop" has been replaced by the new shibboleth, "São Paulo *must* stop." Concern about the concentration of economic power in the metropolis was formerly expressed only by leaders of peripheral states; now the concern emanates from the Paulistas themselves. Rather than denying the virtue of growth, the Paulista elite is preoccupied with such diseconomies of scale as congestion, pollution, increasing crime (and probably the scarcity of domestics associated with it). The future of São Paulo will turn on how these problems are handled, or ignored.

NOTES

1. *See, e.g.*, Baldwin, *The Development of Newly Settled Regions*, 24 MANCHESTER SCHOOL OF ECON. & SOCIAL STUDIES 161 (May 1956); Watkins, *A Staple Theory of Economic Growth*, 29 CANADIAN JOURNAL OF ECON. & POL. SCI. 141 (May 1963); Caves, "*Vent for Surplus*" *Models of Trade and Growth*, in JAMES THEBERGE, ed., THE ECONOMICS OF TRADE AND DEVELOPMENT 211 (NY: John Wiley, 1968).

2. The classic work on central place theory is WALTER CHRISTALLER, CENTRAL PLACES IN SOUTHERN GERMANY (Englewood Cliffs, N.J.: Prentice-Hall, reprint 1967). The most exhaustive review of studies in this area is BRIAN J.L. BERRY & ALLEN PRED, CENTRAL PLACE STUDIES: A BIBLIOGRAPHY OF THEORY AND APPLICATION (Philadelphia: Regional Science Research Institute, rev. ed. 1965).

3. For a recent review and integration of these theories, see Katzman, *The Von Thuenen Paradigm, the Industrial-Urban Hypothesis, and the Spatial Structure of Agriculture*, 56 AM. JOURNAL OF AGRICULTURAL ECON. 683 (Nov. 1974).

4. For case studies and an overview of tropical export economies, see, *e.g.*, JONATHAN LEVIN, THE EXPORT ECONOMIES: THEIR PATTERN OF DEVELOPMENT IN HISTORICAL PERSPECTIVE (Cambridge, MA: Harvard U. Press, 1960); GEORGE BECKFORD, PERSISTENT POVERTY: UNDERDEVELOPMENT IN PLANTATION ECONOMIES OF THE THIRD WORLD (NY: Oxford U. Press, 1973).

5. *See* JEFFREY G. WILLIAMSON, LATE NINETEENTH CENTURY AMERICAN DEVELOPMENT (NY & London: Cambridge U. Press, 1974).

6. At the Stanford Conference (April 1977), David Landes suggested that West Malaysia (formerly Malaya) is another resource frontier which has generated significant industrial urbanization. The West Malaysian rubber and tin export economy, however, has attained levels of industrialization and urbanization significantly lower than Brazil's, or other temperate countries of East Asia, like Taiwan and South Korea. With per capita income comparable to that of Brazil (approximately $400 in 1970), West Malaysia derived only 15% of its income from industry in contrast to 28% in Brazil as a whole, and 40% in São Paulo state. In the late 1960's, West Malaysia was much more of a staple economy, with 40% of its income derived from exports, in contrast to about 7% for Brazil. *See* DAVID C. LIM, ECONOMIC GROWTH AND DEVELOPMENT IN WEST MALAYSIA, 1947–1970, Chap. 1 (Kuala Lumpur: Oxford U. Press, 1973); WOLFGANG KASPER, MALAYSIA: A STUDY IN SUCCESSFUL ECONOMIC DEVELOPMENT (Washington, D.C.: American Enterprise Institute, 1974). Corresponding Brazilian data appear in *As Contas Nacionais*, 24 CONJUNTURA ECONÔMICA 89, at 90, 110-11.

7. The model of "initial advantage and circular and cumulative causation" is most carefully elaborated in ALLEN PRED, SPATIAL DYNAMICS OF U.S. URBAN-INDUSTRIAL GROWTH, 1800–1914 (Cambridge, MA: M.I.T. Press, 1966).

8. For a description of the problems of overgrown primate cities, see LLOYD RODWIN, NATIONS AND CITIES: A COMPARISON OF STRATEGIES FOR URBAN GROWTH (Boston: Houghton Mifflin, 1970). For a critique of the model of circular and cumulative causation, see MARTIN T. KATZMAN, CITIES AND FRONTIERS IN BRAZIL: REGIONAL DIMENSIONS OF ECONOMIC DEVELOPMENT, Chap. 7 (Cambridge, MA: Harvard U. Press, 1977).

9. NATHANIEL LEFF, THE BRAZILIAN CAPITAL GOODS INDUSTRY, 1929–1964, at 168-76 (Cambridge, MA: Harvard U. Press, 1968).

10. At the onset of North American industrialization, the basic industrial processes, particularly sources of power and production technologies, were imported. However, substantial technological modifications, reflective of American factor proportions, were made by the highly skilled craftsmen and artisans in the population. H.J. HABAKKUK, AMERICAN AND BRITISH TECHNOLOGY IN THE NINETEENTH CENTURY (NY and London: Cambridge U. Press); Rosenberg, *American Technology: Imported or Indigenous?* 67 AM. ECON. REV. 21 (Feb. 1977).

11. *See, e.g.*, CELSO FURTADO, THE ECONOMIC GROWTH OF BRAZIL: A SURVEY FROM COLONIAL TO MODERN TIMES (Berkeley: U. of Calif. Press, trans. Ricardo W. de Aguiar & Eric C. Drysdale, 1968).

12. *See generally*, RICHARD MORSE, THE BANDEIRANTES (NY: Alfred Knopf, 1967).

13. J.F. NORMANO, BRAZIL: A STUDY OF ECONOMIC TYPES, Chap. 2 (Chapel Hill: U. of N.C. Press, 1935).

14. *See generally*, SÉRGIO MILLIET, O ROTEIRO DO CAFÉ (São Paulo: Estudos Paulistas, 1938); Katzman, *Industrialization, Agricultural Specialization and Frontier Settlement in South Central Brazil, 1940–70*, 6 DEVELOPMENT AND CHANGE 25 (Oct. 1975).

15. São Paulo became a state in 1889.

16. RICHARD GRAHAM, BRITAIN AND THE ONSET OF MODERNIZATION IN BRAZIL, 1850–1914 (London & NY: Cambridge U. Press, 1968).

17. *See, e.g.*, ROBERT CONRAD, THE DESTRUCTION OF BRAZILIAN SLAVERY, 1850–1888 (Berkeley: U. of Calif. Press, 1972).

18. These census figures were compiled by Douglas H. Graham and Sérgio Buarque de Hollanda Filho, to whom I am grateful.

19. The role the expansion of the coffee frontier played in abolishing slavery is subject to considerable dispute. The "traditional" view is that political and ideological forces resulted in the demise of slavery. "Revisionists" argue, however, that slavery was moribund for demographic reasons (slaves were not reproducing themselves), and that the existence of the institution was an obstacle to attracting free labor from Europe. *See generally*, EMÍLIA VIOTTI DA COSTA, DE SENZALA À COLÔNIA (São Paulo: Difusão Européia, 1966); CONRAD, *supra* note 16. Carvalho de Mello, *The Economics of Labor in Brazilian Coffee Plantations, 1850–1888* (unpublished Ph.D. dissertation, U. of Chicago, 1977), however, notes that the coffee plantations absorbed only one-fifth of the slave labor in the coffee regions, that there were considerable opportunities to expand production under traditional social relations after 1888, and that political and ideological factors played the critical role in abolition.

20. 1889–97 was the peak period for immigration to Brazil, which attracted nearly one-fifth of the immigration to the Americas.

21. *See* Hall, *The Origins of Mass Immigration in Brazil, 1871–1914* (unpublished Ph.D. dissertation, Colombia U., 1969); Graham, *Migração estrangeiro e a questão da oferta de mão-de-obra no crescimento econômico brasileiro, 1880–1930, 3 ESTUDOS ECONÔMICOS* 7 (Apr. 1973).

22. Graham, *supra* note 19; Douglas H. Graham & Sérgio Buarque de Hollanda Filho, *Migration, Regional and Urban Growth and Development in Brazil* (U. of São Paulo, Instituto de Pesquisas Economicas, 1971).

23. Brasil, *Recenseamento de 1920, População*, Vol. 4, Part 4, pp. i-xxv.

24. Graham, *supra* note 16. On the major role of immigrants as entrepreneurs, see WARREN DEAN, THE INDUSTRIALIZATION OF SÃO PAULO, 1880–1945 (Austin, TX: U. of Texas Press, 1969).

25. Nathaniel Leff, *Tropical Trade and Development in the Nineteenth Century: The Brazilian Experience*, 81 JOURNAL OF POL. ECON. 678, at 684, 690 (May/June 1973).

26. In the 1920's, about 70% of all coffee exports emanated from São Paulo. In other words, about 7% of the national income of Brazil was derived directly from São Paulo coffee exports. Thus, if São Paulo's share of national income was 20 to 25%, São Paulo's coffee exports generated directly about 28 to 33% of its own total income.

27. DOUGLASS C. NORTH, ECONOMIC GROWTH OF THE UNITED STATES, 1790–1960, at 6 (NY: Norton, 1960).

28. HARVEY S. PERLOFF *et al.*, REGIONS, RESOURCES, AND ECONOMIC GROWTH (Lincoln: U. of Nebraska, 1960); Lampard, *The Evolving System of Cities in the U.S.*, in HARVEY S. PERLOFF & LOWDON WINGO, JR., eds., ISSUES IN URBAN ECONOMICS 81 (Baltimore, MD: Johns Hopkins Press, 1968).

29. *Id.*

30. *See* Rothstein, *Antebellum Wheat and Cotton Exports: Contrasts in Marketing Organization*, 40 AGRICULTURAL HISTORY 91 (Apr. 1966); BECKFORD, *supra* note 4.

31. *See, e.g.*, LEVIN, *supra* note 4.

32. Baldwin, *supra* note 1.

33. Katzman, *The Social Relations of Production on the Brazilian Frontier*, in JEROME STEFFAN & HARRY D. MILLER eds., THE FRONTIER: COMPARATIVE STUDIES 275 (Norman, OK: U. of Oklahoma Press, 1977).

34. JAMES SCOBIE, REVOLUTION ON THE PAMPAS: A SOCIAL HISTORY OF ARGENTINE WHEAT, 1860–1910 (Austin: U. of Texas Press, 1964).

35. The Turner thesis and alternative hypotheses are discussed and evaluated in Katzman, *The Brazilian Frontier in Comparative Perspective*, 17 COMPARATIVE STUDIES IN SOC'Y & HISTORY 266 (July 1975).

36. *Id.*; Warren Dean, *Latifundia and Land Policy in Nineteenth Century Brazil*, 51 HISPANIC AMER. HIST. REV. 606; Viotti da Costa, *supra* note 15.

37. Douglas H. Graham and Thomas Merrick, *Population and Economic Growth in Brazil: An Interpretation of the Long Term Trend (1800–2000)*, Ms.

38. Krasner, *Manipulation of International Commodity Markets: Brazilian Coffee Policy, 1906 to 1962*, 21 PUBLIC POLICY 493 (Fall 1973).

39. Hall, *supra* note 21; GRAHAM, *supra* note 16.

40. As late as the 1960's, the government expended as much as 2% of the national product in acquiring coffee stocks. Lessa, *Fifteen Years of Economic Policy in Brazil*, 9 ECON. BULLETIN FOR LATIN AMERICA 153 (Dec. 1964).

41. This phrase is from ANDRE GUNDER FRANK, CAPITALISM AND UNDERDEVELOPMENT IN LATIN AMERICA (NY: Monthly Review Press, 1967).

42. Graham, *supra* note 15; PAUL SINGER, DESENVOLVIMENTO ECONÔMICO E EVOLUÇÃO URBANA 28-32, 51-53 (São Paulo: U. de São Paulo, 1968).

43. Katzman, *supra* note 7, chap. 7.

44. The historical stage at which this overtaking and surpassing occurred is of great significance. Since most important industries prior to the 1940's produced bulky consumer goods or processed natural resources, access to the market and raw materials supply area carried great weight vis-a-vis access to capital, political intelligence, or existing suppliers of machine tools and parts. Had the shift of the coffee frontier to São Paulo occurred after the metallurgical and mechanical industries had developed in Rio, São Paulo might have remained as rural and unindustrialized as Paraná, its successor as a coffee frontier. This is because more complicated and roundabout industrial processes depend upon a greater division of labor among firms, and, given the backwardness of communications and transportation, a high degree of proximity. This situation would have favored the largest existing industrial agglomeration, as suggested by the model of circular and cumulative causation.

45. An exception to the rule that little attention was paid to modernization is state support of cottonseed research after the 1920's, which was induced by the search for an alternative to coffee. Love, *External Financing and Domestic Politics: The Case of São Paulo, Brazil, 1889–1937*, in ROBERT E. SCOTT, ed., LATIN AMERICAN MODERNIZATION PROBLEMS 236 (Urbana: U. of Illinois, 1973); Joseph L. Love, *Fiscal Federalism* (Chapter 8 of forthcoming manuscript of São Paulo state under the First Republic). Given its level of income, Brazil had the lowest level of human capital formation of any major nation in the world during the early post-War period. *See* FREDRICK H. HARBINSON & CHARLES A. MYERS, EDUCATION, MANPOWER, AND ECONOMIC GROWTH (NY: McGraw-Hill, 1964).

46. A major debate revolves around whether Brazil's low level of industrialization prior to World War II was an inevitable consequence of its role as a staple economy dominated by a planter class, or was instead merely a distortion caused by ill-informed policy. A subordinate issue is whether the collapse of coffee export during World War I, the Great Depression, and World War II helped or hindered industrialization. Structuralists tend to view staple exports, and the class relations they imply, as an inevitable impediment to industrialization. *See, e.g.*, FURTADO, *supra* note 11. Neo-classical revisionists believe Brazil's low level of industrialization was a result of poorly formulated policy, not invariably in the interests of the dominant planters, and not ameliorated by reducing coffee exports. *See, e.g.*, ANNIBAL VILLANOVA VILLELA & WILSON SUZIGAN, POLÍTICA DO GOVERNO E CRESCIMENTO DA ECONÔMICA BRASILEIRA, 1889–1945 (Rio: Instituto de Planejamento Econômico Aplicada, 1973); CARLOS M. PELÁEZ, A HISTÓRIA DE INDUSTRIALIZAÇÃO BRASILEIRA (Rio: APEC Editora, 1972).

47. For an analysis of the political economy of industrialization, *see* NÍCIA VILLELA LUZ, A LUTA PELA INDUSTRIALIZAÇÃO DO BRASIL (São Paulo: Difusão Européia, 1961); NATHANIEL LEFF, ECONOMIC POLICY-MAKING AND DEVELOPMENT IN BRAZIL, 1947–1964 (NY: John Wiley, 1968); THOMAS

E. SKIDMORE, POLITICS IN BRAZIL, 1930–1964 (London: Oxford U. Press, 1967); JOHN WIRTH, THE POLITICS OF BRAZILIAN DEVELOPMENT, 1930-1954 (Stanford, CA: Stanford U. Press, 1970).

48. The basic facts and bibliography on the expansion and diversification of the hinterland are found in Katzman, *supra* note 14.

49. Ayer & Schuh, *Social Rates of Return and Other Aspects of Agricultural Research: The Case of Cotton Research in São Paulo, Brazil*, 54 AM. JOURNAL OF AGRICULTURAL ECON. 557 (Nov. 1972).

50. Katzman, *supra* note 3.

51. For a more detailed discussion, see KATZMAN, *supra* note 8, chapters 3 and 10.

52. Stan Czamanski & Luis A. Ablas, *A Model of the Industrial Structure of Maturing Economies: The Case of São Paulo* (unpublished).

53. *Id.*

54. Goodman, *Industrial Development in the Northeast* in RIORDAN ROETT, ed., BRAZIL IN THE SIXTIES 231 (Nashville, TN: Vanderbilt U. Press, 1971).

55. Osmundo E. Reboucas, *Interregional Effects of Economic Policies: Multisectoral General Equilibrium Estimates for Brazil* (chap. 5 of unpublished Ph.D. dissertation, Harvard U., 1974).

56. *Supra* note 17.

57. Thus far, no area outside of the São Paulo–Rio axis seems capable of spawning a complete industrial complex, although partial ones exist in Belo Horizonte (steel) and Salvador (petrochemicals). The former has never been able to attract the forward-linked fabricating industries to complete the complex, while the latter hardly has the scale, technical manpower, or resource hinterland to develop completely in the near future.

Intercity Development
and Dependency:
Liverpool and Manchester

JOHN B. SHARPLESS*

THE RELATIONSHIP BETWEEN changes in the economic structure of cities and the evolution of hinterland economies remains obscure.[1] In seeking to delineate the character of such relationships, a return to the empirical setting that has spawned so much of the theoretical work on industrial and economic growth—the northwestern region of Britain—is appropriate. The transformation of nineteenth century Lancashire and Cheshire was not only one of the first but also one of the most intensive cases of urban-industrial development among the Western economies. Of particular importance to this development process was the relationship between Liverpool and Manchester and the changing character of industry in the surrounding Lancashire/Cheshire hinterland.

In many ways, the growth of Liverpool and Manchester closely fits the classical theories of urban economy which emphasize the changing nature of transport technology, the rise of central place functions, and the concentration of industry. Yet the symbiotic character of their demographic growth and economic function appears to violate other basic principles of conventional urban theory. On the basis of central place theory, for example, one would not anticipate the growth of *two* "central" cities, sharing the urban functions which are usually concentrated in a single dominant center. Nonetheless, this did occur. Moreover, this type of development constitutes a significant minority pattern in the Third World today and, therefore, is worthy of more intensive examination.

* Assistant Professor of History at the University of Wisconsin.

I. CITY/HINTERLAND SYSTEMS IN DEVELOPING ECONOMIES: A THEORETICAL FRAMEWORK

A port city is a nexus of two or more marketing systems. On the inland side there is the hinterland, an area assumed to encompass both productive and consumptive activities. Externally, there are foreign regions with which the port has some regular economic contact through trade and commerce.[2] Although some of the world's largest entrepôts are without adjacent hinterlands (Singapore being an obvious example), such cities provide the exceptions rather than the rule. Most port cities are locked into an evolving network of relationships with their surrounding economies. The character of these relationships is reflected primarily in the changing structure of supply and demand for the commodities passing through the port: the supply of exportable goods and products within the hinterland relative to external demand for those products, and the demand within the region for externally produced commodities and services relative to the supply of those commodities and services in foreign areas. Whether the hinterland urbanizes or remains rural, whether the port city industrializes or remains commercial, and whether there is a specialization or diversification of product flows, ultimately depend on the nature of that supply and demand nexus.

Given the wide range of commodity movements, and differences in institutional structure and chronology of development as well as diversity of geographical locations, one would expect a wide range of possible port–hinterland relationships.[3] For heuristic reasons, therefore, it is useful to initiate this analysis by proposing a simple typology of port city–hinterland arrangements.

At the risk of oversimplification, the wide variety of hinterland systems might be reduced to three "ideal-typical" patterns.[4] (Each is represented schematically in Figure I.) The first type is by far the most common pattern both historically and at present. Under this pattern, the regional economic system is marked by a single center of overwhelming commercial and administrative dominance. The hinterland is largely nonurban and nonindustrial. To the extent that demographic concentration does occur in the hinterland, it is to be found at the nodes of the transportation network. These small regional centers simply serve as transfer points in a network designed to move raw materials and agricultural commodities out of the hinterland, and thence to foreign markets. The regional transportation net is, therefore, a "drainage system" for a nonurban economy of primarily extractive activities. Although there is often considerable small-

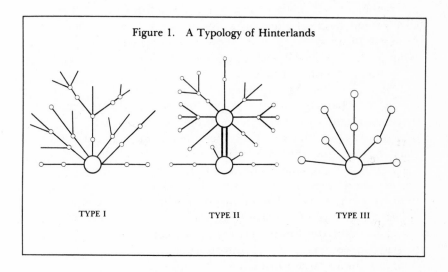

Figure 1. A Typology of Hinterlands

TYPE I TYPE II TYPE III

scale domestic manufacturing scattered across such regions, if modern industrial development does occur, it is most likely to be concentrated in the port city. Moreover, it is not uncommon for the first wave of industrial development to derive from the port's commercial function rather than from independent generation.[5]

Examples of the Type I port–hinterland pattern are legion. In part a manifestation of colonial dependency, much of the urban development in Third World countries assumes some variation of this general form.[6] There are many North American and European examples, however. In the nineteenth century, New York, Philadelphia, and New Orleans all functioned in a manner roughly similar to a Type I form. Such European cities as Bordeaux and London also might be viewed as variants of this type. With so many of the major urban centers falling into this category, it is not surprising that this has become the major prototype for port–hinterland theory. It is not, however, the only form such systems can take.

The second type of regional system outlined in Figure I occurs less frequently than the first. In this category, two major cities grow together, sharing functions usually concentrated in a single coastal center. The British geographer, Richard Momsen, in reference to the relationship between Curitiba and Paranaguá, has used the term "coupled nuclei."[7] Occasionally, there is a demographic balance at each end of the growth axis; over time each center remains roughly the same size and maintains a certain level of political and social autonomy despite its obvious economic dependence. In this setting, competing elite structures can form with distinctive cultural proclivities and political allegiances. More often, however, one city assumes the lead in the growth process and eventually dominates the other in both political and economic activities. In either instance, some specialization of function normally occurs.

Situated at the edge of internal and external markets, the port city is usually characterized by a predominance of mercantile and maritime activity. Industry, to the extent that it exists at all, tends to be supportive or derivative of the commercial function. Both the working class and the elite structure often reflect this commercial/merchantilist dominance. The hinterland center frequently has more diverse economic structure. Hinterland cities of this sort may be industrial centers as well as administrative or religious centers. As the primary city within the hinterland, such centers very often form the major locus of the hinterland transportation network. Outside the two urban centers and the transportation corridor that connects them, the hinterland is often like that of the Type I pattern—nonurban and nonindustrial in character, extractive in orientation.

Since this form of hinterland structure is less common, perhaps it is useful to list some examples:

Africa	Asia
Nairobi/Mombasa	Kyoto/Osaka
Johannesburg/Durban	Seoul/Inchon
Cairo/Alexandria	Hanoi/Haiphong

North America—Europe	South America
Fairbanks/Anchorage	São Paulo/Santos
Birmingham/Mobile	Curitiba/Paranaguá
Houston/Galveston	Caracas/La Guaira
	Santiago/Valparaiso

Brussels/Antwerp
Milan/Genova

As one examines these examples, it is clear that a wide variety of conditions can generate this spatial pattern. Merely because similar patterns are etched on the map does not mean that the social and political implications are always identical. It will be noted that some of these "coupled nuclei" resulted from the imposition of a colonial regime (primarily concerned with extractive commerce) onto an indigenous culture which retained its loyalty to an older religious or administrative center.[8] In other cases, such as in the Birmingham/Mobile or Houston/Galveston examples, there is a clear specialization due to the locational constraints on resources: an industrial processing center develops in proximity to a raw materials site, and a port grows to handle the movement of resources to other domestic or foreign markets.

The last of these hinterland systems (Type III) is the least common, generally limited to the industrialized regions of the northeastern United States and Europe. This pattern involves a large coastal commercial and administrative center surrounded by a cluster of highly specialized manufacturing or processing towns. In contrast to the other two hinterland arrangements, this one is characterized by a transformative function. Initially, the development of these towns may have reflected proximity to a particular natural resource such as water power or coal deposits. Raw materials are brought into the region through the port city, distributed across the industrial towns, processed or converted into finished goods, and finally shipped back through the port to consumers outside the region.

The occupational structures of these satellite cities tend to reflect their single-function character. Professional and financial services are limited or nonexistent; clerical and white-collar occupations are simply adjuncts to the factory system; artisan and petty bourgeois classes are proportionately small compared to those in the port city. The occupational structure of the port, however, complements the truncated occupational structure of the satellite cities. The port provides the professional, wholesaling, and retailing services which are absent in the industrial towns. To the extent that manufacturing is present in the port city, it is supportive of commercial/mercantile interests. The working class in this instance is made up of porters, warehousemen, shipyard workers, and longshoremen. Collectively, these groups may have little affinity with the working class of the industrial centers.

Examples of this kind of hinterland arrangement are few. The most striking case occurs in New England, where a cluster of industrial towns such as Lowell, Lawrence, Fall River, and Lynn surrounds Boston. The relationship between Hamburg and the industrial towns of Northern Prussia or, in the more recent past, the relationship in northern industrial Italy and the port at Venice are other possible cases.

II. UNIQUE CONFIGURATIONS IN TIME AND SPACE:
THE INTERVENING VARIABLES

Such factors as historical circumstance, technological innovation, and political exigency complicate any simple model which automatically equates geographic patterns, economic function, and occupational structure. Since all cities perform a variety of functions, and since these functions are subject to considerable change over time, it is often difficult to discern what functions are highly dependent upon locational variables and which can be considered ubiquitous. Nevertheless, the occupational structures of cities vary systematically with location. Citites and towns in farming areas, for example, take on a set of economic characteristics quite different from those manifested in an iron and steel town proximate to ore and coal deposits.

Viewed as a historical process, one important consideration affecting the distribution of economic activity across the economic landscape is the relative impact of transportation costs on the overall cost structure faced by each firm (whether it be a family-owned shop or a multinational corporation). For most non-service industries, transport costs are directly determined simply by weight and distance. In the most uncomplicated of settings, therefore, the location of production facilities will be determined by the net difference between assembly and distribution costs. If the cost-per-mile of moving the raw materials exceeds that of moving the final product to the consumer, then it makes sense to locate the production process near the source of the raw materials. If, however, the costs associated with shipping the final product are greater than the accumulated costs of transporting the raw materials, then location near the final market is optimal. The nature of the production process, the character of the goods produced, and the modes of transportation available are the key determining variables. Indeed, the most important, yet least studied aspects of the industrial revolution, are the ways in which innovations in techniques and mechanics altered the relationship between distribution and assembly costs. Obviously, the state of transportation technology, as well as the availability of various modes of transport, will affect the pattern of location decisions. The necessity of water transport, for example, had its effect on both the location and subsequent growth of cities in eighteenth century Europe.

One of the classic conceptions of how cities form and grow is based on the notion that populations cluster near raw materials sites. The establishment of a smelting facility near the site of mineral extraction, for example, may initiate a chain of events resulting in the growth of a major settlement. As industries which produce intermediate goods and businesses providing supporting services are attracted to the site, there is a rise in employment opportunities. This clustering of workers and their families increases local demand for retail services. If the process continues, in time the settlement could begin to attract producers oriented to local markets. What was at the outset simply a materials-oriented settlement becomes a market for consumer goods. This is one of the conventional models of how cities are established and prosper. The cities of St. Helens, Wigan, and Blackburn exemplify this pattern in the Lancashire region.

However, settlements which derived their primary growth stimulus solely through a materials orientation are seldom among the largest cities in the Western economies. For cities such as New York, Marseilles, Rio de Janeiro, London and Liverpool, proximity to raw material sources was of secondary consequence to their economic development. Moreover, for cities like Manchester and São Paulo, a mix of resource and market factors interacted to encourage growth. While the role of transportation was obviously important, however, the mechanics of growth were somewhat different from the "classic" pattern outlined above. In each of these latter cases, the city was located at the juncture of various modes of transportation and, over time, became a locus of distribution as well as production. Since changes in conveyance were often required at these points, it was usually advantageous for firms to locate in or near such cities. This was particularly true in industries for which a break-in-bulk involved a certain level of processing, *e.g.*, the milling of grains and refining of animal and mineral oils. For the commercial city, therefore, the geographic situation itself may be the resource.[9]

As a practical matter, however, the production of goods and services are not equally subject to transportation cost considerations. This admission opens the way for considerable modification of traditional location theory in its empirical applications. Most of the complications introduced as one moves from theoretical to actual situations fall into one of two major areas. First, different productive activities are faced with different input requirements; transportation is not the only spatially variable cost factor. Second, real world location decisions are not made in an unchanging space but in economic environments layered with the results of past decisions and the commitments of earlier generations.

Geographic differences in the availability of land, labor and capital are primarily regional phenomena. Although differentials in factor prices are always a short-run consideration, during initial periods of economic development these differences may be sufficiently aggravated so as to dampen or significantly alter the development process.[10] At the very least, such differentials may act to produce interregional variations in the degree of urban concentration quite apart from other accessibility factors.[11] Thus, the location of industries does not, by itself, explain the growth of settlements. It provides but one explanation of why certain economic activities locate in certain places. Continued demographic growth depends, first, on the labor requirements of these activities and, second, on development of an economic environment in which other developing industries will continue to locate at the site.

The development of such a growth environment is not only local but regional in scope. Moreover, it is contingent on the technological and developmental level of the national economy in general. The kinds of economic activities and resources which are distributed across regions serve to impose constraints both on the possibilities for diversity in local enterprise and on the overall growth potential of the cities that lie within regions. Differences in resource availability, the timing of migratory movements, and the implementation of transport improvements cause uneven urbanization between regions. For example, one immediately associates the growth of "textile towns" with the development of the Lancashire/Cheshire/Yorkshire industrial complex. Somewhat later in the century, the growth of the industrial districts of the British Midlands resulted in the population increases of such cities as Birmingham and Wolverhampton. In contrast, we think of East Anglia as organized around small farming villages and quaint market towns. Transport advantage in this setting is less an absolute than the result of a variety of locational and developmental factors concomitant with urban growth.

Throughout the whole of the nineteenth century, the relationship between Liverpool, Manchester, and the surrounding region can be viewed as a hybrid of Types II and III of the port–hinterland typology. The economy of northwestern Britain revolved around an axis of two metropolises functioning in tandem. Although first and foremost the major industrial center in the region, Manchester also served as the regional locus for retailing, wholesaling, and marketing services. A cluster of large manufacturing towns specializing in various aspects of textile production surrounded the city. Manchester, therefore, rather than Liverpool, provided the range of financial, brokerage and management services for the industrializing Northwest. On the other hand, Liverpool merchants controlled the flow of raw cotton into the region as well as the shipment of finished textile products out of the Northwest region as well as the rest of Great Britain. The distribution of raw cotton throughout the region and the gathering of the finished product for shipment was concentrated in Manchester, but entrance into and exit from the system was at Liverpool. A complex set of symbiotic relationships tied the fate of each city to the other, and ultimately both were tied to the worldwide supply and demand for cotton textiles. The development of the Liverpool/Manchester axis in the nineteenth century serves, therefore, as an interesting case study of the evolving relationship between hinterland market structure, transportation development, and urban occupational structure.

III. THE LIVERPOOL/MANCHESTER AXIS: A HYBRID PATTERN

The urban and industrial expansion of South Lancashire in the late eighteenth and early nineteenth centuries was, by any comparison, truly phenomenal. In his classic account of Manchester's industrial proletariat, Engels set the scene as follows:

> What was once an obscure, poorly-cultivated bog is now a thickly-populated industrial district. Lancashire's population has increased ten-fold in 80 years; and many large towns have grown up there. Liverpool and Manchester, for example, have together 70,000 inhabitants. Near at hand are Bolton (50,000 inhabitants), Rochdale (76,000), Oldham (50,000), Preston (60,000), Ashton and Stalybridge (40,000). These and many other factory towns have experienced a mushroom growth. Modern times can show few greater marvels than the recent history of South Lancashire.[12]

At the very heart of this urban industrial growth was the Liverpool/ Manchester axis: at one end the great commercial entrepôt of the British Empire, at the other the manufacturing giant of industrial England. It is significant that Engels combined their population as if they were a single center about which were clustered the smokey factory towns and dismal industrial villages of 19th century Lancashire. Engels predicted that if their burgeoning growth did not cease, "Manchester and Liverpool . . . would meet at Warrington or Newton-Willows,"[13] an urban corridor, a single industrial metropolis, stretching from the docks of Liverpool deep into the heart of Lancashire. The prophecy was fulfilled; the Merseyside agglomerate has now merged completely with the Manchester/Salford urban district.

At Engels' writing, however, they were, physically at least, two separate cities, bound in time and space by the exigencies of the cotton trade and a growing demand for cotton textiles.

Throughout the whole of the nineteenth century, there was a remarkable demographic balance between Liverpool and Manchester. Neither city overshadowed the other in either absolute or relative terms. Table I displays the estimated populations in each city for the first seven decades of the nineteenth century; the proportion of the total Lancashire population residing in each city (by decade) is given as well. Measured solely in terms of demographic concentration, Manchester exhibited a slight tendency to lead in the growth process until the 1830's; however, after the recession of the late '30's, the growth of both centers ebbed, and the roles were reversed. In neither case, however, was the demographic dominance pronounced.

TABLE I. ESTIMATED POPULATIONS OF LIVERPOOL AND MANCHESTER, 1801-1871

Census Year	Liverpool Population	Manchester Population (Including Salford)	Liverpool's Share of Lancashire Population	Manchester's Share of Lancashire Population
1801	82,300	93,400	12.2	13.8
1811	104,100	113,800	12.5	13.8
1821	138,400	158,700	13.1	15.1
1831	201,800	232,800	15.1	17.4
1841	286,500	273,900	17.5	16.4
1851	376,000	388,500	18.5	19.1
1861	444,000	441,200	18.2	18.1
1871	493,400	476,000	17.4	16.8

Note: There are many definitional problems in generating a series of population data for British cities. There are various governmental boundries one can use. Moreover, the governmental divisions need not represent "true" urban areas. These data are no exception. There are a number of series available for these two cities. No two are exactly alike. These data were taken from the 1871 British Census which attempted to develop a series of urban population estimates based on similar areal units over time. Nonetheless, they are estimates, not "true" values. Similar estimates are provided by B.R. MITCHELL & P. DEANE, ABSTRACT OF BRITISH HISTORICAL STATISTICS 24-27. (Cambridge, Cambridge U. Press, 1962).

Manchester's population growth, compared to that of Liverpool, was much more responsive to the vicissitudes of the fluctuating nineteenth century economy.[14] Despite similarities in their growth during the early decades of the century, in the '30's, '40's, and '50's their growth patterns diverged substantially. While the periodic recessions of the era affected both cities, each time the decline in Manchester's growth rate greatly exceeded that of Liverpool. Upward changes in Manchester's population growth were much more responsive to good times as well. Following the trade depression of the late 1830's, for example, Manchester rebounded with unusual resiliency, registering a recovery of more than forty percentage points in its demographic growth. This increase in the city's population growth is particularly surprising given the rather sluggish rise in the rate of growth in industrial output. Indeed, there is evidence that in the region's smaller industrial towns, economic instability persisted throughout the '40's.[15]

The explanation for the relatively greater volatility in Manchester's population growth lies in the character of the city's industrial composition. Cotton textile manufacturing and processing was one of the core industries in the British economy in the early nineteenth century. As such, the employment and capital demands of the industry often anticipated rather than followed the cyclical movements of the economy.[16] The dependency of the Manchester economy on a chain of backward and forward linkages, all leading to the textile industry, might well have served to encourage instability in local labor markets.[17] Although Liverpool's economy was also dependent on the cotton trade, by mid-century it had developed sufficient diversity in its trading interests to cushion the city from the effects of the business cycle. The key, therefore, to understanding the relationship between demographic growth and urban economy in the Lancashire region lies with the occupational structure and economic functions of the cities within that region.

The industrial districts of Lancashire and Cheshire superseded an earlier Medieval system of marketing, religious, and administrative centers. In some cases, the industrial system complemented the old system; in other instances the new hierarchy supplanted established centers of commerce and industry. Some old established marketing centers such as Chester, Warrington, and Lancaster were either left behind in the industrialization process of the eighteenth century, or simply assumed the role of secondary administrative centers. Meanwhile, previously isolated country villages grew to be massive manufacturing districts. Table II provides a listing, according to rank, of the cities in northwest England reporting populations of 20,000 or more at the mid-century mark. A range of supporting data is provided as well. These figures highlight the balanced primacy of Liverpool and Manchester. Over the first fifty years of the century, the growth of the regional towns clusters tightly around a 7% annual increase. Birkenhead, the "suburban" port across the Mersey from Liverpool, was the striking exception to this rule, but its growth would appear to be a case of modern suburbanization rather than an instance of "independent generation." At the other end of the growth spectrum was Chester. Once the major port for the Northwest, by the mid-nineteenth century it was a small market city and governmental center.

TABLE II.   PATTERN OF URBANIZATION IN NORTHWEST ENGLAND, 1801-1851

City	Population in 1851	% of Regional Population	Average Annual Growth Rate 1801-1851	% of Workforce Engaged in Industry	% of Industrial Workforce Engaged in Textiles[a]
Manchester- Salford	388,490	15.6%	6.3%	50%	24%
Liverpool (& West Derby)	386,926	15.5	7.3	29	*
Oldham	72,357	2.9	4.6	63	45
Preston	69,542	2.8	9.4	53	60
Bolton	61,171	2.5	4.8	56	45
Stockport	53,835	2.2	5.2	58	56
Blackburn	46,536	1.9	5.8	61	68
Rochdale	41,513	1.7	4.4	58	40
Macclesfield	39,408	1.6	6.9	52	8
Birkenhead	34,496	1.4	100	26	*
Wigan	31,941	1.3	3.8	50	24
Bury	31,262	1.3	4.8	56	51
Aston- under-Lyne	30,676	1.2	7.6	62	59
Chester	27,766	1.1	1.6	28	*
St. Helens	25,403	1.0	5.3	60	*
Burnley	24,745	1.0	8.2	56	59
Stalybridge	23,387	.9	11.0	N.A.	N.A.
Warrington	22,894	.9	2.0	37	6

* Percentage less than 1.0%.
[a] Data for 1861.
Source: Reports, Censuses of Great Britain, 1851 & 1861.

These data provide some indication of the functional specialization that had taken place in this region. The commercial cities of Liverpool, Birkenhead, and Chester held minority status in a region dominated by industrial enterprise. Outside of the coastal commercial centers, the concentration of the urban work force in industrial activity averaged about 60%, ocasionally reaching 70% in some mill towns. Moreover, this specialization was not only a matter of degree but also of kind. Note the very high levels of concentration of local employment in textiles in these towns on the eve of the Cotton Famine. It is no wonder that the effects of the American Civil War were so immediately felt in this region. St. Helens, despite its lack of textile industry, was no less a factory town, specializing in glass and chemicals.[18] It should also be noted that, in contrast with the other industrial towns in the region, Manchester had roughly a third of its manufacturing sector in textile activity. The remaining portion of Manchester's industrial capacity was devoted to a wide range of supporting activities for both the city and the region.

TABLE III. CONCENTRATION RATIOS FOR SELECTED OCCUPATIONS

Occupation	"Old" Market Towns			"New" Industrial Towns				
	Chester	Lancaster	Stockport	Blackburn	Bolton	Oldham	Liverpool	Manchester
Professional/Semi-Professional								
Doctors	1.53	2.77	1.04	.94	.79	.74	1.56	1.39
	(26)	(25)	(33)	(25)	(28)	(27)	(361)	(339)
Lawyers	4.64	3.05	.57	1.14	.66	.47	1.00	1.00
	(60)	(21)	(14)	(27)	(13)	(13)	(172)	(186)
Surveyors	.34	9.06	.55	.44	1.15	.48	1.00	1.49
	(1)	(14)	(3)	(2)	(7)	(3)	(38)	(62)
Auctioner/Appraiser	1.76	1.10	.41	.12	1.12	.91	1.58	1.40
	(9)	(3)	(4)	(1)	(12)	(10)	(110)	(84)
Accountants	1.46	2.53	1.67	.58	5.16	.21	1.57	1.02
	(13)	(12)	(28)	(8)	(96)	(4)	(191)	(131)
Mercantile								
Merchants	.62	.58	0.0	0.0	0.0	0.0	2.23	1.69
	(14)	(7)	(0)	(0)	(0)	(0)	(679)	(550)
Bankers	2.99	1.40	0.0	.95	.35	.35	1.31	.83
	(4)	(1)	(0)	(2)	(1)	(1)	(24)	(16)
Ships Brokers/								
Shipping Agents	0.0	1.68	0.0	0.0	0.0	0.0	4.35	.23
	(0)	(4)	(0)	(0)|	(0)	(0)	(265)	(15)
Brokerage (general)	0.0	.78	.88	.35	.39	.02	2.35	.94
	(0)	(3)	(12)	(4)	(6)	(8)	(249)	(96)
Dealers (wholesale)	.34	.65	.15	.63	.14	.64	2.08	1.70
	(7)	(7)	(6)	(20)	(6)	(28)	(574)	(496)
Couperage	2.23	1.88	.34	.46	.50	.12	3.48	.84
	(49)	(22)	(19)	(16)	(23)	(6)	(1042)	(266)

Occupation	"Old" Market Towns		"New" Industrial Towns					
	Chester	Lancaster	Stockport	Blackburn	Bolton	Oldham	Liverpool	Manchester
Commercial/Trade								
Agents, factors								
(regional)	.26	.34	.38	1.49	.75	.67	.97	2.96
	(3)	(2)	(8)	(26)	(17)	(16)	(147)	(476)
Salesmen	0.0	.41	.12	.07	.10	.41	.21	4.99
	(0)	(2)	(2)	(1)	(2)	(8)	(27)	(651)
Clerks								
(commercial)	.68	1.28	.13	.39	.13	.64	2.05	1.84
	(56)	(56)	(21)	(50)	(22)	(112)	(2294)	(2179)
Travelers	.81	1.96	.43	.30	.67	.16	1.58	2.75
	(14)	(18)	(14)	(8)	(24)	(6)	(371)	(680)
Local Retail								
Pawnbrokers	1.00	1.63	.84	2.68	1.24	.74	1.79	1.72
	(7)	(6)	(11)	(26)	(18)	(11)	(169)	(171)
Shopkeepers (misc.)	.77	.54	.93	3.73	1.67	1.98	.69	1.12
	(1)	(7)	(43)	(142)	(85)	(103)	(228)	(394)
Hawkers, Peddlers	1.72	.69	.80	2.09	1.55	.91	.89	1.70
	(47)	(10)	(41)	(89)	(88)	(333)	(668)	(53)
Ironmongers	2.41	3.10	.55	1.22	1.09	.77	1.59	1.19
	(19)	(13)	(5)	(15)	(18)	(13)	(171)	(135)
Butchers	1.61	1.54	.46	1.07	1.26	1.03	1.19	1.01
	(104)	(53)	(141)	(108)	(170)	(143)	(1044)	(942)
Greengrocers	.50	.47	1.16	.74	2.32	1.64	.68	1.88
	(6)	(3)	(46)	(14)	(58)	(42)	(112)	(324)
Fishmongers	.62	.71	1.13	2.57	1.98	.64	1.33	1.43
	(5)	(3)	(17)	(32)	(33)	(11)	(145)	(164)
Bakers	2.74	.66	1.45	.45	1.08	.34	2.02	1.80
	(101)	(13)	(101)	(26)	(83)	(27)	(1017)	(957)

Source: These statistics are based on data taken from the Census of Great Britain, 1851, *Occupations of the People* ccxlvi-ccxlvii, ccli, cclv, 648-51.

In order to gain some additional understanding of the functional balance between Liverpool and Manchester, it is necessary to decompose the occupation data beyond the broad categories of "commercial" and "industrial." The data displayed in Table III allows further analysis along this dimension. In addition to Liverpool and Manchester, six regional cities were selected for examination: two old marketing/governmental centers and four "new" industrial towns. A cluster of nonindustrial occupations has been isolated for analysis: professional, mercantile, commercial/trade, and local retail services. The numbers in parentheses are the absolute number of male workers employed in each class in 1851. Of primary interest are the concentration ratios which have been calculated for each occupation in each city. This measure simply divides the town's share of those employed in a given occupation by its share of the total regional population. A value of one would obtain if these proportions were equal. For example, in 1851 Chester had just as many pawnbrokers as one would expect given its share of the region's population. Values less than one suggest that an occupation was underrepresented for a town of a given size. Values greater than one reflect an inordinate concentration of that particular activity locally and, therefore, the suggestion of domination in that activity over other areas.[19]

As one examines these distributions, a number of the occupational patterns anticipated by the port–hinterland typology are evident. First, the "single industry" manufacturing towns experienced what might be called truncated occupational structures. The occupation distribution in these cities was marked by:

1. limited access to professional services;
2. an absence of mercantile elites;
3. very limited commercial/trade services;
4. uneven and occasionally limited local services; and
5. generally adequate local retail services.

As indicated in Table II, the majority of the work force was engaged in industrial activity.

The occupational structure of the old marketing towns provides an interesting contrast. While Chester and Lancaster failed to retain some higher order mercantile services, they did quite well in maintaining a class of professionals larger than one would expect for towns of their size. Perhaps this reflects the continuing "pull" of the governmental functions which each continued to hold. Reflecting the diminishing sphere of their economic influence regionally, their hold on the commercial trades appears to have declined. In all, however, it is impressive that these centers, while failing to respond to the "new" growth of an industrialized economy, maintained most of their basic functions. At the margins of influence by the Liverpool/Manchester axis, these cities remain modest but important centers for specific professional, administrative, and financial services.

Liverpool and Manchester not only "fit" with one another, but their collective economy also "fits" with those of hinterland industrial towns. As one would expect, Liverpool dominated mercantile services; Manchester dominated regional commercial trade activities (agents, factors, salesmen, travelers). They shared a host of professional and semi-professional services at the expense of their adjacent industrial towns. Together these two cities exhibited a "complete" metropolitan occupational distribution.

Despite the impression of balance and reciprocity, however, there was a perennial suspicion among Manchester's commercial and industrial elite that Liverpool exacted an unfair tariff for providing its gatekeeper-brokerage function. Thinly veiled references to Liverpool's use of dock dues to enhance the city treasury were common in

the "pro-Manchester" literature. While few of the Manchester merchants would deny Liverpool's Dock Committee a right to a modest
return on their enormous capital investment, taxation of Manchester
for Liverpool's municipal improvement seemed unfair.[20] Benjamin
Love's *Manchester As It Is* (1839), in commenting on the
dearth of public improvements in Manchester, notes with some cha-
grin that "Liverpool, with her dock dues and wealthy corporations can
afford to deck herself out in external gaiety; and in this respect
[alone], perhaps, she excels Manchester . . . ."[21] Of course, the Manchester industrial aristocracy presumed that Liverpool's prosperity
depended wholly on Manchester's industry.[22]

Manchester consumers, whether purchasing foodstuffs from Ireland or raw cotton from Mississippi, paid for "services rendered" at
the port of Liverpool and for transit to Manchester. However, making
an accurate assessment of total transfer costs is difficult. There was a
wide range of brokerage, porterage, and storage fees in addition to
dock dues and piloting charges. Liverpool was reported to have the
lowest port charges among the major ports in Britain, yet pressure to
reduce the rates mounted. Responding to these complaints, the Dock
Board reduced all rates by a third in 1836 and removed completely
the charges on coastal and Irish trade. Even at these lower rates,
however, the movement of cotton through the port could generate as
much as £70,000 annually in the early forties, about 10% of the total
dues collected. Nonetheless, in terms of the price of cotton at Manchester, the impact was negligible amounting to only about two pence
per 100 pounds of cotton.[23]

More important for the ongoing hostility of Manchester's entrepreneurs was the increasing concentration of economic power in the
hands of a few Liverpool shipowners. In the most vital area, the
cotton trade, the total number of Liverpool merchants engaged in the
trade between 1820 and 1840 declined. Moreover, those who remained active increased their concentration of power; the thirty leading importers controlled less than 40% of the trade in the '20's, but by
1839 saw their share jump to 60%. These cotton importers became
highly specialized in their functions and increasingly exercised considerable control over the trade.[24]

In the 1870's, when trade to Third World areas began to reach
significant proportions, shipping interests at Liverpool formed cartel-
like arrangements to "ensure all companies of a reasonable share of
available cargoes."[25] These "Conference Agreements," as they were
called, established "a classified list of freight charges and offered
merchants a deferred rebate as an inducement to securing loyalty to

Conference ships. In return, the shipowners promised regularity of service and prompt delivery of cargo."[26] Although these agreements merely made "public" what had been standard practice for years, Manchester merchants and industrialists were indignant. The Conference agreement originally regulated only the China trade, but within a few years the Indian, East Indies, African, and South American trade were all brought under the Conference System.

Manchester's commercial elite pushed hard, but unsuccessfully, to keep the Birkenhead dock independent of Liverpool control. In 1857 their hopes died when a reorganization of the Dock Committee of Liverpool incorporated the Birkenhead docks into the "new" Mersey Docks and Harbor Board. It would not be until the end of the century, with the successful agitation for the Manchester Ship Canal, that the Manchester industrialists would feel free of Liverpool domination.[27]

Prior to the construction of the Ship Canal, changes in the character of the transport system, while reducing costs and encouraging further concentration of the textile industry, did not alter the basic pattern of traffic flow in the region. Nonetheless, transport innovation and construction did serve to promote an internal consolidation of the Lancashire/Cheshire economy as well as link it with a growing national system.

Major innovations in the transport system came in two waves. The first was the development of the canal system in the latter half of the eighteenth century. The second, which in part reinforced and rendered more efficient the canal network, was the development of the railway system in the period 1830-1860. (It seems appropriate that the beginnings of both of Britain's "transport revolutions" are to be found in the Liverpool/Manchester "corridor." The first major canal project, the Duke of Bridgewater's Canal, and the first successful railway system in the period 1830-1860. (It seems appropriate that the hanced the development of the Liverpool/Manchester axis.)

The first canal projects, notably the Sankey Navigation (1757) and the Duke of Bridgewater's Canal (1766-1776), reduced the cost of transporting coal to domestic and industrial users. In the case of the Sankey Navigation, two of the major underwriters of the project were directly involved in the salt processing industry in the Merseyside area. Despite public appeals based on the promises of lower fuel costs, the primary intent was to bring coal to the Cheshire salt boilers. Increased flow of coal to the port of Liverpool appears to be an incidental by-product.[28] The Duke of Bridgewater was responsible for an even more impressive venture when he connected his colliery at Worsley with markets in Manchester. Upon completion, the project was an immediate success. Subsequently, the canal was extended to link Manchester with the Mersey, and hence with Liverpool. Although coal remained the major commodity transported on the canal, foodstuffs (primarily from Ireland) and raw cotton dominated an increasing portion of the total traffic.[29]

The success of the Bridgewater Canal encouraged a wave of canal construction throughout England, particularly in the Northwest. By 1800 an impressive system of canals linked Britain's major metropolitan areas with resource producing regions. The returns affected Liverpool most directly, expanding its port hinterland well into the Midlands and Yorkshire. Nonetheless, the advantages to Manchester cannot be underestimated. There can be little doubt that for bulk commodities the transport savings were considerable. One estimate placed the cost of transport by land between Liverpool and Manchester in the 1770's as high as 40s. per ton and by the river system at 12s. per ton. The cost of using the canal system, however, averaged only 6s. per ton.[30] The introduction of steam-driven factory equipment, particularly the power loom, made low-cost coal as important to the Manchester economy as low cost cotton. By the 1830's, Manchester was using more than 25,000 tons of coal weekly for both domestic and industrial purposes. Even after the establishment of the rail system, the canals still hauled a major portion of the coal used at Manchester; in the late '30's nearly 65% of the coal used in Manchester came by barge.[31]

The railway boom, initiated with the successful completion of the Liverpool & Manchester in 1830, was much more intensive and of shorter span than the period of canal construction. While it took nearly forty years to complete the Leeds and Liverpool Canal, a railroad covering the same distance was constructed in less than a decade. If the canal system can be characterized as primarily resource oriented, the rail system could be described as market oriented. The system connected established urban areas and thereby widened the net for consumption of urban goods and services.[32] In general, the rail network, by following markets, recapitulated the older system. Although it did not alter the pattern of migratory or commodity flows generally, the rail system accelerated urban growth and further encouraged concentration of industry.

The establishment of regular train service between Manchester and Liverpool integrated the economies of these two cities even more tightly than did the canals. The Liverpool & Manchester served as the main artery between the two cities. Subsequent construction was either a branching of this main line or merely an extension of it. Apart from the canals and natural waterways which connected the two cities, there was no serious competition to the Liverpool & Manchester. Encouraged further by a series of amalgamations, the rail route held a monopoly throughout most of the nineteenth century. Manchester was the crossroads of the vast inland network of trunk lines; Liverpool (via the rail/canal corridor) was the terminus and trans-shipment point.[33] Indeed, as J. R. Kellett has suggested, the Lancashire rail system was complementary to rather than competitive with the canals.[34]

IV. ESTIMATING "DEPENDENCY" ALONG THE MANCHESTER/LIVERPOOL AXIS

The statistical data suggests a balanced relationship (based on reciprocity and symbiosis) between the two "poles" of the Liverpool/Manchester axis. The contemporary commentary, however, indicates a dependency relationship with Manchester on the losing end. In the absence of financial and commodity data, a direct assessment of "dependence" or "exploitation" is impossible. There are no balance of payments ledgers between cities within nations. Nonetheless, an indirect estimate of dependence is possible, using the occupational data from the published census.

If we assume that changing demand for products results in changing demand for labor, we can estimate the weight of determinants of local (city-level) shifts in occupational structure by changes in the occupational structure of the region and/or the nation.[35] In this particular case, we are also interested in the impact of one city's economy upon another. Two linear regression models were used to estimate this relationship; in each case the variables are the percentage change of the employment in each of 155 major occupations for the decade 1841-1851. There are three independent variables: one for regional effects, one to measure national effects, and one to assess the effects of the "other city." Presumably, the unexplained portion of the variance is due to "local" effects, *i.e.*, factors which may affect local employment apart from non-market (institutional or technological) forces. Given the limiting assumptions, the coefficients attached to the independent variables can be read as the proportion of local structural change attributed to demand shifts in each of the external components.

TABLE IV. "DEPENDENCY" ALONG THE
MANCHESTER/LIVERPOOL AXIS

Dependent Variable	COEFFICIENTS				
	Constant	"Other" City	Region	Nation	R^2
Manchester	.2649	.4613*	.1778*	.0794	.40
	(.0748)	(.0811)	(.0731)	(.0666)	
Liverpool	.1558	.3882*	.2620*	.2471*	.52
	(.0698)	(.0672)	(.0644)	(.0576)	

* Significantly different from zero at the .99 level.

The results of these regressions offer confirmation of earlier suspicions (Table IV). While it appears that Manchester exhibited a greater sensitivity to changes in Liverpool's occupational structure than Liverpool to Manchester's, the coefficients of the city-level variables are not significantly different (statistically). As a commercial entrepôt, however, Liverpool did show a greater responsiveness to structural change at the regional and national levels. The higher constant values for Manchester suggests that this city was more affected by local market conditions than Liverpool. At least for the mid-nineteenth century, then, the complaints of Manchester's commercial and industrial elite do not find justification in the shifting occupational data of the two cities. This does not diminish the importance of their expressions of discontent over what they perceived to be a subservient relationship with Liverpool. Ultimately, they acted on their perceptions by constructing a transportation link to ocean commerce that was independent of Liverpool's control.[36] Although the Ship Canal altered commodity flows within the region, it did not change Manchester's excessive dependence on world supply and demand for cotton textiles.

In the mid-nineteenth century, however, such difficulties lay in the future. Both Liverpool and Manchester were at the height of their economic power, each in its own way profiting from a seemingly ever-expanding British Empire. The Empire provided the British economy with raw materials for production and markets for consumption. The Liverpool/Manchester axis was at the very core of the British economy.[37]

V. POSTSCRIPT:
OTHER TIMES AND OTHER PLACES:
THE SANTOS/SÃO PAULO COMPARISON

The clustering of people in space, *i.e.*, the formation and growth of cities, is more than an isolated demographic event. It is conditioned by a hierarchy of economic and political determinants. At the very least, we must identify the outlines of that hierarchy if we are to understand the city growth process in the world today as well as in our urban past.

The economic development of São Paulo and its relationship to the economy of the port city of Santos provides an interesting parallel to the Liverpool/Manchester experience of the mid-nineteenth century. The railroad linking Santos, São Paulo, and Jundiai in 1867 served as the core for the development of a modern regional transportation system focusing on São Paulo.[38] Unlike the transportation system which converged on Manchester, the Paulista system was oriented toward extraction and only incidentially toward distributive functions. São Paulo performed the function of a regional commercial center, primarily as a point for concentration and trans-shipment of coffee to the coast. Although São Paulo industralized, Brazil's southeast region did not develop the hierarchy of industrial towns which marked the economic geography of Lancashire and Cheshire. Santos, like Liverpool, stood at the other end of the transport axis, serving as the primary port for the region.[39]

In the decades immediately following the completion of the rail link between Santos and São Paulo, these two cities exhibited a relatively balanced development. Rather than competition between the two cities, the region as a whole struggled to escape the traditional domination that Rio exercised over the entire Brazilian hinterland.[40] Santos grew at roughly the same pace as São Paulo , and at one time rivaled the inland center as a locus of commercial activity.[41] By the turn of the century, however, São Paulo emerged as the dominant center with Santos acting simply as a specialized adjunct to the growing inland metropolis. Notably, it was the mercantile elite of São Paulo, not of Santos, which took the lead in the manufacturing revolution of the twentieth century.[42] The initial pattern of balanced duality, once broken, never returned.

The striking difference in developmental sequence for these two city–hinterland systems reveals the necessity of viewing economic structures in a broader developmental context. The Lancashire/Cheshire regional economy was, in many ways, the transformative core not only for the British national economy but also for the British Empire generally. As sensitive as the region was to the fluctuations of the cotton trade, it was locked into a supportive industrial complex and growing internal markets. This relationship was particularly important for Liverpool, which became a major national port with a diversified import/export mix. Santos, by contrast, never developed strong trans-regional marketing links. Since the primary direction of flow was out of region, São Paulo rather than Santos served the "gatekeeper" function ascribed to Liverpool in the early nineteenth century.

What is important, however, is the role of each of the national economies in the evolving world-wide market system. Liverpool and Manchester were at the core of production, consumption, and capital generation in a system of domestic and colonial markets. São Paulo and Santos were situated at the periphery. From this perspective, the primary purpose of the Santos/São Paulo regional system was simply to funnel coffee out to the outside world. Flows of products into the region were comparatively minor. Unlike the Liverpool/Manchester system, the Santos/São Paulo axis was based on an extractive (agricultural) economy with relatively low levels of demand for finished goods. External dependency encouraged internal imbalance along the axis. The relationship between the coffee economy and the world marketing system set limits to urban growth in southeastern Brazil.[43]

The comparison of the Liverpool/Manchester axis with the economic relationship between Santos and São Paulo reveals the necessity of evaluating a city's economy in terms of a wider, yet specifically defined, distribution of cities—regionally, nationally, and internationally. Ideally, once measures of the variant as well as the mean behaviors of urban economies are established, we will have an empirical yardstick to apply to any specific locality of interest. Of equal importance is the idea of a hierarchy of causation which is implicit in the logic of this kind of comparative study. In moving through each succeeding level of analysis, it is assumed that, increasingly, the variance of the behavior of the entities—in this case, cities—is explained. Thus, the demands of national and international markets determine the growth potential of regional economies. In turn, the population and productive capacity of each region defines the opportunities for growth available to the cities and the towns within that region. Finally, within the city, the structure of industry determines the job opportunities for individuals seeking employment.

Our chronic inability to coordinate human needs and economic resources in the great cities of the world suggests a continuing need to identify precisely the dimensions of urban growth and decay during periods of national economic development and industrialization. This effort is necessary not only to increase our historical understanding of urbanization in the "developed" Western economies but also to evaluate whether it is appropriate to apply our experiences to developing countries in the world today. Like it or not, the Anglo-American development experience remains the prototypical model—or anti-model—in the ever-expanding literature on economic development and urban growth.[44] Through cross-national comparison of past and present urban systems, it appears possible to refine current theories of urban development, freeing them from their parochial origins.

NOTES

1. For a review of the theoretical literature, see JOHN B. SHARPLESS, CITY GROWTH IN THE UNITED STATES, ENGLAND AND WALES, 1820-1861: THE EFFECTS OF LOCATION, SIZE AND ECONOMIC STRUCTURE ON INTER-URBAN VARIATIONS IN DEMOGRAPHIC GROWTH 23-47 (New York: Arno Press, 1977). For bibliography, see BRIAN J. L. BERRY & ALLAN R. PRED, CENTRAL PLACE STUDIES: A BIBLIOGRAPHY OF THEORY AND APPLICATIONS (Philadelphia: Regional Science Research Institute, 1961).

2. For reviews of the port-hinterland literature, see generally Weigend, *Some Elements in the Study of Port Geography*, 48 GEOGRAPHICAL REVIEW 185-200 (1958); Britton, *The External Relations of Seaports: Some New Considerations*, 56 TIJDSCHRIFT VOOR ECONOMISCHE EN SOCIALE GEOGRAFIE 109, at 112 (May/June 1965); Robinson, *The Hinterland-Foreland Continuum: Concept and Methodology*, 22 THE PROFESSIONAL GEOGRAPHER 307-10 (Nov. 1970).

3. Weigend, *supra* note 2, at 186-88.

4. This typology is a variation on a suggested temporal typology in Taafe, Morrill, & Gould, *Transport Expansion in Underdeveloped Countries*, 53 GEOGRAPHICAL REVIEW 503, at 503-05 (1963). Unlike Taafe, Morrill, and Gould, I am making no claim for temporal sequence.

5. The idea of industrial dependency in the "mercantile city" is given its greatest defense by ALLAN R. PRED in THE SPATIAL DYNAMICS OF U. S. URBAN-INDUSTRIAL GROWTH, 1800-1914, at 143-215 (Cambridge: M.I.T. Press, 1966). At least for the American urban experience, this view has been subjected to some criticism. See DIANE LINDSTROM, ECONOMIC DEVELOPMENT IN THE PHILADELPHIA REGION, 1810-1850 (New York: Columbia U. Press, 1977); Lindstrom & Sharpless, *The Dynamics of the American Urban Economy*, 3 RESEARCH IN ECONOMIC HISTORY (forthcoming, 1978).

6. A recent review of the "dependency" literature is in Chilicote, *Dependency: A Critical Synthesis of the Literature*, 1 LATIN AMERICAN PERSPECTIVES 4-29 (Spring, 1974).

7. RICHARD P. MOMSEN, ROUTES OVER THE SERRA DO MAR 143-71 (Rio de Janeiro, 1964).

8. EDGAR A. JOHNSON, THE ORGANIZATION OF SPACE IN DEVELOPING COUNTRIES 1-116, 152-207 (Cambridge: Harvard U. Press, 1970).

9. JAMES HEILBRUN, URBAN ECONOMICS AND PUBLIC POLICY 65 (New York: St. Martin's Press, 1974); ALLAN R. PRED, *supra* note 5, at 143-215; O. D. DUNCAN, *et. al.*, METROPOLIS AND REGION 23-26 (Baltimore: Johns Hopkins Press for Resources for the Future, Inc., 1960).

10. Alonso, *Urban and Regional Imbalances in Economic Development*, 17 ECONOMIC DEVELOPMENT AND CULTURAL CHANGE 1 *passim* (Oct. 1968).

11. The history of the textile industry in Lancashire provides a relevant illustration of the relationship between factor costs, location constraints, and production technology. Before the mid-seventeenth century, textile production (both spinning and weaving) was marked by geographically dispersed labor and relatively high transport costs. Under the "putting-out" system (by which raw cotton and wool were distributed to cottage artisans), labor costs were extremely low. With the cost-reduction advantages to concentration minimal, it was feasible to bring the materials to the laborer. With the introduction of power machinery, there was initially a necessity of locating textile factories near water power sites. Indeed, prior to the introduction of steam power, this particular input requirement posed a totally inelastic constraint on the use of the power loom. Material, labor, and transport costs were, by definition, secondary considerations. (For example, with the establishment of the first factories at Lowell, Massachusetts, labor was brought to the productive facilities at some considerable expense.) Later, with the development of more mobile sources of power, the industry was again free to seek locations which minimized other input costs. Today, the industry is considered "labor-cost oriented." Heilbrun, *supra* note 9, at 67. For a discussion of the industry in the nineteenth century, see generally ALFRED P. WADSWORTH & JULIA DE LACY MANN, THE COTTON TRADE AND INDUSTRIAL LANCASHIRE, 1600-1780 (Manchester: Manchester University Press, 1931); PHYLLIS DEANE, THE FIRST INDUSTIAL REVOLUTION 84-99 (Cambridge, Cambridge University Press, 1965).

12. FRIEDRICH ENGELS, THE CONDITION OF THE WORKING CLASS IN ENGLAND 16 (Stanford, Stanford U. Press, trans. & eds. W.O. Henderson & W.H. Chaloner, 1968, first published 1845).

13. *Id.* at 29.

14. These observations are based on a comparison of city growth rate data and United Kingdom manufacturing output data from B. R. MITCHELL & PHYLLIS DEANE, ABSTRACT OF BRITISH HISTORICAL STATISTICS (Cambridge, Cambridge University Press, 1962).

15. ASA BRIGGS, THE MAKING OF MODERN ENGLAND, 1783-1867: THE AGE OF IMPROVEMENT 295-96 (New York: Longman, Green, 1959).

16. Rostow, *Cycles in the British Economy: 1790-1914*, BRITISH ECONOMIC FLUCTUATIONS, 1790-1939, at 83-84 (London: Macmillan-St. Martins, eds. D. H. Aldcroft & P. Fearon, 1972).

17. WILBUR R. THOMPSON, A PREFACE TO URBAN ECONOMICS 139 (Baltimore: The Johns Hopkins Press, 1968).

18. T. C. BARKER & J. R. HARRIS, A MERSEYSIDE TOWN IN THE INDUSTRIAL REVOLUTION: ST. HELENS, 1750-1900 (London: Frank Cass, 1954).

19. For a detailed discussion of such measures, see WALTER ISARD *et. al.*, METHODS OF REGIONAL ANALYSIS 245-308 (Cambridge: M.I.T. Press, 1960).

20. FRANCIS E. HYDE, LIVERPOOL AND THE MERSEY: AN ECONOMIC HISTORY OF A PORT, 1700-1970, at 89 (Newton Abbot, England: David & Charles, 1971); *see also* Mountfield, *Liverpool Docks and the Municipal Commissioners' Inquiry of 1833 for Liverpool*, 115 TRANSACTIONS OF THE HISTORIC SOCIETY OF LANCASHIRE AND CHESHIRE 163 (1963); STUART MOUNTFIELD, WESTERN GATEWAY: A HISTORY OF THE MERSEY DOCKS AND HARBOUR BOARD (Liverpool: Liverpool U. Press, 1965).

21. BENJAMIN LOVE, MANCHESTER AS IT IS 19-20 (Manchester: Love & Barton, 1842).

22. *See, e.g.*, A SURVEY OF THE HISTORY, COMMERCE AND MANUFACTURES OF LANCASHIRE at 83–85 (London: 1897): "No better register of the growth of Manchester can be found than the following figures exhibiting the increase of the commerce of Liverpool, *which is simply a reflex* of the prosperity of the great industrial area of which Manchester is the commercial imporium (*sic*)."

23. These estimates are based on dock rate information and piloting charges provided by J.R. McCULLOCH, A DICTIONARY OF COMMERCE AND COMMERCIAL NAVIGATION 490-503 (London: Longman, Rees, Orme, Brown, Green & Longman, 1843). Data on cotton traffic at Liverpool for the 1840's are taken from the same source.

24. *See* Williams, *Liverpool Merchants and the Cotton Trade, 1820-1850*, LIVERPOOL AND MERSEYSIDE: ESSAYS IN THE ECONOMIC AND SOCIAL HISTORY OF THE PORT AND ITS HINTERLAND 182-211 (London: Frank Cass & Co., ed. J. R. Harris, 1969).

25. HYDE, *supra* note 20, at 104.

26. *Id.*

27. *Id.* at 132-39.

28. *See* Harris, *Early Liverpool Canal Controversies*, LIVERPOOL AND MERSEYSIDE: ESSAYS IN THE ECONOMIC AND SOCIAL HISTORY OF THE PORT AND ITS HINTERLAND 78-80 (London: Frank Cass & Co., ed. J. R. Harris, 1969).

29. *See* Chaloner, *The Birth of Modern Manchester*, MANCHESTER AND ITS ORIGINS 131, at 131-32 (Manchester: Manchester U. Press for the British Ass'n for the Advancement of Science, 1962).

30. RAMSEY MUIR, A HISTORY OF LIVERPOOL 257 (Liverpool: Williams & Norgate for the U. of Liverpool Press, 1907).

31. LOVE, *supra* note 21, at 25-26.

32. *See* A.D. GAYER, W.W. ROSTOW, & A.J. SCHWARTZ, 2 THE GROWTH AND FLUCTUATION OF THE BRITISH ECONOMY, 1790-1850, at 650 (Oxford, Clarendon Press, 1953).

33. FRANÇOIS VIGIER, CHANGE AND APATHY: LIVERPOOL AND MANCHESTER DURING THE INDUSTRIAL REVOLUTION 159-60 (Cambridge: M.I.T. Press, 1970).

34. JOHN R. KELLETT, THE IMPACT OF RAILWAYS ON VICTORIAN CITIES 191-92 (London: Routledge & Kegan Paul, 1969).

35. Using occupational data to measure "interaction" or "dependence" relationships requires some strong limiting assumptions. It is necessary to assume that capital requirements are relatively equal across all sites within any industry. Moreover, it is necessary to assume that employment is responsive to market pressures in the *product* market. Finally, since *occupational* rather than *employment* data are used, it is necessary to assume that the former is an unbiased indicator of the latter. In all, one must look upon these results as merely *indicators* of direction and force, not precise estimates of flows. I wish to thank Professor David Landes for his helpful comments on an earlier presentation of these results.

36. HYDE, *supra* note 20, at 115-41.

37. *See generally* DEANE, *supra* note 11, at 84-99.

38. *See* MOMSEN, *supra* note 7, *passim*. *See also* Mattoon, *Railroads, Coffee and the Growth of Big Business in São Paulo, Brazil*, 57 HISPANIC AMERICAN HISTORICAL REVIEW 273, at 274-75 (May 1977).

39. *See generally* JANET D. HENSHALL & RICHARD P. MOMSEN, JR., A GEOGRAPHY OF BRAZILIAN DEVELOPMENT 39-43, 61-69, 88-93, 149-89 (London: G. Bell & Sons, 1974).

40. *See* Mattoon, *supra* note 38, at 277. *See also* WARREN DEAN, THE INDUSTRIALIZATION OF SÃO PAULO, 1880-1945, at 84 (Austin: U. of Texas Press for The Institute of Latin American Studies, 1969).

41. *See* Mattoon, *supra* note 38, at 277-78.

42. *See* DEAN, *supra* note 40, at 19-33.

43. The idea of urbanization being tied to the evolution and fluctuation in world markets is developed by BRINLEY THOMAS, MIGRATION AND URBAN DEVELOPMENT (London: Methuen & Co., 1972). Also useful is ALBERT H. IMLAH, ECONOMIC ELEMENTS IN THE PAX BRITANNICA (Cambridge: Harvard U. Press, 1958).

44. The development literature which assumes the Anglo-American experience to be the archetype experience is extensive; *see, e.g.*, United Nations Department of Economic and Social Affairs, *Processes and Problems of Industrialization in Under-Developed Countries* (U.N. Doc. E/2670/ST/ECA/29, 1955); THE EDITORS OF THE SCIENTIFIC AMERICAN, TECHNOLOGY AND ECONOMIC DEVELOPMENT (New York: Alfred A. Knopf, 1963); WALT W. ROSTOW, THE STAGES OF ECONOMIC GROWTH (Cambridge: Cambridge U. Press, 1960). One of the classic critiques of this viewpoint can be found in ALEXANDER GERSCHENKRON, ECONOMIC BACKWARDNESS IN HISTORICAL PERSPECTIVE (Cambridge, Belknap Press of Harvard U. Press, 1962). Also useful is JOHN H. KUNKEL, SOCIETY AND ECONOMIC GROWTH: A BEHAVIORAL PERSPECTIVE OR SOCIAL CHANGE (New York: Oxford U. Press, 1970).

Legal Institutions and
Early Industrial Growth

ROBERT W. SHIRLEY*

THIS ARTICLE COMPARES the industrial development and subsequent forms of urbanization of Manchester between 1756 and 1911 and São Paulo between 1872 and 1945. During these periods, the population growth and industrial development of the two cities followed similar patterns. The main focus is on the administrative responses, especially of the legal apparatus, to the first great industrial impulse in both regions.

In Manchester during the target period, one finds a rapidly growing industrial plant, based largely on cotton textiles and metal works, developing within the framework of a world market system founded on the overseas expansion of the British Empire at its zenith.[1] In São Paulo, a similar industrial plant developed mainly to supply textiles and foodstuffs to a pre-existing national market economy founded on the exportation of coffee to the world market. The two plants were of roughly similar pattern and size, but were mirror images of one another in relation to the world economy: Manchester's market was mainly external (destroying India's textile industry as it grew), whereas São Paulo's was mainly internal. The two cities thus form a textbook example of the problems of primary and secondary industrialization.[2]

A comparative chronology based upon population size provides a reasonably useful way to compare administrative forms under primary and secondary economic situations, especially when the administrative entities involved are culturally and politically very different. Such a chronology allows a comparison not only of administrative growth and development in the face of increasing urban needs, but also of the capacities of the different local governments to meet such needs. The chronology I have constructed for this paper may be found in Table I.

* Associate Professor of Anthropology at The University of Toronto.

TABLE I.   A COMPARATIVE CHRONOLOGY
OF URBAN POPULATION

| MANCHESTER | | SÃO PAULO | |
Year	Population	Year	Population
1756	16,530		
1773	22,481		
1788	42,821	1872	31,385
1811	79,459	1890	64,934
1821	108,016		
1832	142,026		
		1900	239,820
1842	311,263		
1845	360,000		
1851	420,716		
1861	492,720	1920	579,033
1882	c.750,000	1930	c. 750,000
1961	661,041	1950	2,198,096
		1970	5,924,615

Sources: ARTHUR REDFORD, MANCHESTER MERCHANTS AND FOREIGN TRADE, 1794-1856 (Manchester: Manchester U. Press, 1938); SHINA D. SIMON (LADY SIMON OF WYTHENSHAWE), A CENTURY OF CITY GOVERNMENT: MANCHESTER 1838-1939 (London: George Allen & Unwin, Ltd., 1938), FRANCOIS VIGIER, CHANGE AND APATHY: LIVERPOOL AND MANCHESTER DURING THE INDUSTRIAL REVOLUTION (Cambridge, MA: M.I.T. Press, 1970); ANUÁRIO ESTATISTICO DO BRASIL, 1975.

Note: In making such comparisons, one must use relevant and similar definitions of the urban unit. In this case, the population shown for São Paulo is that of the *município*, whose boundaries have been largely fixed since Imperial times. (Its area is over ten times that of the borough of Manchester.) For Manchester, the population shown is for the township before 1842, and the municipal borough after that date. The "real" urban population of Manchester is difficult to define after 1890, because improved transportation integrated the city with its suburbs.

In Manchester, the historical record clearly shows the local industrial and commercial bourgeoisie creating an urban administration from nothing but an ancient feudal Court Leet.[3] Only in 1846 was the city of Manchester able to buy the manorial rights to its own territory from the baronial Mosley family.[4] In São Paulo, on the other hand, the new industrial system had to develop within a pre-existing political and economic infrastructure of considerable scale, organized during the Imperial period by the powerful coffee planter families. Ironically, early industrial São Paulo had a vastly more efficient administration than did early industrial Manchester.

I. GENERAL ADMINISTRATIVE HISTORIES

A. *Manchester*

The development of urban administration in Manchester is a tale of vast confusion and improvisation, in large part because the city's demographic and economic growth rapidly outstripped the capacities of the local government until nearly the end of the nineteenth century. Manchester's urban services grew by trial-and-error and crisis management, and only toward the end of the Victorian era did the city develop an effective municipal administration. Throughout much of its early history, the city did not have transportation networks and other basic infrastructural elements of sufficient size to support and even feed its people, and the dominant groups of the time were only slightly interested in developing them. Periodic economic crises coupled with the generally squalid conditions produced the constant threat of famine and food riots among the workers until well into the nineteenth century.

The township was initially governed by means of the medieval Court Leet of the Manor of Manchester. This body met twice yearly and was presided over by the Steward of the Manor Lord, who appointed the jurors for each year. The jurors in turn appointed the town officials. These officials served largely without pay, but were responsible for the entire administration of the town. Besides the Boroughreeve, the town's chief officer, the officials were mainly marketlookers, searchers, appraisers, guards of the town market and water supply, scavengers, and distributors for Poor Relief. The only paid officials were the Deputy Constable and a beadle; the two regular constables were unpaid.[5] Administrative funds generally did not exist. As late as 1770, when the town already had a population of 20,000, the Court Leet appointed 140 officials, but the total municipal expenditures amounted to only 409 pounds.[6]

Although the Court Leet functioned well into the nineteenth century, such a flimsy administrative structure could not realistically support an industrial city of several hundred thousand people. A series of *ad hoc* solutions developed for various individual problems as each of these reached a crisis point. The only municipal funding came from borrowing from the Poor Rate funds, a form of tax on assessed valuation of property which dated from the time of Elizabeth I, or from specific capital grants from the national government through private bills for the city's improvement, nearly all of which were used to improve canals and highways.[7]

In 1792, social order in Manchester almost completely broke down. Political mobs even attacked the home of the liberal Borough-reeve.[8] The Tory elite of Manchester supported a bill creating a system of Police Commissioners, who included not only the local church and Leet officials, but any person owning property or income with a value in excess of 30 pounds. This act potentially permitted some members of the local middle class to participate in local government. In addition, the commissioners now possessed a considerable tax potential, since they were authorized to levy a rate of seven and one-half percent on assessed property valuation. Unfortunately, little of this potential power was utilized, since the new commissioner system simply paralleled and did not displace the older church and Leet administrations. Each of these guarded its own prerogatives, and general administrative paralysis was only narrowly avoided by the fact that usually the same men headed all three systems in a small oligarchic circle. Manchester, moreover, remained under fairly tight oligarchic control despite the efforts of some powerful reformist elements within the middle class. In 1829, despite significant improvements, only 2.6 percent of the population was eligible to vote.[9]

The city was granted borough status in 1838 (confirmed with a charter in 1842). But the immediate reaction to the new Borough Council was not favorable. The existing administrative systems continued to maintain their privileges and to insist on their own control. The Church wardens refused to produce their rate books, and the Police Commissioners even denied the new corporation access to the town hall.[10] In 1838, there were five overlapping administrative organizations in the town, with six layers of local taxation (county, highway, poor, police, magistrate, and church) collected by three different groups.[11] Four hundred fifty streets were unpaved. Over one-half the population relied on rain, well, and river water for drinking, which precluded the building of sewers in the town. Over 20 different committees struggled to govern Manchester.[12]

By 1842, however, taxation and administration became fully centralized in the hands of the Borough Council. The purchase of the Manorial rights in 1846 eliminated the powers of the Court Leet. A series of Parliamentary acts and judicial decisions gave the Council complete administrative control, and it functioned thereafter in a more rational manner. The general administration of the city developed slowly but steadily through the Victorian era. By 1938, Lady Simon, by no means an uncritical observer, stated that the city administration was one of the best in England.[13]

B. *São Paulo*

In contrast to Manchester, the administrative development of São Paulo seems like a model of efficiency. Two factors explain the difference: coffee and the state. The municipal government was not unimportant, but the active administration for almost all critical activities in the city was the state government with its powerful President and Secretaries.

The State of São Paulo, after the fall of the Empire in 1889, inherited an administrative system which had developed during nearly 70 years of Imperial government. This system entailed a high concentration of formal power in the hands of the State President. The President, the Provincial Chief of Police, and all judges were appointed by the government in Rio de Janeiro.[14]

Politically, agrarian Brazil, like eighteenth century England, was dominated by a handful of powerful commercial and landed families. This was generally true from Colonial times until the 1930's, with sporadic attempts at government centralization during the later years of the Empire.[15] The collapse of the Imperial government and the failure to institute a central military government led to the presidency of Campos Salles in Rio de Janeiro and the "Política dos Governadores" from 1898 to 1902. This policy of giving state governors free internal control in exchange for their support of the nation allowed the major Brazilian states to build their own public administrations without serious interference from the federal government. The State of São Paulo, the center of the coffee economy, took full advantage of this opportunity.

Ironically, the Paulista Campos Salles, noted for his policies of decentralization as President of Brazil, was strongly centralist as President of São Paulo. The following comment reflects the general attitude of the São Paulo agrarian ruling class: "Campos Salles, like the majority of historical Republicans, detested parliamentarianism, and defended the theory of a strong government supported by a strong party, without admitting, however, that the government should be totally dominated by the party leadership."[16]

The government of São Paulo during the Old Republic (1889-1930) generally represented only one interest group, the coffee planters. The coffee elite desired and built a small but efficient state administration catering to their needs. Transportation, police control, water supplies, and elite education were some of the basic services which the landed families demanded from their state administration. To get them, they were willing to relinquish almost dictatorial powers,

to a series of very strong administrators whose interests, particularly
the maximization of coffee income, usually coincided with theirs.
The result was one of the most honest and effective state governments in Brazil, but one which was almost totally uninterested in the
general problems of the country, the "social problem" of agrarian and
urban poverty, or even the development of industry, except when it
served the interests of the planters by reducing their costs.[17]

The coffee interests, moreover, had the money to pay for an
effective state government. The state administrators had two important advantages in financing government activities. First, although
they collected revenues throughout the entire state, they could
spend at their complete discretion. Thus, they were able to concentrate expenditures on the central urban unit in a way which Manchester's leaders could not. Second, they shared in the coffee income, and
the coffee economy was a large one. Exports of coffee through Santos
quadrupled from $40,000,000 in 1892 to $170,000,000 in 1912.[18] In
1904, 68 percent of the state's income came from the coffee planters.
They were powerful enough to persuade the Brazilian federal government to pay for the support of coffee prices, thereby increasing
their income still further.[19]

In sum, the State of São Paulo offered much greater economic
capacity and concentration of wealth, as well as much more direct
control over spending, than did the Borough of Manchester. This
political and economic condition greatly influenced administrative
development, especially of the police and judicial systems.

II.   DEVELOPMENT OF THE POLICE FORCES

For the sake of comparison and analysis, I have distinguished
four basic police functions as comparative variables. The first three
variables are indicators of a "legitimate" regime, whereas an increasing use of repression (variables three and four) signifies greater social
conflict.

(1) *Administrative public services: e.g.*, fire protection, finding lost children, helping the sick.
(2) *Petty judicial decisions: e.g.*, resolving family disputes,
traffic control, settling fights, dealing with alcoholics.[20]
(3) *Individual repression:* the social control of individual
members of society who deviate from social norms,
whether these be customary or state-mandated. This function is commonly known as "criminology" or "crime

control," which is seen as a public service by many people, but in cross-cultural and cross-class perspective, is more usefully classified as a separate function.

(4) *Mass repression:* the control of groups of people in street riots or, in more general form, of entire classes of people. This is the hallmark of authoritarianism.

By comparing the sizes of the police forces of the two cities with the comparative chronology based on population, we see dramatic differences in the administration of the two regions. At any given point in the urban growth of the two cities, the police capacity of São Paulo (*i.e.*, the number of trained professional policemen available to the government) was eight to ten times greater than in Manchester.[21] Throughout most of its history until 1930, at least half of the police force of São Paulo had been formed as military police or tactically mobile forces. There was always a considerable reserve force above that necessary for daily administration. This reserve was at times used for class repression, and it also served as a military defense for the state against external threats.[22]

I do not mean to imply that the municipal government of Manchester had no repressive elements. The comparative weakness of its police forces meant that mass repression, when it occurred, was transferred onto another level of government. Manchester authorities, particularly in the early part of the nineteenth century, regularly called on the regular British Army for assistance when their own forces failed. This had important political consequences, as will be noted below.

A. *The Manchester Police Force to 1911*

Throughout most of its urban history, the Manchester police force was notoriously weak, especially in view of the poverty of the city workers and the continual food crises and other riots. Vigier notes a riot in 1757 which started over the price of a sack of potatoes. The rioters were dispersed by " 'the magistrates and principal inhabitants of the town who armed themselves with Stout Sticks,' and by the high Sheriff of the county, who came into town 'attended by fifty of his tenants, neighbours, and friends well armed.' "[23] Under the administration of the Court Leet, only two unpaid constables and the paid Deputy Constable and his beadle were responsible for all aspects of policing the town. The Leet also contracted for police services on a piecemeal basis. The general lack of funds, however, limited the number of people whom the town could hire.

TABLE II. COMPARATIVE SIZE OF POLICE FORCES

URBAN POPULATION	SIZE OF POLICE FORCES (AND YEAR) Manchester	São Paulo
50,000	30 (1789)	429 (1872)
150,000	131 (1830)	
250,000	155 (1837)	4,408[a] (1900)
300,000	398 (1842)	
450,000	522 (1855)	
600,000	1,037 (1898)	8,814 (1920)
700,000	1,000 (1903)	9,216 (1926)

Sources: FRANCOIS VIGIER, CHANGE AND APATHY: LIVERPOOL AND MAN-CHESTER DURING THE INDUSTRIAL REVOLUTION (Cambridge, MA: M.I.T. Press, 1970); SHINA D. SIMON (LADY SIMON OF WYTHENSHAWE), A CENTURY OF CITY GOVERNMENT: MANCHESTER 1838-1938 (London: George Allen & Unwin, Ltd., 1938); WILLIAM EDWARD ARMYTAGE AXON, THE ANNALS OF MAN-CHESTER (London: J. Heywood, 1886); HELOISA RODRIGUES FERNANDES, POLITICA E SEGURANÇA (São Paulo: ed. Alfa-Omega, 1974).

By 1800, under the Police Commissioners, the new Boroughreeve organized the urban services and increased the number of watchmen to 43, with 22 firemen and a paid fire chief.[24] The number of paid watchmen gradually increased to 121 in 1834, although the population of the city had grown to almost 300,000. The organization of the watchmen was complicated by a dual system: the day watch was controlled by the Court Leet and the night watch by the Police Commissioners.

It seems likely that these few men in an industrial city over one thousand times their size could provide little more than a minimum of protection in the center of town. Indeed, by 1842, the police force was in a state of crisis, undermanned and sharply divided amongst themselves. The new Borough Council soon realized that the force, which had now grown in number to almost 300, was inadequate for its task. However, organization and pay scales were gradually improved, and the first inspection report of the British government, published in 1861, stated that the force consisted of 522 officers and constables, "a remarkably fine and effective body of men, most of them in the prime of life and health."[25]

Manchester was a highly radicalized and polarized city, with a huge and oppressed working class, some of the largest factories in England, and some of the richest industrial capitalists. It was also a strong Socialist center.[26] Major working class riots swept through the streets of the city every few years. The Annals of Manchester lists nine of them between 1800 and 1842.[27] At times, the city was completely taken over by the rioters.

In order to cope with these riots, the police force had to be supplemented with substantial contingents of military men. Manchester was a garrison town with barracks for a regiment of troops in Salford, on the other side of the river. Early in the nineteenth century, 2,000 troops were stationed there, and their ranks could be increased in times of emergency. The best-known incident of overt repression was the "Peterloo massacre" of 1819.[28] In 1881, Manchester was also the site of the King's Liverpool Regiment (562 officers and men), and two militia battalions of 903 officers and 678 men.[29]

According to Simon,

> Gradually a police force was built up which was capable of keeping order without the aid of the military. It is interesting to recall that when, in 1890, the War Office decided to remove the troops which were stationed at the Hulme Barracks, the City Council protested on the grounds that although difficulties very seldom arose in Manchester, 'the very fact that a troop of cavalry could sweep any of our streets in a few minutes had certainly a wholesome influence.' The venerable Alderman Heywood . . . supported the War Office's proposal. He pointed out that cavalry had not been used in Manchester since 1848, when they had been called in to clear the streets of working men's demonstrations in favor of political representation. Since that had been granted, he could see no further necessity for keeping the military in Manchester.[30]

Thus, by the end of the nineteenth century, the local and national governments had reached such a degree of legitimacy that mass police repression was no longer used in Manchester.

B. *The São Paulo Police Force to 1930*

In contrast to the police force of Manchester, which developed haphazardly from a series of watch patrols, the police forces of the State of São Paulo had been consciously planned as a para-military force controlled by the plantation elite of the state. Since the beginning of the Republican period in 1892, the state government built a powerful force, both to keep internal order and to aid in external defense. The police were a major factor in the tough political infighting which kept São Paulo the most powerful state in the Brazilian Federation.

A crucial difference between the two urban areas of Manchester and São Paulo was the vastly greater financial resources available to the latter. Until the 1830's, Manchester operated on a municipal budget of a few thousand pounds sterling per year.[31] On the other hand, the state budget of São Paulo, from the beginning of the Republic, was over 1,000,000 pounds, and exceeded 15,000,000 pounds in 1926.[32] Furthermore, the Paulista budget was not tied, like Manchester's, to specific groups or organizations, such as the Church. Thus, the Secretariat of Security received about 15 percent of the total budget, reaching a peak of 30 percent in 1932 (with the revolt) and declining thereafter.[33]

The traditional police force of the Province, developed during the Imperial period, was led by a professional police chief, trained in law and appointed directly by the Imperial Government. He in turn appointed a number of *delegados*.[34] In addition, a permanent police corps served as a mobile tactical force to watch over the capital city or to be sent wherever trouble might break out. In 1888, there were seven companies of infantry and one of cavalry, with 1,480 men (an increase from only 530 the year before).[35] There was also an urban guard with 243 members in 1886.[36]

The period after the fall of the Empire represented an era of extreme political instability in Brazil in general and São Paulo in particular. In 1892, the new state police force consisted of five infantry batallions, one cavalry corps, and a fire corps, with a total of 3,933 men. All of these were directly under the central authority of the state President.[37] In the next few years, the police were increasingly militarized, as was partly manifested in the adoption of military titles for officers. In 1900, there were 2,251 men in the civil guard of the interior of the state, 538 in the capital city, and a military brigade of 1,619 men.[38] These forces were combined into the famous Força Pública, which remained the principal police force of the state until recent times. In 1926, a Civil Guard was created for the city of São Paulo "without military character."[39]

The complex Brazilian system of local power known as *Coronelismo*[40] was common in São Paulo for much of its history. In this system, effective policing (repression) was handled by private gunmen (*jagunços*) in the pay of the local commercial planters. The military police was also mainly at the service of the planters, but served principally as an urban and emergency force. The vigorous São Paulo presidents, however, feared the danger of schism and disorganization with many private police forces. They fought for a powerful, centralized military force which could dominate the state. Jorge Tibiriça, President of the state in 1906, contracted with the French Army to train the Força Pública of São Paulo. This succeeded in installing military discipline into the police force. By 1924, the Força Pública had become a model of military police organization. According to its members: "The religion of a solider of the Força Pública is order, and its Bible, the Law."[41]

This "Brazilian Prussia" began arming itself with machine guns and took on the apparatus of a small modern army, with a hospital corps, artillery corps with heavy guns, and even a small squadron of airplanes.[42] The purely police functions of the Força were being lost in its role of defender of the Paulista coffee interests against insurrection by the working class of the city. At least six times, the Força was mobilized to handle labor disputes.

The high point, as well as the collapse, of the Força Pública as a military unit came in 1932 when it formed the core of the Constitutionalist revolt by São Paulo against the "revolutionary" government of Getulio Vargas. Despite heroic statewide efforts and the recruitment of thousands of civilians, the federal and other state forces under General Góis Monteiro defeated the Paulistas in four months, and the independent military capacity of the State of São Paulo was broken. The Força Pública was federalized and lost its heavy weapons. The state, however, maintains a strong military police force even in modern times.

III. THE JUDICIARY

The judiciary of any society is very important to the development of its political and administrative structures. Besides the immediate influence that judges have in mediating conflict and, in some societies, determining the legitimacy of other political mechanisms, the judiciary is frequently viewed as the preserver of cultural traditions and norms. Thus, it is normally a force for stability and conservatism.[43] Because the social rank of judges grants them influence and authority exceeding their nominal political resources, the role of the judiciary in society is very complex,[44] and cross-cultural comparisons become all the more difficult.

Despite these caveats, a study of the judiciaries in developing Manchester and São Paulo demonstrates that the true social effect of a judiciary is not necessarily determined by normal measures of professionalism and formal power. On the face of it, the São Paulo judiciary would have seemed a much more significant institution than its British counterpart. The Paulista judges were university-trained professionals with life tenure who tried all cases without a jury, except in cases of alleged homicide. There was an adequate number of them, though their proportion among the population declined over time.[45] On the other hand, the British judiciary was composed of unpaid rural lay magistrates, assisted until 1834 by only one professional judge for both Salford and Manchester.[46] Even though these rural magistrates were appointed by the Crown, they would not seem to have the same prospect for social importance as the Paulista judges.

These formal powers, however, were outweighed by other determinants of the judiciary's social role. Simply put, the Paulista judges were captives of the rural coffee aristocracy, frequently drawn from the ranks of the aristocracy and protective of its interests. The Paulista judiciary reached its lowest ebb during the Old Republic. The judges were underpaid and dependent on local political leaders, serving merely as juridical aides to the coffee families.[47] Thus it was that in the tumultuous history of the state from 1900 to 1930, practically no reference was made to the power or influence of the judiciary. There were few laws governing labor relations, and the police and Secretariat of Justice were able to implement their desires directly, bypassing the judiciary. The great majority of the urban population never saw a judge. As a result, the moral authority of the Paulista judiciary was sharply limited.

The British magistrates, however, were much more influential than their formal position would cause them to appear. First, because the British judges were normally Tory landowners, they were members of the local elite rather than subordinate to it. As Redford noted, "the magistrates, the principal officers of the Court Leet, the principal officers of the Parish, and the leaders of the Police Commissioners were all, or nearly all, members of a closely knit oligarchy . . . ."[48] Thus, the judges were individually very influential. Second, the judiciary actually benefited from the incredibly confusing and overlapping patterns of political administration discussed above. As the local agents of the Crown, the Manchester judges were able to fill the power vacuum created by the weakness of the city government and its police force. For example, the British magistrates had the power to employ and arm special constables, and to request military assistance. In these ways, the judiciary was able to exercise considerable authority.

Finally, while both countries had some exceptional judges, the general role of the judiciary in both societies was to provide a structure for social control, and to support the domination of a landed elite over rural and urban workers. The liberal ideal of universal justice had little relevance in these cities. As a result, the judiciary did not effectively legitimate the social order for the urban masses. This shortcoming aggravated perceptions of repression among the urban poor and contributed to the development of several severe social crises.

From the longer historical perspective, we see that there was a strange inversion of institutional roles. In nineteenth century Manchester, the magistrates were the key repressive agency while the new police forces tended to exercise a legitimizing effect. The opposite trends were discernable in São Paulo.

IV. LEGAL INSTITUTIONS AND WORKERS

The most striking parallel in the comparative histories of the two cities is the reaction by the state to the developing industrial urban working classes. In both cities, tight oligarchical control over all aspects of the politics and economics of the two countries produced fierce resentment on the part of the workers. This often exploded into open rebellion which the state authorities found difficult to contain. In both countries, the agrarian-commercial ruling class was confronted with a new and seemingly dangerous element—an industrial proletariat. The initial reaction by the authorities in both cities was massive repression. This caused greater resentment, which eventually grew into incidents of such magnitude that the national governments were shaken into attempts at new legitimation through social reforms.

A. *Manchester and "Peterloo"*

Manchester, with its large urban population and its under-developed social and economic infrastructure, was a major center for civil unrest. "Peterloo" was the classic confrontation between the Manchester workers and the local government authorities. Although the affair did not cause many deaths, it had considerable political importance. What began as a peaceful protest turned grimly violent as a result of the overreaction of the authorities.

Britain had just emerged victorious from its long struggle with Napoleon after the battle of Waterloo in 1815, but the war with France had several severe consequences in Manchester. The government authorities were so greatly frightened by the ideas of liberty, equality, and fraternity that the city was nearly placed under a state of siege during the wars. In addition, the cost of the wars led to constantly spiralling living costs. The radical reform movement grew rapidly despite efforts by the country magistrates to prevent its organization.

On August 16, 1815, the radicals led by Henry Hunt planned a mass meeting on St. Peter's fields in Manchester. The local magistrates reluctantly permitted the meeting, but because of their general fear of the workers, they enrolled several hundred special constables to guard the city, and called up two troops of the local Yeomanry, 400 of the Cheshire Yeomanry, two squadrons (300 men) of the 15th Hussars, and a troop of the Royal Horse Artillery with two artillery pieces. These troops, together with the 31st Infantry Regiment and part of the 88th Infantry, were all hidden in various streets of the city.[49]

The total number of participants in the meeting was variously estimated at 150,000 (by Hunt) and 60,000 (by the magistrates). They were largely unarmed at the insistence of their leaders, who apparently expected no violence. It was probably the sheer size of the meeting rather than its organization which frightened the magistrates. Thirty justices signed a warrant for the arrest of Henry Hunt and others. The deputy constable requested aid in serving the warrant, and troops were sent into the field. Colonel L'Estrange, in charge of the Army contingent, refused to send his infantry, thereby saving many lives. Unfortunately, the local Manchester Yeomanry, half drunk, arrived first. Poorly led and organized, they soon became blocked by the crowds and both sides panicked. Wellington's Hussars, using the blunt edge of their swords, cleared the field in minutes, sweeping all before them, workers, constables, and Yeomen. By official estimates, 11 people were killed and about 400 injured.[50]

This violent reaction to nothing more than a large, peaceful radical meeting created still more hostility among the workers and more anxiety on the part of the local officials. On the same night, another riot broke out in the city. During the next four days, five serious riots occured. On August 23, the London Times wrote: "Manchester now wears the appearance of a garrison, or of a town conquered in war."[51] Eleven persons, including Henry Hunt, were imprisoned on major charges and 30 others jailed on lesser ones. Hunt served three years in jail and became a folk hero, eventually being elected to Parliament.[52]

One notable effect of these massive labor movements was their gradual acceptance and incorporation into the British political scene.

Peterloo was important because it shocked the established order, gave new support to the radical groups, and helped solidify the working groups. Workers gradually organized, and their organizations were accepted by the governing classes. Manchester became the center of the British Socialist movement.[53] Riots were gradually replaced by strikes. In short, despite extraordinary efforts at government repression during the first part of the nineteenth century, the city gradually developed into a major center of social reform and labor organization, with lasting effects on British politics.

B. *São Paulo and the General Strike of 1917*

São Paulo was also a powerful center for labor activity in the first part of this century. The city was paralyzed by three general strikes, in 1906, 1917, and 1919. It was the headquarters for the development of syndicates, cooperatives, and other organizations at a time when such activity was emphatically discouraged by the state.[54]

The labor movement in São Paulo seems to have been organized in a much more sophisticated way than that in Manchester at a similar period of industrial development. The many immigrant workers were able to look to established European models of labor organization.[55] Unfortunately, the repressive mechanisms, principally the state police, were equally sophisticated for the period.

The most important and dramatic labor confrontation in São Paulo during the Old Republic was the General Strike of 1917. It involved a violent reaction by the state government and a violent counter-reaction by the striking workers. The strike started in June, 1917, and by July 4, some 40,000 workers were out. Pressures on the workers had been building for some time because of the increasing costs of food due to the war in Europe. The strike began quietly, and the requests of the workers were modest. Some powerful newspapers, such as the *Estado de São Paulo*, supported the movement, citing the "miserable" conditions of the factory workers.[56]

As in Manchester, the sheer size of the Paulista labor movement caused panic among members of the local elite.[57] When the workers finally marched, they crippled the city. Violence was prevalent in all districts of the city. The police responded with its full force. Throughout the strike, police movement was enormous. The workers held out for a long time, despite police attempts to disperse them. The strike finally ended in a partial victory for the workers.[58]

During this time, the "harmonious relationship" between the employers and the police was first noted.[59] According to Warren Dean,

[After the strike,] the police picked up several hundred
"agitators," not always "in a manner prescribed by law,
however justifiable from the standpoint of expediency."[60]
Finally it was decided to deport several of them. . . . Once
[a] blacklist was established, it became very difficult for an
organizer to find a job within a factory. As soon as one was
identified within a plant, the General Secretary (of the São
Paulo Confederation of Industries) simply called the police
and had the man jailed.[61]

The spontaneous anarcho-syndicalist labor movements in São
Paulo and Brazil reached their peak during the period from 1917 to
1920, when they were generally defeated in direct confrontations
with government forces. Thereafter, the movement went into a long,
slow decline, although it was never fully crushed. In fact, it was later
picked up and used by the national government after 1930.

V. CONCLUSIONS: REPRESSION AND REFORM

It appears that in both cities, a powerful, thoughtful, and generally capable commercial-agrarian elite found itself in a brutal struggle
with a newly developing urban industrial proletariat. The initial reaction in both cases was government repression, but the capacities and
reactions of the various groups involved were very different.

In Manchester, a feeble, archaic administrative structure was
barely able to contain a massive series of uprisings. The well-trained
British Army was thrown into the gap to maintain internal order. The
Army itself, however, was badly weakened by budgetary crises, and
was sometimes unwilling to raise weapons against its own country-
men.[62] Furthermore, the Army was needed for the expansion of the
British Empire abroad and defense against growing European
competition.

A double economic and political pattern was thus established. It
became increasingly important for the British rulers to legitimate
themselves to the working class and to try to unify the nation. Productivity and the great expansion of British commercial and imperialist
power abroad had to be maintained. Second, the very expansion of
the Empire gave Britain the resources it needed to integrate the
workers into the national government.

The Reform Bills of 1832 and 1867, simultaneously radical and
conservative, brought the British working class into the government
to a degree unusual in almost any capitalist country. The Imperial

commercial expansion gave Great Britain great economic prosperity. Police or military repression became an unnecessary force because of the general growth of the economy.

The Victorian government, although eminently aristocratic, succeeded in legitimating itself to most of its people (with the exception of the Irish) by constantly improving wages and working conditions, allowing unions to develop, and awarding universal male suffrage.[63]

In São Paulo, on the other hand, the industrial establishment exerted much less influence on the international commercial scene. As Warren Dean has shown, the original Paulista industrialists enjoyed a closely integrated relationship with the powerful landed coffee planter families.[64] The agrarian commercial state preferred to put its great resources into repressive mechanisms, at least up to 1930, rather than attempt to legitimate itself to the urban or rural workers.

The great series of popular and military disturbances of the decades of 1910 and 1920 helped cause the government's downfall in 1930.[65] The highly flexible and pragmatic Getulio Vargas took power. One of his foremost skills was a capacity to balance the needs of various interest groups. He gave the Paulistas a constitution, after defeating them in open warfare in 1932. He was able to divide the old agrarian elite, while still aligning himself at various times with parts of it to maintain his own support.

At first his policies were basically conservative, and he continued violent repressive measures against the workers' movements, particularly the Communist Party.[66] On the other hand, he was very aware of the potential force of the labor movement, and decided to bring it under his direct control. Social laws and workers' syndicates had existed before in Brazil,[67] but Vargas introduced much new social legislation in favor of the workers (most notably a minimum wage), and created federally controlled syndicates in almost all areas of urban work.[68] In 1943, all of the laws relating to working conditions and labor organizations were brought together into one unit, *A Consolidaçao das leis de trabalho*.[69]

Perhaps more important in the social sense was the creation of several institutions to enforce these laws, most notably a separate series of tribunals to decide labor disputes.[70] These were called the Courts of Conciliation and Judgment (*Juntas de Conciliação e Julgamento*), which aptly reflected their function. The results, however complex politically, had considerable effect on the country in the long run as many of the social laws were applied.[71] In this way, Vargas succeeded in gaining enormous popular support, especially in the larger cities.

Once again the patterns of the two cities seem somewhat reversed. Victorian social legislation was aimed at admitting working people into the governmental process through electoral reforms. It has been a tradition in England, only recently questioned, for the government to "abstain" in matters affecting unions and labor relations.[72] These subjects were considered personal and contractual matters. The workers were allowed to develop their own organizations and political parties after the late nineteenth century. The growing political force of labor in government helped resolve the "social question" for over a century.

In Brazil, on the other hand, the state was continually and directly involved in labor problems. Except for a few brief instances, the workers have rarely participated in government decision-making. The Brazilian government, since the time of Vargas, has attempted to reduce labor unrest and legitimate itself in the eyes of the workers through paternalistic labor legislation and strongly centralized control over all labor organizations. All advances in workers' conditions were decreed by the government. Meanwhile, the state had continued to maintain a considerable repressive apparatus through various state and federal institutions. This repression has, at least to date, effectively excluded the workers from real organization or government participation.

NOTES

1. *See generally* ERIC J. HOBSBAWM, INDUSTRY AND EMPIRE (NY: Pantheon, 1968); ARTHUR REDFORD, MANCHESTER MERCHANTS AND FOREIGN TRADE, 1794–1856 (Manchester: Manchester U. Press, 1934).

2. *See generally* CELSO FURTADO, THE ECONOMIC GROWTH OF BRAZIL (Berkeley: U. of Calif. Press, trans. Richard W. de Aguir & Eric C. Drysdale, 1963).

3. ARTHUR REDFORD & IRA RUSSELL, THE HISTORY OF LOCAL GOVERNMENT IN MANCHESTER (NY: Longman's Green, 1940).

4. FRANÇOIS VIGIER, CHANGE AND APATHY: LIVERPOOL AND MANCHESTER DURING THE INDUSTRIAL REVOLUTION 193 (Cambridge, MA: M.I.T. Press, 1970).

5. WILFRED HARRY THOMSON, A HISTORY OF MANCHESTER TO 1852 at 81-82 (Altrincham, Eng.: John Sherratt & Son, 1967).

6. VIGIER, *supra* note 4, at 106-07.

7. *See id.* at 108.

8. *Id.* at 115.

9. *Id.* at 149.

10. *Id.* at 191.

11. SHINA D. SIMON (LADY SIMON OF WYTHENSHAWE), A CENTURY OF CITY GOVERNMENT: MANCHESTER 1838–1938 at 61-63 (London: George Allen & Unwin, 1938).

12. *Id.*

13. *Id.* at 334.

14. For an excellent and extended discussion of these problems, *see* RAYMUNDO FAORO, OS DONOS DO PODER (Porto Alegre: Editora Globo, 2d ed., 1975) and VICTOR N. LEAL, CORONELISMO, ENXADA E VOTO (São Paulo: Editora Alfa-Omega, 2d ed., 1975).

15. FAORO, *id.*

16. RODRIGO SOARES JR., JORGE TIBIRIÇÁ E SUA ÉPOCA 396 (São Paulo: Companhia Editora Nacional, 1958).

17. *See* WARREN DEAN, THE INDUSTRIALIZATION OF SÃO PAULO, 1880–1945 (Austin: U. of Texas Press, For the Institute of Latin American Studies, 1969).

18. *Id.*

19. FURTADO, *supra* note 2.

20. Even Kelsen gave the police this latitude. *See* HANS KELSEN, GENERAL THEORY OF LAW AND STATE (NY: Russell & Russell, trans. Anders Wedberg, 1961).

21. While the Paulista force was larger partly because it was a state police and thus responsible for an area much larger than the city proper, I believe the comparison is still sociodynamically valid because the best measure of overall police capacity is the total force that can be mobilized at any time and place.

22. An example of this was the 1932 Constitutionalist rebellion against the Federal Government of Brazil.

23. VIGIER, *supra* note 4, at 100.

24. *Id.* at 122-23.

25. SIMON, *supra* note 11, at 330-34.

26. WILLIAM E. A. AXON, THE ANNALS OF MANCHESTER, (London: John Heywood, 1886).

27. *Id.*

28. In addition to the regular army garrison at the Hulme Baracks in Salford, Manchester supported a number of militia groups. Axon lists 13 of them in 840 with a total of about 5,500 men, though with no indication of their armaments. *Id.* at 134.

29. HISTORICAL RECORD OF THE KING'S LIVERPOOL REGIMENT OF FOOT. . . . TO 1881 (London: Harrison & Sons, 2d ed., 1883).

30. SIMON, *supra* note 11, at 333.

31. VIGIER, *supra* note 4, at 204.

32. 25 REVISTA BRASILIERA DE ESTATÍSTICA 4, at 205-06 (1971).

33. ORÇAMENTO DO ESTADO DE SÃO PAULO, DIÁRIO OFICIAL for the years after 1831.

34. HELOISA RODRIGUES FERNANDES, POLÍTICA E SEGURANÇA 108 (São Paulo: Editora Alfa-Omega, 1974).

35. *Id.*

36. *Id.* at 101.

37. *Id.* at 151.

38. *Id.* at 152.

39. *Id.* at 154.

40. LEAL, *supra* note 14; MARIA SYLVIA DE CARVALHO FRANCO, HOMEN LIBRES NA ORDEM ESCRAVOCRATA (São Paulo: Instituto de Estudos Brasileiros, U. de São Paulo, 1969).

41. CARVALHO FRANCO, *id.* at 193.

42. *Id.* at 162.

43. *See generally* WILLIAM J. CHAMBLISS & ROBERT B. SIEDMAN, LAW, ORDER & POWER (Reading, MA: Addison-Wesley, 1971).

44. *See* KELSEN, *supra* note 20, at 279.

45. *See generally Lei da Organização Judificária*, DIÁRIO OFICIAL (São Paulo) for 1892 to the present.

46. RUSSELL, *supra* note 3, Volume II at 33.

47. JULIO CESAR DE FARIA, JUIZES DO MEU TEMPO (São Paulo: Editora Autor, 1952).

48. REDFORD & RUSSELL, *supra* note 3, Volume I at 258.

49. DONALD READ, PETERLOO (Manchester: Manchester U. Press, rev. ed., 1973); JOYCE MARLOW, THE PETERLOO MASSACRE 118–44 (London: Rapp & Whiting, 1969).

50. READ, *id.* at 139–40; MARLOW, *id.* at 152–56.

51. READ, *id.* at 140–43.

52. MARLOW, *supra* note 49, at 200.

53. AXON, *supra* note 26, at 182, 202, 213.

54. AZIS SIMÃO, SINDICATA E ESTADO: SUAS RELAÇÕES NA FORMACÃO DO PROLETARIADO DE SÃO PAULO 201–02 (São Paulo: Dominus Editora, U. de São Paulo, 1966).

55. BORIS FAUSTO, TRABALHO URBANO E CONFLITO SOCIAL (São Paulo: Difel, 1977).

56. LEÔNCIO RODRIGUES, CONFLITO INDUSTRIAL E SINDICALISMO NO BRASIL 144 (São Paulo: Difusão Européia do Livro, 1966).

57. *Id.* at 142–44.

58. *I2.* at 146.

59. DEAN, *supra* note 17, at 165.

60. *Id.* at 166.

61. FAUSTO, *supra* note 55.

62. J.W. FORTESCUE, 12 A HISTORY OF THE BRITISH ARMY 56 (London: MacMillan & Co., 1930).

63. *See generally,* MICHAEL HILL, THE STATE, ADMINISTRATION AND THE INDIVIDUAL 28 (Totawa, NJ: Roman & Littlefield, 1976).

64. DEAN, *supra* note 17.

65. EDGARD CARONE, REVOLUÇÕES DO BRASIL CONTEMPORÂNEO, 1922–1938 (São Paulo: Coleção Buriti, 11, 1966).

66. *Id.* at 137, 138, 141, 170.

67. *See* SIMÃO, *supra* note 54.

68. JOHN SAUNDERS, MODERN BRAZIL, NEW PATTERNS OF DEVELOPMENT 137 (Gainesville: U. of Florida Press, 1971).

69. Decreto–lei No. 5,452 de 1–5 1943, in JOSÉ SERSON ed., CONSOLIDAÇÃO DAS LEIS DE TRABALHO (São Paulo: Sugestões Literárias S/A, 11th ed., 1975).

70. ORLANDO GOMES E ELSON GOTTSCHALK, CURSO DO DIREITO DE TRABALHO (São Paulo: Forense, 6th ed., 1975).

71. *Id.*

72. CHARLES D. DRAKE, LABOUR LAW 10 (London: Sweet & Maxwell, 2d ed., 1973).

Two Religious Movements: Protestantism and Umbanda

PETER FRY*

The stress of the transition [to industrial society] falls upon the whole culture. . . . And this culture includes the system of power, property-relations, religious institutions, etc., inattention to which merely flattens phenomena and trivializes analysis. [1]

I. INTRODUCTION

This essay will examine the religious dimension in nineteenth century Manchester and twentieth century São Paulo, focusing on Methodism in the first case and what is usually termed the Afro-Brazilian religion of Umbanda in the second. Both of these movements emerged with notable clarity from the general "noise" of religious activity in the two situations, growing apace with industrialization and exciting the comments of contemporaries and historians. By looking at the growth, organization, cosmology, and moral systems of these two movements and by observing the ways in which they made sense in, sprang from, and became integrated with the societies in which they thrived, questions will be raised concerning essential differences between the two industrializing experiences.

The argument which will be developed takes into consideration the questions raised by previous research concerning the parallel growth of Umbanda and Pentecostalism in São Paulo.[2] The coexistence of these two religious movements is problematic in that, while it has been impossible to distinguish sociologically the membership of the two movements, they differ markedly in terms of organization and cosmology, representing two quite distinct ways of interpreting and dealing with the afflictions generated by the contradictions of the urban environment. Previous authors have argued that both these religions have been successful largely because they functioned as

* Assistant Professor of Anthropology, Universidade Estadual de Campinas.

institutions which "integrated" the rural migrant into urban life.[3] This argument carries the implicit premise that urban society exists as a functioning whole, and that new members may be "integrated" into it by establishing primary links with religious congregations and by commitment to a cosmology which offers a coherent interpretation of the facts of urban social life. However, conversion to any social movement, whether or not it may be defined as religious, involves commitment not only to that movement's cosmology, but also to a set of social relationships which will demand investment of time and money, thereby reducing other investments. Clearly, therefore, such conversions "integrate" the new convert not into the town as such, but into a new field of social relationships either as a substitute for, a reinforcing of, or an escape from other primary relationships, such as kinship.

This interpretation of integration is unsatisfactory also because it fails to consider the distinctive natures of the two movements. Umbanda is essentially congregationalist in that it proliferates via the spontaneous fission of existing groups, spreading through the urban landscape like an acephalous tribe. Pentecostalism grows through the proselytization of great preachers and forms large congregations whose autonomy is constrained by effective federations. Umbanda presents a highly eclectic cosmology with as many variants as there are practitioners; it is oriented to the short-term ritual solution of pressing problems. Pentecostalism presents a unified cosmology with clearly enunciated notions of good and evil, defining a rigorous moral ethic, mapping out the path to ultimate salvation after death, and setting the believer apart from non-believers during life. These two religious forms correspond to two different and indeed contradictory ways of perceiving Brazilian society and operating within it. While Umbanda lays emphasis on the achievement of defined social goals in the short term through the manipulation of social relationships, sometimes called "clientage," Pentecostalism represents the celebration of the kind of bureaucratic rationalism which accompanies the growth of modern industrial capitalism and state formation.

One could argue that strong parallels exist between present-day Pentecostalism in São Paulo and Methodism in nineteenth century England: both are evangelizing movements, both stress a rigorous moral discipline as the way to salvation in a future world and both share a concern with large-scale organization and hierarchy. However, since it is the increasing vigor of Umbanda which marks the radical difference between the two cities, it is on the properties of this movement that this essay will concentrate. The central difference between the religious movements in the two cities under comparison is that there was no structural equivalent to Umbanda present in nineteenth century Manchester. On the contrary, what we conveniently call "magic" declined during seventeenth and eighteenth century England, clearing the way for the Industrial Revolution and the marching puritanism of that period. Keith Thomas has demonstrated that the "cunning men" who experienced something of a revival after the Reformation had become insignificant as a viable institution before the religious and industrial changes which were to characterize the late eighteenth and nineteenth centuries.[4] In the Brazilian case, the sequence is reversed, for instead of declining with industrialization and the growth of cities, Umbanda appears to thrive where industrial sophistication is greatest.

At first sight, it may appear absurd to attempt to compare a religion whose cultural origins can be traced to Roman Catholicism, European Spiritualism, and the religious systems of indigenous Brazilian and African populations, with another whose roots lie in the Reformation and seventeenth century puritanism. After all, the cultural history of Brazil is dramatically different from that of England. However, by concentrating on the structure of the organization and cosmology of these two religious forms and relating these to the structuring of social relationships in the two situations, comparison becomes possible. By taking the emphasis away from the cultural genealogies of the two religions and placing it on their basic structural principles, it will be possible to raise questions concerning the way in which social experience is structured in the two situations.

II. THE GROWTH AND ORGANIZATION OF UMBANDA

A. *Development*

The earliest accounts of Afro-Brazilian religious groups describe the situation in Salvador and Rio de Janeiro at the turn of the century.[5] In both cases, ignoring subtle differences of style and ritual, the general picture was one of small communities, called *candomblé* in Salvador and *macumba* in Rio, made up of blacks under the leadership of a *pai* or *mãe de santo* (father or mother in sainthood). Ritual was centered on the worship of and possession by deities derived from the West African cultural traditions which were hidden behind the masks of the Catholic saints. These community groups were oriented toward maintaining the well-being of their members and helping outsiders who seek their aid in times of affliction. Cult organization was complex, but was based on the authority of the fathers and mothers over their children in sainthood. Conflict was present both

within and between cult centers and this led occasionally to fission and
the founding of new centers. This process was controlled by the
requirements that a person complete a number of expensive and
time-consuming initiation rituals in order to acquire legitimacy as a
cult leader.

Over time—probably in the 1920's[6]—this tightly controlled organizational structure began to break down, with several changes
appearing simultaneously. New leaders established themselves without necessarily having passed through all of the required *rites de
passage*, more males entered the cult, and new spirits, the *caboclo*,
appeared, believed to represent dead members of indigenous ethnic
groups. Something of the old order gave way and the overall organization became more fluid, perhaps as a result of the greater fluidity in
society as a whole during these years of rapid industrialization in São
Paulo.

It is at this time also that elements of Kardecist spiritist doctrine,
and in particular the notion that spirits pass through successive rein-
carnations earning promotion and final perfection, began to be incorporated by some cult groups. Diana Brown has documented this
process for Rio de Janeiro, where the term Umbanda first appeared.
Simultaneous with the adoption of spiritist doctrine, these groups
began to play down the more "African" aspects of doctrine and ritual,
such as animal sacrifice, in an attempt to make their religion more
"respectable," a development Brown has termed "the whitening process."[7]

From their earliest existence until the end of the Estado Novo, the
Afro-Brazilian cults were repressed by the police, being regarded as
deviant by the dominant class. After the Second World War, however,
Umbanda began to burgeon in the great cities, not least in São Paulo.[8]
It spread spontaneously as centers split up and new ones were formed
by ambitious mediums who felt they had the necessary number of
followers and financial support, rather than under the overall control
of any one charismatic leader. The rivalry and competition between
mediums within cult centers, which led to their fission, are also a
feature of the relations between cult centers. Some ambitious leaders
have established federations of cult centers in an attempt to establish
ritual and political hegemony over this rapidly expanding religion.
However, rivalry is even more intense at this level of organization,
and no single federation has succeeded in penetrating effectively the
jealously guarded political and ritual autonomy of the individual cult
centers.[9]

B. *Social Composition and Relations With Society*

At the turn of the present century, the *candomblés* and *macumbas* were made up of the descendants of slaves, amongst whom the cults had originated. To mitigate the repression on the part of the white elite, the gods of Africa were concealed behind the façade of the Catholic saints. The relationship between the cults and the ruling elite, however, was ambiguous. While the bourgeoisie repressed the cults, it also recognized their ritual power. The politically and economically weak were perceived to wield supernatural power. In Salvador, members of the white elite were recruited as officials (*ogans*) of the *canomblés*. As such, they were given ritual protection in exchange for their political protection of the cults. In other words, the very elite who repressed the cults was also responsible for their protection.[10] In Rio the situation was similar. The journalist João do Rio described how the wealthy depended on the *macumbas* for ritual help in political, business, and amorous problems and how the *macumbas* depended on the wealthy for their "very existence." "It is we," and here João do Rio is surely referring to the members of the middle class who consult the *macumbas*, "who assure their very existence with the love of a businessman for his actress lover."[11] His metaphor was well chosen, for while the middle- and upper-classes were espoused to the Catholic religion, they maintained clandestine relations with the *macumbas*.

Over the past three decades, Umbanda has not only grown exponentially, but the social composition of its membership has also changed. Although it is almost impossible to gauge with accuracy the sociological nature of Umbanda practitioners, most recent work indicates that it has ceased to be the monopoly of blacks and has penetrated all social classes.[12] This "whitening process" has applied not only to ritual, but also to the social composition of Umbanda. To a certain extent, Umbandistas have come out of the closet; those who in the past maintained semi-clandestine relations with the cult are now found acting publicly as fully committed mediums.

With these changes in social composition, relations between the cult and the state have also changed. Whereas in the past politicians sought the support of cult members through discreet visits to their rituals in exchange for votes, the state government of São Paulo has recently manifested public support for the cult. The Secretary of Tourism sponsors the annual *Festa de Ogum* (Feast of St. George) in the center of Ibirapuera, and local municipal officials are an important presence at the even larger annual *Festa de Iemanjá* (Feast of the Goddess of the Sea) at Praia Grande. It is almost as if the actress lover were being transformed into a legitimate spouse.

The most feasible interpretation of this new policy on the part of the State of São Paulo is that sponsorship of the cults leads to a greater visibility of cult activity and, therefore, greater controllability. But such public wooing might also be seen as a way in which unelected state governors, appointed by the federal president, seek to find some semblance of public legitimacy. As a former State Deputy elected on an Umbanda ticket for Rio Grande do Sul explained: "Today Umbanda is important for national security. Look at the population of Brazil—110,000,000—and we have, according to official statistics, 20,000,000 Umbandistas. Of course the government cannot ignore such an enormous mass."[13]

However, while politicians may see fit to establish a stake in the success of Umbanda, it does not follow that all sectors of the population have ceased to regard the cult as "deviant." The *Estado de São Paulo*, whose editorials can usually be relied upon to represent the interests of the São Paulo bourgeoisie, presents a consistently critical posture. In one 1973 editorial, the cults were described as "hives of perversion and corruption," and the growth of the cult was seen as being counter-evolutionary.[14] The argument was that it was iniquitous to encourage practices that were barbarous, immoral, and culturally retrograde in the context of a sophisticated nation state. Blaming in large part the Catholic hierarchy, which they accused of being basically Marxist, the *Estado de São Paulo* lamented that the government could lend support for this "grotesque cult," "where physical, economic, moral and educational misery reign. The law cannot protect either superstition or credulity; it cannot authorize immorality, crime and corruption which usually accompany the fetishistic practices of the cult groups."[15] Thus, the feeling is expressed that the growth of Umbanda is contrary to the growth of a modern industrial state. This view also reflects the positivist thinking which postulates a fundamental incompatibility between "magic" and the "science" necessary for industrial evolution. But Umbanda's cosmology, in palpable denial of the evolutionist tenet that "magic" is inappropriate to advanced industrialization, appeals to a steadily growing number of people in São Paulo.

C. *Cosmology*

It will be clear by now that, with the highly independent nature of individual cult centers, where each cult leader recognizes himself as the true interpreter of doctrine, the cosmology of Umbanda is highly eclectic. Underlying this eclecticism, however, certain common strands are discernible.

The cult is monotheistic in name only. The godhead is otiose and is approached through a panoply of lesser spirits believed to make themselves known to the living through spirit mediumship, dreams, and omens. These spirits are organized in a sort of para-military hierarchy of lines and phalanxes. The hierarchy is led by the following saints or *orixás*: St. George, *Ogum*; St. Sebastian, *Oxossi*; St. Jerome, *Xangô*; St. Barbara, *Iansã*; Our Lady of the Immaculate Conception, *Oxum*; Jesus Christ, *Oxalá*; Our Lady of the Glory, *Iemanjá*; Saints Cosmos and Damian, *Ibeji*. Each of these leading saints has under his or her control a number of lesser spirits of various types. The main species are old blacks *pretos velhos*, indians *caboclos*, and children *ibeji*. The old blacks are believed to be the spirits of dead African slaves. They are quiet and reserved, and cause their mediums to stoop and to walk with difficulty. They are famed for their healing powers. The *caboclos* stand erect and are valiant and powerful. Their mediums wear colored feathered head-dresses modeled more on the American Far West than the Amazon. The *ibeji*, led by Saints Cosmos and Damian, are playful and also famed for their curative powers. All these spirits respond to their clients' appeals for help as long as such requests are deemed morally sound. They may be classified, therefore, as moral spirits. They contrast with two types of spirits, the *Exús* and the *Pombagiras*, who have no moral sense, *juizo*. The Exús are believed to be spirits of deceased "marginals," *i.e.*, robbers and evil farmers. Their female equivalents, the Pombagiras, are considered spirits of dead "loose women," many of whom claimed to be of Spanish ancestry and to have had no less than seven husbands. These two groups of spirits are believed to be immensely powerful and most effective in producing desired effects on Earth. Unlike the moral spirits, they do what they are told in exchange for presents. However, if the presents are not forthcoming, the client can expect to suffer the consequences he intended for his victim.

Traditionally, the Exú spirits were the Mercuries of the Afro-Brazilian cults. Even now they are associated with boundaries, crossroads, and danger. No ritual may commence without a prior offering to the Exús. The iconography of the Exús depicts them in classic Mephistophelian shape, and many identify them quite closely with the Devil, although other cult members deny this association.

Quite clear oppositions can be established between the Orixás and the Exús:

Orixás Saints	Exús and Pombagiras
Spirits of light	Spirits of darkness
Right-hand side	Left-hand side
Moral	Amoral
Spirits "descend" to their mediums, who are termed "horses" (*cavalos*).	Spirits "ascend" to their mediums, who are termed "asses" (*burros*).

It is important to notice in these oppositions and ambiguities that the cosmology of Umbanda, while distinguishing between good and evil and between morality and the absence of morality, does not condemn the Exús and Pombagiras. The spirits of darkness are as fundamental to ritual efficacy as are the spirits of light. Their power and force are necessary and are continually invoked to help solve the problems which beset their clients in day-to-day life.

The cult centers, then, enable common men and women to meet the divinities, to seek their help in the solution of problems, and to help smooth out the difficulties of urban living. Problems range from ill health to unemployment, signs of mental difficulties, frustrations in love, and business affairs. Such difficulties are attributed either to the sufferer's unwholesome relationship to the spirits, or to the attack of an enemy through the intermediary of an Exú spirit. In no event is misfortune attributed to personal responsibility, as it was in English culture as a result of the Reformation, and later Methodism. Affliction is perceived as an interpersonal affair, involving spirits and enemies. Its solution, therefore, rests with the effective manipulation of ritual which can be ordained by mediums in trance.

Umbanda cosmology, as in all thaumaturgical movements,[16] is essentially particularistic. Each person is the center of his or her quite private universe of spirits and mortals, and any explanation of misfortune will be constructed from these variables. Indeed, the particularism of the cults is a recurring theme. Each center is a law unto itself; each cult member has his or her specific ritual obligations to certain spirits; and Umbandistas as a whole do not commit themselves to any single all-embracing moral or even ritual code. This vision of the world effectively denies social responsibility and interprets human suffering in terms of the constellation of social and spiritual relationships which encompass the individual. The death of a child is not to be related to the infant mortality rate, nor is losing a job to be related to the unemployment rate. Poverty is not considered a function of exploitation and government income policy, but rather one of individual misfortune. In essence, Umbanda markets a service within cities by which socially generated misfortune is interpreted in individualistic terms, and treated accordingly.

III. THE GROWTH AND ORGANIZATION OF METHODISM

A. *Development*

Unlike Umbanda, which emerged almost surreptitiously and spread without centralized direction into a constantly proliferating number of centers, Methodism grew out of the proselytizing first of John Wesley and later of chosen ministers and preachers. In 1775, Manchester was referred to in the House of Lords as "a center of the growing—and to the speaker [the Earl of Carlisle], alarming—faith."[17] The newly converted became members of classes, which were in turn incorporated into chapels, circuits, and districts, and, finally, the Conference. Wesley has been called a "superlatively energetic and skillful organizer, administrator, and law-giver [who] succeeded in combining in exactly the right proportions democracy and discipline, doctrine and emotionalism."[18] But the democratic element would appear to have been delusive, for indirectly Wesley controlled the classes, "ran them on inquisitorial lines, and expelled many for failure to conform."[19] In contrast with the Umbandista movement, Methodism was run almost dictatorially by Wesley until his death in 1791. This tradition was continued under his successors, not the least of whom was Jabez Bunting. The Buntingites believed in the priestly power of the pastoral office and felt that power in the movement should be "in the hands of those distinguished by their *mind, character, station*, property and influence."[20]

However, Wesley and his philosophy could not escape the consequences of his own spiritual egalitarianism. "If Christ's poor came to believe that their souls were as good as aristocratic or bourgeois souls then it might lead them on to the arguments of the *Rights of Man*."[21] Indeed, the tension of authoritarian rule led to the appearance of secessionist groups and fission within the Wesleyan organization.

The first secession from the Wesleyan fold came in 1797 with the Kilhamite New Connexion. This was to be followed by other secessions such as the Bible Christians in 1819, the Primitive Methodists in 1820, and the Tent Methodists in 1822. These seceding groups challenged what they saw as "the extremely arbitrary and inequitable government under which we labour as Methodists."[22] Such secessions also tended to follow class lines. "The dividing line between Confer-

ence men and reformers repeatedly [ran] between different levels of
education, wealth, and fame. During 60 years a mere handful of
Wesleyan ministers and Conference laymen supported movements
which, by 1857, had the allegiance of 45 percent of Methodists."[23]

While the process of secession tended to siphon off large numbers
of poor from the Wesleyan fold, fission of chapel congregations led to
a spatial separation of rich and poor within the mother organization.
As the rich moved out of the industrial centers to their suburban
villas, they built newer, bigger chapels and established new districts
and circuits, leaving the old central chapels without their financial
support.[24]

Although, as E.P. Thompson so cogently argued, the Methodist
movement "obtained its greatest success in serving *simultaneously* as
the religion of the industrial bourgeoisie . . . and of wide sections of
the proletariat,"[25] it seems likely that secession and city flight tended
to result in a denominational and spatial separation of believers along
the lines of social class.

B.   *Methodism and the State*

Both in Conference and from the pulpit, the Wesleyan church as
a whole explicitly underlined its allegiance to King and Country. This
is the crucial factor in the formal relations between Wesleyanism and
the English state. When government voiced its concern about the
potentially subversive character of Methodism, the reaction was definitive. In 1811, a resolution of the Manchester District attributed
"the preservation of this happy country from the horrors of that
revolutionary frenzy which has so awfully desolated the nations of the
continent . . . to the high degree of religious liberty"[26] which England enjoyed. Orthodox Wesleyans were relieved to see a radical wing
break away in the Kilhamite Secession, and in 1812 John Stephens
held a purge of radical church members in Manchester. So closely
identified was the Methodist church with the state that in 1820 the
Manchester Observer classified preachers as "hireling sycophants," and
in many parts of Lancashire, "Wesleyan preachers moved in fear of
their lives, such was their unpopularity with the working class."[27]
There were moves taken to restrict Methodist preaching, but these
had never been promulgated. Although, as Thompson has argued,
"Methodists were seldom admitted by the Establishment to audience—and then only by the back door," and although they were
"never decorated with the honours of status,"[28] the annual conferences, as loyal defenders of the status quo, never ceased to cry out

their thanks to a tolerant government. In 1812, commenting on the repeal of the Conventicle Act and the Five Mile Bill, the Conference thanks government "for the effect [the repeal] will have upon the happiness of the religious poor." Methodism was a religion which "soothes them under poverty and distress, and, by the grace of God, makes them content under the apparently adverse dispensation of Divine Providence, and teaches them to wait with patience for the 'inheritance which is incorruptible.' "[29] The government of England in the early nineteenth century could hardly have been displeased at the burgeoning of a religion which so vociferously reaffirmed its "unfeigned loyalty to the King and sincere attachment to the Constitution."[30]

Turning now to the cosmology of the Methodists, we may see more clearly why it was not repressed by government and why, in the words of Thompson, Methodism and Utilitarianism, "taken together, make up the dominant ideology of the Industrial Revolution."[31]

C. *Cosmology*

Methodist theology has been described as a form of "promiscuous opportunism."[32] Abandoning the Calvinist notion of "election," grace was to be available to all.

> Any man who came to a conviction of sin might be visited by grace and know himself to be ransomed by Christ's blood. . . . But Christ's ransom was only provisional. Wesley's doctrine here was not settled. He toyed with the notion of grace being penitent; and thus a dejected form of Calvinism (the "elected" being now the "saved") reentered by the back door.[33]

Grace might be maintained in three ways: through service to the church, through continuous religious experience, and "through a methodical discipline in every aspect of life. Above all, in labor itself."[34] Unlike the Umbandistas, the Methodists could not be saved by ritual alone; faith implied the adoption of a way of life marked by methodical discipline "combined with the strict avoidance of all spontaneous enjoyments."[35] A catalog of sins, composed by the secessionist Bible Christians in 1850, contained prohibitions over the ballroom, card table, village wake, racecourse, bowling green, cricket ground, gin palace, and ale house. Dancing was seen to be as wicked as football; novel reading and the theater were evil, and there were, of course, the most severe controls over sexuality.[36] Submission, humility, the avoidance of spontaneity, and hard work were virtues considered theologically in opposition to the Devil and Hellfire. The repentant sinner who hoped to save himself was expected to spend his entire life in a battle against the temptations of Satan and the punishments of Hell.

> There endless crowds of sinners lie
> And darkness marks their chains!
> Tortured with keen despair they cry,
> Yet wait for fiercer pains.[37]

Just as the Devil was opposed to Christ, so the Methodist fold was opposed to the sinful world. One was either with Christ or with the Devil; you were either a Methodist or you were not. The boundaries were marked with the greatest clarity, and indeed John Wesley hoped that his Methodists would be "peculiar people," ready "to abstain from marriage outside the societies; to be distinguished by their dress and by the gravity of their speech and manners; to avoid the company even of relatives who were still in 'Satan's kingdom.' "[38] Those who sinned could expect exclusion not only from future heavenly bliss, but also from their church community—a somewhat more tangible punishment. Moral and ritual behavior was heavily policed among the classes and the chapels; those who erred were mercilessly removed from what might be "the only community group they knew in the industrial wilderness."[39] This could be serious indeed, for the Methodists did provide earthly compensation for the costs of commitment. "[F]or many people . . . the Methodist 'ticket' of church membership acquired a fetishistic importance; for the migrant worker it could be the ticket of entry into a new community when he moved from town to town."[40] Membership in a Methodist chapel was also to the outside world a sign of sobriety, dependability, and the capacity for hard work. "Actuated by interest, proprietors of factories . . . chose sober and pious men for their foremen and overlookers."[41]

In overall contrast to the particularistic belief system of Umbanda, Methodism put forward a universalistic vision of the world. All persons were capable of being saved, but only by obeying the same established rules in the same prescribed manner. Through obedience to these rules, Methodists gave public testimony of their religious conversion with its long-term promise of final salvation.[42]

D. *Interpretations of the Rise of Methodism*

Explanations of the rise of Methodism vary with the way in which the Industrial Revolution is perceived theoretically. Semmel, in optimistic vein, sees Methodism as "the theological form taken by the liberal ideology of the time,"[43] a mediation between a "static, agrarian, traditional society" and a "competitive progressive industrialism."[44] He asks whether the sects of Old Dissen or the Established Church could "have made 'new men' of the lower classes and presided over their non-violent rites of passage into modern society? It was Methodism, the facts show, not Unitarianism or Quakerism, which attracted hundreds of thousands of the lower classes to its standards during the critical time of transition."[45]

Bryan Wilson emphasizes the breakup of traditional community structures and increased individuation as conditions leading to such conversionist religions as Methodism.

> This process of heightened individuation was, in the eighteenth century, considerably reinforced by the social disruption of the industrial revolution. In this situation, men had been both dramatically detached from stable social contexts, and had acquired the independence of mind and the degree of emotional control to respond to a new and orderly system of psychic security and intellectual explanation. The system which Methodism introduced went further, as a secondary socialization process, in the extension of their system of order and in the diffusion of its influence beyond its own boundaries, into wide ranges of public and social life. . . . Having challenged Calvinist elitism by Arminian Free Will teachings, Methodism was at once much less restrained than earlier nonconformity. Its emphasis on free will in conversion amounted to an implicit tenet of equality of opportunity for salvation (although Methodism rejected democracy in this world, and even in its own chapels and band-meetings)."[46]

E.P. Thompson, in his own far from optimistic analysis, sees Methodism in the context of a new kind of exploitation brought about by industrial capitalism, taking into account the important fact that Methodism was a religion not only of the proletariat, but also of the industrial bourgeoisie. Its organization and doctrine, therefore, served two ends. In the case of the bourgeoisie, it functioned as an ideological stimulus to the accumulation of capital. In the case of the proletariat, Methodism played an important role in forging the work discipline which was necessary to the new factory system. Through the schools, the prohibitions, the inquisitorial classes, the threat of Hellfire, the repression of sexual pleasure and spontaneous joy, and

through the emotive reenactment Sunday after Sunday of the drama
of conversion from unproductive sinfulness to productive methodical
discipline, the Wesleyan church contributed to the transformation of
the "traditional" laborer into a committed and devoted factory hand.

Having established the relation between Methodism and the in-
culcation of work discipline, Thompson then asks the more difficult
question, ". . . why so many working people were willing to submit to
this form of psychic exploitation. How was it that Methodism could
perform with such success this dual role as the religion of both the
exploiters and the exploited?"[47] Thompson adduces three reasons:
indoctrination, mainly through the Sunday schools, the Methodist
"community sense," and the "psychic consequences of counter-revo-
lution."[48]

The first two reasons seem plausible enough in view of the evidence. The aim of the Sunday schools was "moral rescue" rather than
education in any broader sense; after all, Jabez Bunting succeeded in
prohibiting the learning of writing until the late 1840's[49], and children were subjected to what Lecky called "religious terrorism."[50] The
Methodist community sense was also very strong and the importance
of Methodist group membership has already been mentioned. However, as was argued above, all social movements involve some kind of
community, so although it is revealing to discover how each movement develops its own rules ensuring community involvement, such
discovery does not necessarily help one understand why people
should be so attracted to one particular kind of community and
ideology rather than another. Thompson addresses this concern with
his hypothesis that Methodism in the period 1795-1830 was essentially a refuge for political frustration on the part of the working class—
what he terms the chiliasms of despair.[51] He suggests that orthodox
Methodism and the revivalist groups advanced as political radicalism
declined, thus inverting Hobsbawm's prior hypothesis that Methodist
expansion accompanied upsurges in radical political activity.[52] The
evidence for either side is confusing and complicated by the subtleties
of local context and the existence of various types of Methodism.
Ward, for example, claims that urban revivalism in Manchester was
rampant before Peterloo, but that after the massacre the "wildfire"
never returned.[53] Stigant, another writer interested in testing
Thompson's hypothesis, argues that it holds in the case of the Primitive Methodists.[54] Whatever the verdict more detailed research might
indicate on this issue, the fact remains that Wesleyan Methodism and
its ramifications did have its conversional heyday during the period
after the French Revolution, a period which also witnessed the growth

of industrial capitalism in the north of England. Given the form of organization, the emphasis on submission and diligence, and the absolute polar opposition of Christ and Satan, the Methodist advance appears to be not only consistent with but intimately linked to social and intellectual changes occurring in nineteenth century England, a period which saw radical transformations in the pattern of social and economic relations effected through continuous reform rather than abrupt revolutionary transformation.

IV. METHODISM AND UMBANDA

A. *A Functionalist View of Belief Systems and Industrialization*

The description and analysis of Methodism by the writers cited above imply that its ideals would be almost a necessary feature of any society in which industrialization takes place. But this merely illustrates the dangers of analysis with a functionalist bent and the frequent results of the alchemy of sociological explanation *a posteriori*. For returning to the São Paulo situation, it can be seen that, at least so far as religious institutions are concerned, the picture is radically different. It is true that the rise of Pentecostalism can be analyzed in much the same way as that of Methodism. Like Methodism, it possesses a complex hierarchical structure supporting a belief system which stresses conversion and a constant battle against Satan and his works. Like the English Methodists, the Pentecostalists of São Paulo are set apart from nonbelievers as a result of their dramatic taboos against drink, television, football, and the like. They also enjoy a reputation for hard work and honesty. The Pentecostal movement differs from nineteenth century Methodism primarily in that it is not also a religion of the bourgeoisie.

But what can make sense of Umbanda, which, in many respects represents the antithesis of Methodism and Pentecostalism (see Appendix), and yet which also thrives in a situation of industrial expansion and urbanization? Umbandistas, with the exception of the leaders of the federations, have few moral pretentions, and indeed the opponents of Umbanda perceive it as a locus of vice and anarchy. Nothing in Umbanda organization, belief, or ritual would appear to be "functional" in the context of the growth of industrial capitalism, except that it can be seen as at least a sedative taken by those who suffer most from capitalist exploitation. After all, Umbandistas' beliefs exalt many of the values to which Methodism and industrial capitalism are so violently opposed, such as dancing, drinking, and, worst of all, the ritual invocation of the "spirits of darkness." Just as

Brazilian Pentecostals see Umbanda as their arch enemy, so it surely would have been defined as a stronghold of Satan by either John Wesley or Jabez Bunting. What differences can be detected, then, between the industrializing processes in Manchester and São Paulo which might suggest reasons for, in the former case, a near monopoly of puritan and utilitarian ideals and practices, and, in the latter the spread of a belief system which spurns long-term notions of universalistic rules in favor of short-term particularistic ritual solution to ills perceived as essentially unique to the individual concerned?

B. *The Intellectual Backgrounds of Methodism and Umbanda*

In an attempt to set forward some answers to this question, a number of factors may be suggested. First, it must be remembered that Methodism was the fruit of 200 years of post-Reformation religious activity. In a sense, it is the final blooming of ideas that first took root at the time of the Reformation.

> [T]he Reformation had initiated advance in a fundamentally new direction. For the people were now taught that their practical difficulties could only be solved by a combination of self-help and prayer to God. . . . The substitute action involved in the practice of magic was condemned as both impious and useless. The strong emphasis upon the virtues of hard work and application which was to become so pronounced a feature of the religious teaching of the sixteenth and seventeenth centuries, Catholic as well as Protestant, both reflected and helped to create a frame of mind which spurned the cheap solutions offered by magic, not just because they were wicked, but because they were too easy. Man was to earn his bread by the sweat of his brow.[55]

Thus, in England, magical elements of religion were dying out *before* the Industrial Revolution. Thomas acknowledges that magic had never really died out and that spiritualism, automatic writing, astrology, and the occult were important in nineteenth century England, as they are now. However, during the sixteenth and seventeenth centuries, there was a change of mood which was itself a necessary condition for the development of the technology which led to the Industrial Revolution.

> [T]he paradox is that in England magic lost its appeal before the appropriate technical solutions had been de-

vised to take its place. It was the abandonment of magic which made possible the upsurge of technology, not the other way round. . . . The rationalist tradition of classical antiquity blended with the Christian doctrine of a single all-directing Providence to produce what Weber called "the disenchantment of the world"—the conception of an orderly and rational universe, in which effect follows cause in a predictable manner. A religious belief in order was a necessary prior assumption upon which the subsequent work of the natural scientists was to be founded.[56]

Until the Second Vatican Council, the Catholic Church in Brazil had been largely a "magical" institution with less emphasis on the moral life and a greater stress on the short-term solutions through Mass, discreet vows to saints at times of misfortune, and a regular cycle of feast days where food, drink, and dance were the order of the day.[57] In spite of the importance among the Brazilian elite of positivist philosophy at the turn of the century, the religious experience of most Brazilians, including the Italian immigrants to São Paulo, was that of folk Catholicism and the Afro-Brazilian cults.

But important as these facts were, they are of little help in understanding the Umbanda movement, for, with the introduction of modern technology and a growing educational system designed in part to teach the fundamentals of that technology, the beliefs in question have merely grown in public acceptance. This only appears paradoxical if one adheres to the ethnocentric premise that "magic" necessarily evolves into what we call science. In the first place, there is no logical reason to suppose that men in society tend towards consistency in their beliefs and practices. Second, there is no reason why a belief system such as that of Umbanda should not flourish simultaneously with other explanatory systems.[58]

It is for this reason that I cannot agree with those who attribute the rise of Umbanda to its claimed capacity to cure sickness and to resolve the myriad problems of urban life.[59] After all, there are other possible solutions to these problems, and the purpose here is to discuss why Umbanda in particular should be perceived to be effective. To move towards an understanding of this question, it is necessary to consider those aspects of social experience in Brazil and São Paulo which lend particular plausibility to Umbanda belief and practice.

C.   *The Manipulation of Spirits and Social Relationships*

It was noted earlier that Pentecostalism bears strong structural similarities to Methodism, and that both may be seen to perform similar functions in relation to the formation of a society based on industrial capitalism where magic would be inappropriate and in which hard work and abstemiousness among the working class would be to the benefit of the system and those who dominate it. It could be argued that those who convert to Pentecostal Churches perceive society in these terms and choose to forge their life strategies accordingly. The Pentecostals lose no love for the Umbandistas, whom they regard as the people of the Devil.[60] That Pentecostals identify the Umbandistas with the devil demonstrates dramatically that these two religions are in most ways structurally opposed. While Pentecostal belief, like that of the Methodists, is universalistic and posits that all men are equal before Christ, Umbanda belief emphasizes the immediate short-term magical solution to problems as they arise. These coexisting yet contrary ways of interpreting misfortune derive their plausibility from conflicting perceptions of the rules which operate in contemporary Brazilian society. Pentecostalism derives its plausibility from official ideology, articulated by the state and subsidiary institutions, that Brazil is essentially democratic and that economic success is the just reward of those who study and work. Umbanda derives its plausibility from the less explicit, but nevertheless equally present ideology, that success in life is to be gained not only through the official channels of work and study, but also by the studied manipulation of personal relations on a particularistic basis.

The coexistence of these apparently contradictory modes of operating within Brazilian society has its roots in the nineteenth century, before the abolition of slavery in 1888. The colonization of Brazil produced three classes in society, the landowner *latifundiário*, the slave, and the "free man" *homem livre*. Roberto Schwarz argues that the favor was the mechanism by which these "free men" were able to survive.

> Thus, under thousands of names and forms, the favor permeated and affected national life, while the basic relation of production [slavery] was guaranteed by force. The favor was omnipresent and was combined with all manner of activities which were more or less subject to its operations, such as administration, politics, industry, commerce, urban life, the Court, etc. Even liberal professions such as medicine, or skilled labor such as printing, which to Euro-

pean eyes owe nothing to anyone, were governed, in
Brazil, by the favor. And so, just as the professional man
depended on the granting of favors in order to be able to
exercise his profession, the small property owner depended on this for the security of his property and the civil
servant for his very job. *The favor is an almost universal
mediation.*[61]

Dependent politically and economically on the European
economic powers, Brazil adopted the liberal universalistic ideology
developed in Europe, which was quite antagonistic to the particularism inherent in the institution of the favor. Thus, those who promulgated these liberal ideas in Brazil were themselves beneficiaries of a
system based on slavery and the granting of favors.

The same thing happened at the institutional level; for
example, the bureaucracy and the judicial system. Although these were run on the basis of clientelism, they
proclaimed the forms and the theories of the modern
bourgeois state. . . . This resulted in an established coexistence which is worth studying. Here is the novelty: *once
European ideas and reasons were adopted, they were able to serve
and very often did serve, as a nominally "objective" justification
for the moment of arbitrariness, which is the essence of the
favor.*[62]

The coexistence of the favor and the liberal European ideology
outlived the colonial period and was only solidified by the increasing
power of the centralized state and the spread of industrial capitalism
over a social system which had been characterized by regional autonomy in which local leaders vied with one another for power, exchang-
ing protection and resources for the political support of their
"clients." It was during Getúlio Vargas's first period in power (from
1930 to 1945) that this process was most marked. However, the new
centralized government, ostensibly observing the rules of a rational
bureaucracy, in practice used the favor as a means of securing political power in exchange for bureaucratic posts.

The federal executive gained enormous patronage power,
both in the sense of federally controlled jobs and in the
sense of the favoritism or discrimination inherent in the
exercising of the growing administrative powers.[63]

Since Vargas's death, and especially since the military coup of
1964, succeeding governments have continued to consolidate the

federal hegemony, but the bureaucratic apparatus that has developed has continued to be used by those in power as a fund of resources exchangable for political support. In the day-to-day running of social and political life, principles of advantage based on merit operate simultaneously with clientelistic principles, and both are used situationally depending on their relative strategic benefits. This was clearly demonstrated in the election for State Governor of São Paulo in 1962, in which the two principles were personified in the two candidates, Adhemar de Barros and Jânio Quadros. Although both were populist politicians, their styles were quite different.[64] Adhemar projected himself as a progressive man of action, a patriarch whose election slogan was "I steal, but I get things done." His supporters, Weffort argues, "hoped to rise individually, making use of their fissures in the social structure and living off the crumbs of power."[65] Jânio Quadros, on the other hand, presented himself as a moralist and a puritan, determined to sweep away corruption. His supporters projected "through an identification with the rigorous asceticism of their leader, the aspiration for an abstract State which the followers of Adhemar could in no way even conceive."[66]

My interpretation of the viability of Umbanda, then, is that it expresses and ritualizes the "other face" of industrial capitalism in Brazil, as represented by the ideas of Adhemar de Barros.[67] Umbanda is plausible because the particularistic relations which are established with the spirits in the hopes of the granting of favors are homologous with the real relationships established for the benefit of men in society. I would question, for example, whether there is really a great difference between the supplicant elector who promises to exchange his vote for a council house (state-subsidized housing) and an Umbanda client who makes a contract with an Exú spirit in order to gain employment. In neither case does the initial vow inevitably lead to its consummation, and even if it does not, the beliefs which oriented the taking of the vow do not seem to be impaired.

Indeed, the very words used in Umbanda terminology support this interpretation. It is surely not by chance that rituals enacted in order to achieve a given end are called *despachos* when this same word is also used to describe bureaucratic dispatches. Going further, it is perhaps not too far fetched to note that a derivative of this same word, *despachante* (he who makes dispatches), is used to describe the hoards of pseudo-lawyers whose function it is to mediate between the man in the street and the overwhelmingly complicated bureaucracy on which his very existence depends. A *despachante*, in exchange for a cash payment which is partially used for bribing officials, can succeed in obtaining in a short time those documents which are essential for access to medical services, employment, and other necessities which would normally take months to acquire through "normal" channels. The *despachantes* and the local politicians mediate between the state and the common man the way the spirits of Umbanda mediate his relationship with a distant and disinterested God.

Umbanda is, in its doctrine and organization, a ritual dramatization of rules and relationships that govern life in large towns in Brazil but are unrecognized by official government ideology. As was noted above, the "spirits of darkness" are as fundamental to ritual as the "spirits of light." As one Umbanda hymn expresses it:

> Exú of midnight
> Exú of the crossroads
> The people of Umbanda
> Without Exú achieve nothing

While the figure of Exú immediately calls to mind such historical figures as the henchmen of rural landowners (*capangas*), their present-day structural equivalent is most probably found in certain police officers. Nowhere is this made more startlingly clear than in Hélio Bicudo's recent book on the Esquadrão da Morte (The Death Squad)[68], in which he documents the way the "heroes" of the regime, those who assassinated or arrested leading members of militant groups opposed to the regime, were also involved with the trafficking of hard drugs and the annihilation of their underworld rivals. Perhaps it is pushing the analogy too far to suggest that the importance of Exú dramatizes the power of "marginal" men in the political life of the country, but other aspects of belief associated with these spirits lend sufficient weight to the argument.

It is now commonplace to note that Umbanda practitioners are "folk psychiatrists." But it is significant that in the majority of cases, Umbanda mediums interpret the ills of their clients in terms of a mystical attack of enemies through the intermediary of an Exú spirit. Ritual antidotes are prescribed to eliminate the spell and to guarantee the protection of the client against future attacks. If Umbanda can be seen as folk psychiatry, then it could be argued that Umbanda tends to reinforce feelings of paranoia in its clients, emphasizing elements of fear and mistrust which are inherent in everyday life. Fear is real in São Paulo. "It is not by chance that one of the most heartfelt popular complaints is about security."[69] A public opinion poll commissioned by the *Journal da Tarde* in November 1975 showed that out of every 10 persons, no less than seven live in fear of being arrested and six of

being assaulted.[70] Based on these statistics, Camargo has put forward
the hypothesis that "it is the necessity for security that frequently
underlies the search for religious experience as a refuge from the
harshness and cruelty of human society."[71] This argument is attractive, but as suggested towards the beginning of this article, it is
perhaps more interesting to go further and to try to ascertain what
kinds of refuge are constructed and why. Umbanda does purport to
supply protection; the word *proteção* is a constant in Umbanda terminology and the shops that sell ritual paraphenalia have shelves full
of incense, bath fluids, and talismans for protection. But the supplying of protection not only responds to a need, it also exacerbates that
need by reinforcing fear, mistrust, and insecurity.[72] Its very organizational structure, characterized by fierce competition between leaders
and the frustrated attempts at effective federation, exemplifies the
same principles at work. No Umbanda leader feels that he and his
center are safe from the jealousy of others, and elaborate ritual
precautions are taken to offset possible spiritual attacks. Within the
Umbanda movement, the fear and mistrust experiences in the outside
world are reproduced in the form of accusations and counteraccusa-
tions of mystical aggression.[73]

If it is correct to argue that Umbanda dramatizes principles which
are present in society as a whole, then when the *Estado de São Paulo*
expressed its shock and horror at the growth of Umbanda,[74] it was, in
fact, expressing shock and horror at the whole social and political
order. In classifying Umbanda as counter-evolutionary, it was failing
to appreciate, or unwilling to acknowledge, that the establishment of
industrial capitalism does not in itself necessarily eradicate "magic,"
either in religious movements or in the mechanisms for the allocation
of power and privilege in society. It is the vitality of the favor, the
"magical" manipulation of social relations, which allows the magic of
Umbanda to be attractive and plausible in São Paulo. The particularism of Umbanda, its high rate of rivalry and schism, its emphasis on
the short-term solution of problems, and its manifestations of fear
and insecurity make sense in the context of a social system in which
the rise of industrial capitalism and the spread of multinational
corporations has not eliminated the vitality of "magic" in social relations, even though these phenomena might have been expected to
induce the dominance of a more "rational" and universalistic order.
Umbanda thrives as "magic" thrives in social relationships; this "magic" apparently thrives in these relationships even where formal power
is wielded autocratically and arbitrarily over people lacking any dem-
ocratically institutionalized forms of political expression. In such a

situation, one of the few ways of achieving certain goals is by cunning manipulation of personal relations. The favor, which was an integral element in the existence of a colonial Brazilian society based on slavery, continues to be important in the existence of the present regime. That the State of São Paulo should have deemed it fit to sponsor Umbanda festivals is not only symptomatic of a politically shrewd attempt to undermine the cults' independence and to cull their favor, but also a recognition that they are all playing basically the same game. Umbanda in its ritual and dramatic aspects is a metaphor reflecting social and political reality in Brazil. The lesson in all this is that what might be called "magic" does not die with purely intellectual changes, nor necessarily with the advent of industrial capitalism *per se*, but only with the institutionalization and legitimacy of universal rules governing the relations between men and groups. It is just this, one could argue, that took place during the nineteenth century in England.

Could it not be argued that the growing stability of the English state was intrinsically related to the manner in which the bourgeoisie managed to establish a stable hegemony over the country as a whole in much the way they directed a religious movement which included large numbers of the working class, something which has not yet happened in Brazil, except perhaps during the pre-1964 populist politics when members of all classes were temporarily swept up into Jânio Quadros's almost puritan ethic?[75]

NOTES

1. Thompson, *Time, Work-discipline, and the Industrial Capitalism*, 38 PAST AND PRESENT 58 at 80 (Dec. 1967).

2. Fry & Howe, *Duas respostas à aflição: Umbanda e Pentecostalismo*, 6 DEBATE E CRITICA 75–94 (1975).

3. CANDIDO P. F. DE CAMARGO, KARDECISMO E UMBANDA (São Paulo: Pioneria, 1961). *See also* EMILIO WILLEMS, *Religious Mass Movements and Social Change in Brazil*, NEW PERSPECTIVES OF BRAZIL 224–25 (Nashville, Tenn.: Vanderbilt U. Press, Parthenon Press, ed. Eric N. Baklanoff, 1966).

4. Umbanda appears to have profited from recent trends in the Catholic Church, such as the decline in ritual which resulted from Vatican II and the expulsion from sanctity of such popular figures as St. George and St. Barbara, both of whom are amongst the most important of the Umbanda saints. Many Umbandistas express the feeling that the ritual they felt effective in the Catholic Church can now be found only in Umbanda centers. *See* KEITH THOMAS, RELIGION AND THE DECLINE OF MAGIC (Harmondsworth: Penguin, 1973).

5. NINA RODRIGUES, O ANIMISTO FETICHISTA DOS NEGROS BAHIANOS (Rio de Janeiro: Civilização Brasileira, 1935); JOÃO DO RIO, AS RELIGIÕES NO RIO (Rio de Janeiro: Edição da Organização Simoes, 1951).

6. Landes, *A Cult Matriarchate and Male Homosexuality*, 35 J. OF ABNORMAL & SOCIAL PSYCHOLOGY 386 at 392 (19—).

7. Brown, *O papel histórico da classe média na Umbanda* (paper presented at the tenth meeting of the Associação Brasileira de Antropologia, Salvador, 1976).

8. O ESTADO DE S. PAULO 27 (June 12, 1975), — (Sept. 12, 1975), — (Nov. 12, 1975).

9. Most federations came into being in order to act as intermediaries between Umbandistas and the police. By joining a federation, a cult leader could obtain permission to hold rituals and a degree of protection from arbitrary police interference. For a detailed analysis of the internal politics of one such federation, *see* A. Vergolina, *O tambor das flores* (unpublished Master's thesis, Campinas, 1975).

10. N. RODRIGUES, *supra* note 5, at 70–71, notes: "Because of the persecution of the *candomble* and because of the ill repute of the magicians, the people of the *candomble* had to look for strong and powerful protectors who could guarantee police protection. These protectors may or may not be cult initiates, but they believe in magic or they have some other interest in the *candombles*, being given, in recompense, the title and honours of *ougans* [sic] . . . . The protection they afford is real and effective. The most rigorous and harsh police prohibitions melt away as if by magic before the power of the *ougans*." (translation supplied by the author of this article, Peter Fry).

11. JOÃO DO RIO, *supra* note 5, at 26.

12. Landes, *supra* note 6.

13. Conversation with Moab Caldas at Praia Grande, Nov. 1976.

14. O ESTADO DE S. PAULO (Apr. 4, 1973).

15. *Id.*

16. BRYAN R. WILSON, MAGIC AND THE MILLENNIUM 24–25 (NY & London: Harper & Row, 1973). In such thaumaturgical movements, "The individual's concern is relief from present and specific ills by special dispensations. The demand for supernatural help is personal and local: its operation is magical . . . . The evils feared are all highly specific, and it is from their particular incidence (not from their universal operation) that salvation is sought. Miracles and oracles, rather than the comprehension of new principles about life, are the instruments of salvation in this case."

17. L. S. MARSHALL, THE DEVELOPMENT OF PUBLIC OPINION IN MANCHESTER 1780–1820 at 42 (Syracuse: Syracuse U. Press, 19—).

18. E. P. THOMPSON, THE MAKING OF THE ENGLISH WORKING CLASS 41 (Harmondsworth: Pelican, 1968).

19. ROBERT CURRIE, METHODISM DIVIDED: A STUDY IN THE SOCIOLOGY OF ECUMENICALISM 19 (London: Faber & Faber, 1968).

20. *Id.* at 41.

21. THOMPSON, *supra* note 18, at 46.

22. ROBERT CURRIE, *supra* note 19, at 77, quoting EXPOSITION 8 (Manchester, 1815).

23. *Id.* at 82.

24. WILLIAM R. WARD, RELIGION AND SOCIETY IN ENGLAND 1421-42 (London: B. T. Batsford, 1972).

25. THOMPSON, *supra* note 18, at 391.

26. *Resolution of the Methodist Ministers*, quoted in BERNARD SEMMEL, THE METHODIST REVOLUTION 132 (NY: Basic Books, 1973).

27. Stagnant, *Wesleyan Methodism and Working Class Radicalism in the North, 1792–1821*, 6 NORTHERN HISTORY 98, 109 (1971).

28. THOMPSON, *supra* note 18, at 386.

29. *Minutes of the Methodist Conferences* (1812), quoted in SEMMEL, *supra* note 26, at 134.

30. THOMPSON, *supra* note 18, at 45.

31. *Id.* at 441.

32. *Id.* at 398.

33. *Id.* at 399.

34. *Id.* at 401.

35. *Id.* at 406.

36. CURRIE, *supra* note 19, at 132.
37. *Id.* at 117.
38. THOMPSON, *supra* note 18, at 41–42.
39. *Id.* at 400.
40. *Id.* at 417.
41. WELLMAN JOEL WARNER, THE WESLEYAN MOVEMENT IN THE INDUSTRIAL REVOLUTION 178 (NY: Russell & Russell, 1967).
42. Following the terminology of Wilson, *supra* note 16, Methodism can be defined as a conversionist movement.
43. SEMMELL, *supra* note 26, at 7.
44. *Id.* at 8.
45. *Id.* at 183.
46. WILSON, *supra* note 16, at 39–40.
47. THOMPSON, *supra* note 18, at 411–12.
48. *Id.*
49. *Id.* at 389.
50. *Id.* at 415.
51. "There is a sense in which any religion which places great emphasis on the afterlife is the chiliasm of the defeated and the hopeless." *Id.* at 419.
52. Hobsbawm, *Methodism and the Threat of Revolution in Britain*, 7 HISTORY TODAY 115 (No. 2, Feb. 1957).
53. WARD, *supra* note 24, at 83.
54. Stagnant, *supra* note 27, at 116.
55. THOMAS, *supra* note 4, at 331.
56. *Id.* at 786. Even though Keith Thomas's argument is more than convincing, it is difficult to document the incidence of "magic" or its decline. Such phenomena tend to leave little in the way of written records, especially if they are stigmatized and repressed. E. P. THOMPSON, *supra* note 18, at 446, claims that in "south Lancashire, the Potteries, the West Riding and the Black Country local customs, superstitions, and dialect were neither severed nor transplanted . . . ."
57. For an excellent discussion of Folk Catholicism in Brazil, see Alba Maria Zaluar Guimarães, *Os homens de Deus, un estudo comparativo sobre o sistema de crenças e práticas do catolocismo popular em algumas áreas do Brasil rural*, Master's dissertation, Museu Nacional, Rio de Janeiro.
58. *See generally* MAX GLUCKMAN, CUSTOM AND CONFLICT IN AFRICA (Oxford: Blackwell, 1955).
59. *See, e.g.*, CÂNDIDO P. F. DE CAMARGO, *supra* note 3. *See also* BEATRIZ M. DE SOUZA, A EXPERIÊNCA DA SALVACÃO: PENTECOSTAIS EM SÃO PAULO (São Paulo: Duas Cidades, 1969), for a similar argument in relation to Pentecostalism.
60. Author's informants, Campinas, Brazil, 1973.
61. ROBERTO SCHWARZ, AO VENDECOR ÀS BATATAS (1), at 16 (São Paulo: ——, 1977) (Fry's translation; emphasis in the original).
62. *Id.* at 17 (Fry's translation; emphasis in the original).
63. THOMAS E. SKIDMORE, POLITICS IN BRAZIL, 1930–1964: AN EXPERIMENT IN DEMOCRACY 35 (NY: Oxford U. Press, 1967).
64. My understanding of this election is based on Weffort, *Raízes sociais do populismo em São Paulo*, 1 REVISTA CIVILIZAÇÃO BRASILEIRA 39 (No. 2, May 1965).
65. *Id.* at 57–58 (Fry's translation).
66. *Id.* at 59 (Fry's translation).
67. There is no shortage of admirers and critics of Adhemar de Barros who affirm that he was himself a fervent Umbandista. Significantly, similar stories do not circulate about Jânio Quadros.
68. HÉLIO P. BICUDO, MEU DEPOIMENTO SOBRE O ESQUADRÃO DA MORTE (São Paulo: Comissão Pontífica de Justiça e Paz de São Paulo, 1976).

69. CÂNDIDO P. F. DE CAMARGO *et al.*, SÃO PAULO 1975: CRESCIMENTO E POBREZA 149 (São Paulo: Ediçoes Loyola, 1976) (Fry translation; emphasis in the original).

70. Poll, JORNAL DA TARDE 4 (Dec. 11, 1975) quoted in CAMARGO, *supra* note 69, at 149 n. 89.

71. *Id.* at 149 (Fry translation).

72. It would be interesting to investigate a personal hunch that as Umbanda grows, the "spirits of darkness" grow in popularity at the expense of the "spirits of light." In one factory which produces statues of the spirits, the two "sides" are produced in equal proportion.

73. For a description and analysis of this phenomenon in the town of Marilia, São Paulo, *see* Mott, *Caridade e demanda* (Master's thesis, Campinas, Brazil, 1976).

74. See text at notes 14 and 15, *supra*.

75. The observation about this parallel between Methodism and the populist politics of Jânio Quadros was made by Michael Hall. I do not hold him responsible for the way in which I have used it.

APPENDIX.

A COMPARISON OF THE RELIGIONS OF UMBANDA AND METHODISM

	UMBANDA	METHODISM
Organization	Small, autonomous congregation. Authority of leaders essentially charismatic. Loose federations. No proselytization.	Large congregations linked to efficient and autocractic hierarchy. Tension between democratic ideals and autocracy. Proselytizing.
Membership	Largely urban poor with growing middle-class membership. Potentially infinite number of real and potential clients. Women outnumber men 2:1.	Both bourgeoisie and working-class, although the latter tend to concentrate in secessionist groups and central chapels. After 1820, orthodox Wesleyanism becomes less working-class and more bourgeoisie and middle-class.
Beliefs and Morals	God otiose, host of lesser saints and spirits. Eclectic variation from one group to another. Ritual use made equally of "spirits of light" and "spirits of darkness." Little or no relation between being an Umbandista and everyday behavior. Each Umbanista fulfills his own particular ritual obligations, in order to secure well-being in this life. Particularistic.	One common system of belief and ritual codified for all centralized organization. Strongly enforced taboos against certain behavior in everday life as necessary to achievement of ultimate salvations and escape from Hellfire. Satan and his works totally rejected. Universalistic.
Relation to State	Originally repressed, later wooed openly by federally appointed State Governors. Not having any clearly defined leadership, Umbanda has no political "platform."	Original suspicions of Jacobin potential alleviated by constant insistence of total loyalty to King, country, and constitution.

Association Football and the Urban Ethos

LINCOLN ALLISON*

I. AN ACADEMIC BLINDSPOT: SPORT AS A NEGLECTED STUDY

TRAVELING IN NORTH AFRICA in 1969, I was often asked where in England I was from. "Colne" seemed an incomprehensible answer and "Burnley" scarcely more likely. So I used to say "Manchester," which did excite a response. The students whom I met in cafes might have thought of Manchester as the first great industrial city, the shock city of the first half of the nineteenth century. They might have associated the name of that city with a school of political economy or regarded it as a city whose high culture aspired to global significance. They might have talked about a great university at which important scientific discoveries had been made. But they did not. Instead, almost to a man, they asked "Connaissez-vous Bobby Charlton?" By the end of the journey, I knew him well.

All over the world, and to many in England, "Manchester" means "football." Organized games, of which the most pervasive is soccer or Association Football, represent to many people in industrial and urban societies a focus for self-expression, ambition, and loyalty. In England, at the peak period of the 1940's, over a million spectators were attending Saturday matches in the Football League alone and perhaps twice as many again were involved in watching and playing in lesser competitions. Rowntree and Laver showed in 1951 that 49.5 percent of the households in England, including 53.3 percent of working class households, were gambling on football through the football pools.[1]

Soccer, along with such other great organized games of the world as lawn tennis and Rugby Union, evolved into a recognizable form in the third quarter of the nineteenth century in England. These games were among the most abiding of Victorian creations; there are many places in the world where Mill and Smiles are rejected if not actually

* Lecturer, Department of Politics, University of Warwick (Coventry, England).

forgotten, and where the Victorian conceptions of parliament and religion have died, but where they play football. Yet, it is possible to open a large and scholarly collection like Dyos and Wolff's *Victorian Cities* and find nothing about organized sport.[2] In Rowntree and Laver's 1951 survey of English social institutions there are chapters on gambling, sexual promiscuity, honesty, cinema, stage, broadcasting, dancing, reading, adult education, and religion.[3] Sport, however, is mentioned only in the chapter on gambling and in some of the individual case studies; football is discussed only in its implications for the football pools. In a recent textbook on social history, Rundle's *Britain's Economic and Social Development Since 1700*, football is mentioned only in a very cursory way.[4] Only in the 1970's has there been any serious academic attempt to analyze the social and ideological implications of modern sport.[5]

Football is an important aspect of life for many people in diverse societies. It has been treated as insignificant, however, by people who consider themselves analysts of society. There are numerous possible explanations for this lack of discussion. The major reason is that the orthodox analytical approach assumes that sports make little difference to the overall development of society. Traditional and Marxist social historians have been preoccupied with political attitudes and the social relations of the workplace. The intellectual style represented by Rowntree and Laver can be described as the "moral philosophy and social work" tradition of social understanding, preoccupied with the morality of the working classes in the most limited sense. Thus, there is an understandable blindspot to sport.

Additional problems have faced those scholars who have sought a social understanding of sport. First, a young scholar has not only the orthodoxy to overcome, but also the suspicion on the part of his seniors that a young scholar who wishes to research football (rather than industrial conditions and attitudes, for example), may be something of a dilettante. Second, if he is a football enthusiast personally, he must overcome "the gentleman's law": No man should make an object of analysis of the thing he loves. He realizes that what is interesting about football exists at a different cultural level from academic study. English football fans, including many academics, want to be part of the "inside" language of football. On Saturdays, pens and typewriters tucked away, they want to absorb themselves in the records, legends, personalities, and emotions of the game. In short, they are interested in the folklore and techniques of the game.

The only exception to this "academic blindspot" concerning football is the sociology of leisure, which has treated the subject as having more than mere peripheral importance. But the sociology of leisure is itself a poorly developed discipline with few major theories or debates, drawing widely and eclectically upon many sociological traditions. In the words of Joffre Dumazedier, a leading French researcher, "The sociology of leisure also exhibits a great methodological variety; it is not marked by adherence to any particular method, but by use of any and all available methods."[6] The drawbacks of the discipline are compounded by the fact that the vast majority of sociologists of sport have been Americans, and have therefore drawn upon a tradition and history of sport which are more clearly separated from the rest of the world than are the traditions and history of sport in any other industrial country.

II. AN ACADEMIC CONTEXT FOR THE STUDY OF SPORT

The first half century from the 1840's to the 1890's was the period in which modern football evolved. It was also a period in which a major consolidation of social institutions and a reform of social forces took place in England. Visitors to Manchester in the forties, including Disraeli, Dickens, Engels, and Faucher, all remarked on two things. The first was the sheer squalor of conditions in Manchester, a squalor which was difficult to relate to either their experience or their reading. The second was the emergence of a new class, the industrial proletariat, which was substantially excluded from English society. It was a class which G.M. Trevelyan was later to describe as unschooled, undoctored, unpoliced, and ungoverned. Half a century later that class, though only slightly healthier, was schooled, policed, and governed, and was voting, in substantial numbers, for the Conservative Party.

There were several factors which aided the process of the incorporation of the working class[7] in Victorian Lancashire. Certainly religion and laissez-faire ideology were significant. Another important element was an awareness of Britian's elevated station in the world as an imperial and industrial power. Lancashire's role in the maintenance of this status was regarded as crucial. Even in the 1950's I was taught to chant "England's bread hangs by Lancashire's thread" by an aged primary school mistress, although by then the proposition was manifestly false. Another element favoring incorporation was that the concept of class was different in Lancashire than it was in London. The working classes of Lancashire always retained vestiges of their two great alliances: with the liberal bourgeoisie against the old

Tory and Whig establishments, and with the aristocratic Tory reformers against the bourgeoisie. On the other side of the equation, the
upper and middle classes of Lancashire did not look upon their
workers with the same degree of fear and contempt as did their
London counterparts.[8] Finally, civic pride played some part in the
incorporation of Mancunians. In the period after 1845, Manchester
entered a phase which can best be described as "dignification." In
1846 the city acquired three parks, in 1847 a bishop, in 1850 a public
library, in 1851 a university, and in 1858 the Halle Orchestra.[9] From
being a mere slum in the forties, by the 1860's Manchester had
become a slum with trappings.

A caveat is in order. I have discussed the period of incorporation
as if the process began and ended in a fixed time. But no incorporation can be achieved unless the foundations already exist. It is worth
remembering that when Queen Victoria visited Manchester in 1851,
she recorded in her diary that, though the citizens looked "painfully
unhealthy," they were, to judge from their enthusiastic welcome, the
most loyal of her subjects.

That this process of incorporation of the working class did in fact
occur has been significant for the development of political theory.
Marx and Engels got it wrong. They considerably overestimated the
revolutionary potential of the English working classes.[10] This error
does not necessarily destroy their worth as social theorists, but it does
cause one to be suspicious of their judgment. Disraeli, on the other
hand, got it right. He saw that the new class must and could be
incorporated into the mainstream of society. This perception became
a constant theme of his work both as a novelist (in *Sybil* and *Coningsby*)
and later as a Tory reformer.

Marxism has been modified subsequently to take account of Disraeli's insight. Perhaps the most impressive modification is Antonio
Gramsci's theory of the hegemonic power of the bourgeoisie.[11]
Gramsci distinguishes two forms of power: "dominance" based on
force and sanctions, and "hegemony" which is close to the traditional
political theorists' concept of legitimate authority. Hegemonic power
is dependent upon the existence of a culture which inculcates an
acceptance of the existing social structure. The nature of hegemonic
culture differs among countries. In Italy, Catholicism is its central
feature. In the United States, it is a combination of the Protestant
work ethic and the elevation of market forces to the level of absolute
law which Gramsci calls "Fordism." In England and Holland, Protestantism also plays a large part. Gramsci's concept of hegemony virtually abolishes the materialism in Marx. Italian Catholicism is portray-

ed not as the consequence of economic forces, but as an independent force in itself. The would-be revolutionary does not necessarily have history on his side; he must act decisively to create a counter-hegemony.

Gramsci's theory is the corollary of Disraeli's action. This is not to say that incorporation and the establishment of a hegemonic culture are the same thing. Gramsci would argue that hegemony had, as one of its consequences, an apparent incorporation: To Disraeli, though, they would be the same thing: apparent incorporation was real incorporation. If the workingmen of Lancashire in the 1880's identified themselves with English society, then they were part of that society.

There is a remarkable parallel between this analysis of Victorian England and Richard Morse's account of twentieth century Brazil. Morse contrasts the awareness of exclusion from society of workers in nineteenth century Europe with the incorporation of twentieth century Brazilians who have moved from the country to the city. He claims that "[t]he Brazilian migrant to São Paulo, on the other hand, soon feels himself part of a national society in transition . . . ."[12]

III. THE MEANING AND SIGNIFICANCE OF ASSOCIATION FOOTBALL AS AN ASPECT OF INCORPORATION

How does the development of football fit into the account of incorporation presented above? Ultimately, the contribution of any given institution must be a subject for speculation. But to fit it into the pattern seems a much stronger hypothesis than to exclude it. After all, to play modern football is to learn to work with a team, to accept a limited and often specialized role, and to accept discipline, all of these qualities being virtues in terms of learning a place in a hierarchical society and an industrial process. To play football is also to take a place in what John Foster describes as a "small scale success system," to aspire to victory and to accept, but never welcome, defeat.[13] To support football is to become involved in a pattern of local loyalties which transcend, but do not eradicate, the social and economic divisions in society. At the international level, this pattern of loyalty serves to reinforce patriotism. However, a broad analysis of the meaning of modern football must wait until after examining the process whereby football becomes an important working class activity.

A. *The Development of English Football*[14]

The development of football can be clearly divided into three phases: traditional, transitional, and modern.

1. *Traditional football.*

Defined broadly, football is a very ancient game, at least as old as
the Roman Empire. There are long-standing indigenous traditions of
football in England and in Italy.[15] Medieval football in England
consisted of a variety of local traditions. Normally games lasted for a
day or more, usually on a public holiday. The terrain was enormous, a
mile or more from goal to goal. Most of these traditions involved
neither rules nor a concept of "team"; an indeterminate number
played on each side. There were, however, instances when the game
was played with limited teams of ten.

The skills required to pay traditional football varied enormously.
In some cases, very little skill was involved. In other areas, the established practice was to get to the river and swim or row the ball to the
goal. In yet other places, the game developed from one of skill and
strength into one of deceit and cunning, tactics being employed like
cutting up the ball and smuggling it to the goal under a woman's
petticoats. Football was called "camping" in many parts of East Anglia, and was a close relation to the West Midlands event of bull-
running, in which a wild bull, not a ball, was to be driven to the goal.

There was always opposition to traditional football. One oft-cited
reason for this is that it was detrimental to archery practice.[16] But
there were objections at least as serious which outlived the need for
skilled archers. Football was riotous; indeed it *was* a riot on occasions.
Moreover, it was a great nuisance to property, particularly in the
towns. In Manchester, for instance, the Court Leet ordered in 1608
that:

> . . . a companye of lewde and disordered persons usinge
> that unlawfull exercise of playinge with the ffotebale in ye
> streets of the said towne, breakinge many mens windowes
> and glass at their plesures, and other inormyties, There-
> fore Wee of this Jurye does order that no maner of persons
> hereinafter shall play or use the ffootebale in any street
> within the said towne of Manchester . . . .[17]

In the 1620's, Manchester employed two constables whose job was to
prevent football from occurring.[18]

Traditional football survived this opposition for many centuries.
It was firmly rooted in the customs and culture of the common
people. It embodied their freedom, both in terms of their rights to the
land and their rights to holidays. It was an expression of their
communal identity and of their needs for myths and heroes. It was

often remarked that in some villages local people could tell tales of games played before they were born. Malcolmson argues that there was a ". . . conservative, gregarious and ritualistic morality which was represented in the pastimes of the common people."[19]

The survival of football was also facilitated by the indulgence of some sections of the aristocracy, particularly after 1660. To the eighteenth century gentleman, the sport of the lower orders was a manly display and an opportunity for a wager. Perhaps some were also shrewd enough to see the advantages to themselves of the common people having absorbing recreation. This instinct was made explicit by Robert Slaney in 1824:

> In order that poorer classes should be happy and content-ed it is not enough that they should have adequate wages . . . they should have the reasonable hope of relaxation from toil before them, and look to a holiday occasionally for amusement. This is of the utmost consequence, not merely to the poor, but to the security of the great.[20]

However, in the growing urban societies of the industrial North, traditional football had little chance of survival. In the first place, there was insufficient space to play it. Moreover, the long-standing traditions of rural villages and market towns had no place in a large and rapidly growing industrial city. Long hours of work left little time for recreation, and both the sanitary conditions and the work situation left the population ill-fitted for violent exercise. The traditionally religious and agricultural rhythms of the countryside had left ample time for holidays and occasions; the demands of the new industrial system left almost none.

In addition, the very spirit of football was deemed to be at odds with the industrial ethic. Even where they had no religious objections to popular entertainments, many members of the bourgeoisie saw football, fairs, and the like as enemies of the effective work discipline that had to be inculcated in order to compete commercially. As early as 1786, Henry Zouch argued that traditional popular occasions were the enemy of industry:

> It is . . . found by long experience that when the common people are drawn together upon any public occasion, a variety of mischiefs are certain to ensue: allured by unlaw-ful pastimes, or even by vulgar amusements only, they wantonly waste their time and money, to their own great loss and that of their employers. Nay a whole neighbor-

hood becomes thereby unhinged in such a manner, that
there is a general stagnation of labour for many days
. . . .[21]

With the growth of public police forces after 1826 as a greatly more
efficient means of social control, "unlawful pastimes" were easier to
eradicate.

Even in the countryside and small towns, traditional festivities
such as football were in decline. Religion played no small part in this.
Puritanism, formally defeated in the seventeenth century, achieved a
slow and stealthy, but very real, victory in the nineteenth century.
This was true not only of Methodism which formally separated from
the Anglican church after the death of John Wesley, but also of the
evangelical tendencies within the established church. William Wilber-
force expressed the Puritan attitude toward popular recreation when
he said that "the people can only innocently recreate themselves on
[Sunday] by attending to their religious duties."[22] Puritanism generally opposed most popular recreations, but it abhorred Sunday recreations. Where the mass of the people had no free time except on
Sunday, the new religious spirit was the death of sport. Many rural
sports died out in Lancashire and the West Riding of Yorkshire under
the influence of Methodism, and cricket was deliberately killed by
evangelical Anglicanism in the East Burnham in 1842 and 1843.[23]

A final enemy of the old football was enclosures, so much so that
in 1840 William Howitt speculated that "Football . . . seems to have
almost gone out of use with the enclosure of wastes and commons,
requiring [as it does] a wide space for its exercise."[24] In fact, this was a
considerable exaggeration both of the cause and the effect. In the
mid-forties, the magistrates of Derby were renewing an old struggle
against the local game, reputedly one of the biggest in the country,
with over one thousand men on each side. They argued that Derby,
with a population of 40,000, had become too big for football. They
persuaded the leading players to cancel the game on the condition
that alternative amusements would be provided. However, they
welched on the promise; the game was revived and, in fact, survived
into the twentieth century to become a byword in football for any
game involving intense local rivalry.[25] There were other survivals of
traditional sports in the area which Neville Cardus used to describe as
"the great hinterland of Manchester." In Bolton, Colne, and Burnley,
where the cotton-town was much closer culturally and physically to
the countryside, a number of ancient sports have survived to this day.
They include bowls, knur, spell and, if rumor is to be believed, cock-

fighting. Traditional football had never been prominent in this area, though, partly because of the rough nature of the terrain.

In contrast, in a big new industrial city like Manchester, the old game was a plant which could not take root: there was neither the time, space, energy, tolerance, nor tradition for it. The literary tourists who went to Manchester in the 1840's would not have seen football in the streets or on the waste ground. For the new proletariat, the tradition of football was dead, to be revived through the agency of a set of institutions of which they could scarcely have had the remotest knowledge.

2. *Transitional football.*

The English public schools of the early nineteenth century were few in number. They were outmoded, inefficient, and decadent institutions rapidly falling out of line with their times. After 1780, they became predominantly upper class institutions, drawing on the social groups of the aristocracy and landed gentry whose sub-culture was predominantly hedonistic and cavalier. The masters, often men of a slightly lower social order with no great vocation to teach, were generally held in contempt by the boys. The boys, left alone, exhibited behavior which might be described as similar to that of the tribal adolescent male: a sub-culture of ritual, dominance, violence, and sensuality. Their games, superficially like those of the peasants, were more violent manifestations in the hands of the adolescents. There were frequent rebellions: six of them occurred at Winchester between 1780 and 1818, requiring the military to restore order. In the great rebellion at Rugby in 1797, led by Willoughby Cotton, the headmaster's door was blown down with gunpowder.

There were considerable outside pressures on these schools to reform. Evangelical Christianity regarded them as undisciplined and immoral. The bourgeoisie coveted the social status which they still represented, but disliked their immorality and inefficiency. As time went on, governments looked to them to provide a more disciplined and educated administrative class for the home and colonial civil services.

No one man personified these pressures on the schools more clearly than Thomas Arnold, headmaster of Rugby from 1828 until 1841. It is tempting to elevate Arnold's status to that of a prophet, and to say that Arnold found, in late Georgian Rugby, a testing ground for the establishment of hegemony in urban society. One of his referees to the trustees of Rugby, Dr. Hawkins, wrote that if appointed ". . . he would change the face of education all through the public

schools of England."[26] Later appraisals have been scarcely less generous. The reality of Arnold's career was only slightly less dramatic. A
great deal of what he did followed from his theological and moral
principles. The specific message of Arnold's Christianity was that
theology applied to all situations and to every minute of the day. He
believed in a solidarity of the whole of nature moving together if it
moves at all. This implied the necessity of a personal devotion to
Christ; it also meant that a man's devotion (particularly a young
man's) would be corrupted by contact with base and fleshly things.
That the body was the temple of the Holy Spirit, as Arnold often told
his boys, was not a metaphor but literal truth worthy of their constant
awareness.

The implementation of these prinicples required radical reform.
In a sense, Arnold was lucky in finding Rugby, a school which had
developed from a humble grammar school. It lacked the great traditions and established character of Eton, Harrow, or Winchester,
where he had received his own education. He taught the classics with
emphasis on their linguistic, literary, and moral implications. He
introduced the "modern" studies of history, mathematics, and living
languages. More important, for the purposes of this argument, he
modified and established games as an essential part of education.

Games at Rugby changed in their essential nature: They evolved
from barbaric celebrations into organized and disciplined activities
which offered boys the opportunity to develop and demonstrate the
virtues of endeavor, discipline, and self-control. In part, this was the
application of a shrewd political instinct. Arnold saw that it was easier
and more effective to mold and modify a tradition than to destroy it.
From having no great enthusiasm for games, he came to regard them
as an essential part of education. Thus, Christianity and organized
games served together as instruments of a rising middle-class morality.

By 1845, there were written rules for the game played at Rugby
which barred a number of dangerous and violent practices. Within a
year rules had been written at Cambridge University. The idea of
organized games as part of a boy's education thus spread steadily
through the schools of England. It affected not only the established
public schools, but also the grammar schools and the new wave of
public schools founded after Arnold's death. In the 1850's, organized
games of football became common practice in the universities and
then among the professional classes. By 1864, the Clarendon
Commission was reporting that games ". . . hold . . . a distinct and
important place in public school education."[27] A handling form of the

game was established in The Royal Grammar School, Lancaster by the early 1860's.[28]

There were no national rules; team captains agreed upon the rules for each game with like-minded opponents. Naturally, this led to considerable disputes. The most extreme argument was between those who favored a game with a substantial amount of handling (loosely, the game played at Rugby) and those who wanted a predominantly kicking game such as was played at Harrow. In 1863, a group of the kickers formed the "Football Association" to define a set of rules for the kicking game. An immediate consequence of this was the formation of the Blackheath Club (still called "the club" in Rugby circles) to preserve the handling game. The national Rugby Football Union was not formed until 1871.

Until the late 1870's, football remained a predominantly middle and upper class recreation. When the first national competition, the Football Association Challenge Cup, was started in 1871, it drew 15 entrants. All of them consisted entirely of players from the professional and leisured classes. Fourteen of these teams were from South Eastern England and one, Queen's Park, was from Glasgow, Scotland. For a decade the cup was won exclusively by teams of this kind. The Wanderers, Royal Engineers, and Old Etonians were the most prominent.

Football began to be disseminated among the working classes in the 1870's. For the most part, it was taught and organized by middle-class missionaries—clergymen, schoolteachers, and businessmen. There may have been many motives in this activity, but the most pressing and immediate seem to have been internal to the sport; it was a question of wanting to play and needing other men with whom to play. It was a question of wanting to win and needing to recruit the best physical talents available.

The game's movement down the social pyramid caused important changes. In the first place, there was a change of tactics. The lower orders tended to be smaller and less robust than their social superiors. To win, they had to introduce new skills of close control, dribbling, and passing. When the predominantly working class Blackburn Olympic team of 1883 travelled to London and won the cup by beating Old Etonians 1-0 after extra time, they did so because of their superior skills. The Old Etonians was a robust, physical team which had shaken Blackburn Rovers with its speed and strength the previous year. Olympic won by their superior passing and positional play. As small men accustomed to the division of labor in a cotton mill, they held their positions and passed with great accuracy.

It was the end of an era. The southern middle classes never again offered a serious challenge in top-class football. So greatly did the balance of power shift that in 1888, when the Football League was founded, six of its twelve teams were from Lancashire and none was located south of Birmingham. None of the original entrants to the Football Association cup was a founding member of the Football League.

In short, the 20 years from 1870 to 1890 involved the transition of football from an upper class pastime into a modern, urban, mass sport. Several aspects of this transition require further analysis: The most important was that football became a working class game. Other changes including the establishment of professionalism (acknowledged by the Association in 1885), the change in tactics, and the shift in power from South to North were consequences of this tendency.

The game became working class in a very strong sense. The vast majority of its players, spectators, and officials were of working class origins. Thus began a substantial snobbish retreat of the middle class from the game, the most important long term aspect of which was the establishment of Rugby Union as the sole winter game in the majority of public and grammar schools. That the middle class educational institutions should adopt the much more robust and physical code of rules was captured in the popular saying that "Football is a game for gentlemen played by ruffians, while Rugby is a game for ruffians played by gentlemen." Even within the Association code, the middle class began to develop its own competitions confined to amateurs. The Football Association Amateur Cup, which was instituted in 1895, was the most important of these, but the Arthur Dunn Cup, restricted entirely to the former pupils of public schools, was the most exclusive.

This nearly complete shift of power on the terraces and on the field should not be taken to mean that the middle classes lost contact with the game. They remained important as owners, shareholders, and reporters of the game. Nor is it possible to produce an objective and definitive account of the effects of the proletarianization of football on class consciousness. On the one hand, it was an early exercise in the democratization of an important national institution, an aspect which might be stressed by social democrats.[29] On the other hand, we must give at least some credence to the familiar picture of football as a palliative to the emotions and ambitions of the working class, an aspect which has been stressed by many Marxists.

It should be stressed, however, that the rapid emergence of mass spectator support for football stemmed from the inherent ethos of the game rather than from changes in its class composition. As

Harold Hobson has said, football is theater where the audience consists of actors. The combination of passion and technical insight which characterized involvement in modern sport applied to both spectators and players. The experience of support is vicarious to that of participation: not only do spectators identify with what happens on the field but, for the most part, they are or have been, at some stage and at some level, players themselves.

3. *The modern game*.

The half century from 1840 to 1890 marked the evolution of football from a declining rural tradition to a thriving professional game which drew its workers and customers substantially from the urban working class. In England it had become, and still remains, the dominant game of urban areas, only seriously challenged by professional rugby in limited areas of South Lancashire and West Yorkshire, and by amateur rugby in Warwickshire and the Bristol area. With the introduction of a second division to the Football League in 1892, all the major institutions of English Football were established: two major competitions and two separate organizations to run them, a system of promotion and relegation between divisions, and an acceptance of professionalism limited (through compromise with the scruples of the Football Association) both in terms of wages and profits.

Soccer contrasts quite sharply with other modern professional sports. There was never a break between the middle class amateurs and the working class professionals in soccer as there was within rugby in 1895. Football was lucky in this respect; there was power on both sides. A successful sport needed the resources of the educational system and the traditions of the southern establishment just as much as it needed the crowds and players of the northern industrial areas. Deprived of these resources, Rugby League has survived rather than thrived.

Of the six clubs in Lancashire which were founders of the Football League, only Everton could be described as a big city club. Professionalism and the second division brought with them a number of clubs from the big cities: Ardwick (later to be called Manchester City), Newton Heath (Manchester United) and Liverpool. Liverpool was an exceptional institution. Of the major Lancashire clubs, only it was founded as a profit-making corporation with professional players.

Remarkably, many of the details of modern football have survived from the Victorian period. The major clubs, their grounds, even their colors would be recognizable to a supporter of the 1890's.

The rules which govern the game, both on and off the field, have changed less than those of any other major sport. Even cricket has modified considerably to suit the changing commercial and social context of the twentieth century, while Rugby Union is still struggling to incorporate the demands of competition and the commercial pressures stemming from the existence of the gate-taking clubs.

4. *A Case Study: Football in Blackburn.*

Harry Berry wrote of the Blackburn Rovers:

> Blackburn and the cotton trade have always been synonymous. The town once had a glut of mills and by far the most important benefactors of the club have been directors of mills in the town, just as for a long time the main body of spectators were weavers and doffers. It has given the club a working class air of blunt honesty and steadfast dependability. It remains today as true as it ever did, but the founders of the club were not working men but the intelligensia of the town.[30]

Working class football in Lancashire began not in a city or even a town, but in a village. In Turton, a village on the moors between Blackburn and Bolton, J.C. Kay, the son of the Lord of the Manor, and W.T. Dixon, the village schoolmaster, founded a football club in 1871 for the men of the village. Until 1874 they played according to the Harrow rules, but in that year they changed to Association rules. The popularity of the game spread rapidly. On November 5, 1875, John Lewis and Arthur Constantine, both old boys of Shrewsbury School, held a meeting in the St. Leger Hotel, Blackburn. The club they founded was destined for a rapid rise in the world of football, winning the F.A. Cup three successive times in 1884-86.

Rovers began as a substantially middle class team, the majority of their players being fairly wealthy men and old boys of Blackburn Grammar School. It was to remain so for some time, although the club was fortified by the addition of a number of dubiously amateur Scots in the 1880's. Nevertheless, football spread rapidly through the workers of the town and, by 1878-79, there were eight teams in the Blackburn Association Challenge Cup. None of these included Rovers, who instead had their eyes set on national competition. The competition was won by Blackburn Olympic.

It is interesting to speculate on this rapid spread down the social pyramid and on the relationship between classes in a stratified society who met each other on the field of play. Two factors seem to have prevented snobbery from intervening. In the first place, there was an assumption among both classes that social difference ought not to apply on the field. A story which emerged from an early Rovers game against the miners of Haslingden was that Walter Duckworth, a wealthy bourgeois Rovers player, had been kicked unceremoniously around the field by a pit worker. Eventually, Duckworth was driven to ask whether the man had anything personal against him. "Well, I 'ave to kick some'at"[31] was the unbiassed reply. A second factor was what might be called the autonomous dynamics of sport. In plain English, footballers want to play football and they want to win. If a man cares about a game, he is unlikely to scruple over either a teammate's or an opponent's social class. Moreover, the working classes of Blackburn were, of course, far more numerous than the middle classes.

In some cases, the attitudes of the middle class players went beyond more tolerance and became positive enthusiasm. A.N. "Monkey" Hornby, the captain of Lancashire Cricket Club and son of a wealthy Cheshire industrialist, chose to play with the cotton workers of Olympic in the 1880's in order to try to keep the club alive.[32] In the course of the eighties, despite Hornby's gallant intervention, the resources and mass support of the competing Rovers killed Olympic as a top class club. Even so, the team holds a place in the history of English football as the pioneer of a new style and a new class.

Professionalism was the great moral issue of football in this period. Many of the middle class amateurs objected that paying players was an offense to the traditions of sportsmanship. But even Lord Kinnaird, the most successful of the amateurs, saw that professionalism, if contained by a maximum wage, could have a useful role in raising standards and spreading the game.[33] Rovers occupied a middle position on the issue, which was often cast as the broader issue of the eligibility of players for specific clubs. The team had four Scottish players, of whom all but one had jobs outside football. Rovers came in for some criticism for their attitude toward eligibility. On the other hand, they were critical of clubs like Burnley and Preston North End who were more or less openly professional.

An important dimension of the game in this period was the geographic rivalry which took on two distinct forms: a bitter rivalry between the teams from Lancashire which were struggling for national eminence, and a far more gentlemanly rivalry between North and South. The feud between Rovers and Darwen erupted on November 22, 1880, into a fist fight among the 10,000 supporters. The game was forced to be abandoned.

Playing against the gentlemen of the South, however, Rovers were subject to a different kind of attack. When they reached the cup final for the first time in 1882, an article in the *Pall Mall Gazette* described them as "The Northern Horde."[34] The *Gazette* was owned by Lord Morley, and the article was written by C.R. Morley, his nephew, and the son of Dr. Morley, an important figure in the Rovers Club itself. The article was, therefore, an act of treachery by a young man trying to cut a dash in London society. It was received as such. But what is interesting is that the same phrase, "Northern Horde," was used to describe Olympic, the working class team, when they made the journey south a year later. In the terms of southern snobbery, notherners were a "horde" irrespective of social class. This attitude was reciprocated by the Lancastrians whose local loyalty transcended class.[35]

B. *Football in Brazil*[36]

Football spread through the world on the wide-ranging tentacles of British capitalism. The late nineteenth century was a period in which many Englishmen and Scotsmen left their native countries and sought fortune overseas as bankers, entrepreneurs, and engineers. These men taught the world to play the organized games they had learned in English schools.

The normal pattern consisted of three stages. First, British emigres would establish clubs for playing games among themselves. Normally, cricket was at least as important as football in such clubs. Then, the indigenous upper classes would be introduced to these games. They gained status from association with the British social institutions while the emigres in turn gained much-needed manpower. Finally the game would develop among the indigenous lower classes. In almost all cases, football completed this three-stage transition while cricket did not.[37] One suspects this was partly because football is a much simpler game; but it might also be argued that cricket is culturally a more exclusively English game.

In some cases the middle stage of this process was omitted and the game was taught directly to the workers by their English bosses. For example, there is evidence that English capitalists did this in Russia with specific regard for the advantages of teaching the peasantry discipline, teamwork, and the division of labor.[38]

Brazil is clearly an example of the classic pattern. Association Football was played in São Paulo as early as 1864 by some British sailors. But it did not begin to take root for a generation. When it did, its immediate expansion was largely due to Charles Miller.[39] Miller was born in São Paulo of English parents. He was educated in England and played football for Southampton in their very early years. When he returned to Brazil in 1890, he found that the game was virtually unknown. He was instrumental in establishing a number of clubs. He persuaded the São Paulo Athletic Club to play soccer as well as cricket and he was involved in the raising of teams under the auspices of the English Gas Company, São Paulo Railways, and the London Bank.

Within a decade, there were a number of teams of Portuguese-speaking Brazilians. The first predominantly native team was Mackenzie College in 1898. In 1914, a Brazilian national team played for the first time and beat Argentina 1-0. By the 1920's, the game had spread to the middle and lower classes in the cities.

The standard of play was raised enormously, but the game was subject to two conflicting pressures. On the one hand was the desire for individual clubs and the national team to utilize the intensely-practiced skills of the lower classes. Against this was social prejudice by the classes who had established the game against the lower orders, and racial prejudice against black players.[40] Manteiga of America F.C. was the first black player in a major team and his inclusion caused many supporters to desert to Fluminense.[41] Games were played between blacks and whites, but this could cause trouble also. Friedenrich, a mulatto, was very upset when picked for the blacks.[42]

As the middle classes resisted professionalism, Brazil began to lose many talented lower-class players to Europe and Argentina. In order to stem this loss, professionalism was permitted in 1933. Even so, it was some years before racial issues finally faded. When Brazil played Italy in the semi-final of the 1938 World Cup in Paris, they lost 1-2, but there were many who argued that Brazil would have won if they had not mysteriously excluded their two best black players, Tim and Leonidas. Leonidas returned as captain for the third place match, in which Brazil beat Sweden 4-2. By 1950, when the World Cup started again, 80 percent of the top Brazilian players were lower-class, and blacks were fully accepted. The rest is well-known history: Brazil won the championship three times out of four from 1958 to 1970 and a black player, Pele, established himself almost indisputably as the world's finest player.

Soccer has become a major focus for popular culture in Brazil in much the same way that it has in England. But there are important differences. First, the Brazilian national team represents not merely the progress of Brazil as a society, but also the flair and style of Brazil.

Brazilian fans contrast the brilliance and individualism of their players with the methodical and efficient style of the Europeans. The
Brazilian way represents to them almost a kind of magic which sym-
bolizes their national culture. In England, the national side is almost
peripheral to the game, though this might not be the case if it were
more successful.

A second difference is that the "club" is a very different kind of
institution in Brazil. English clubs are almost exclusively concerned
with what their first teams do in competition. They have no "members" as such and the social life that surrounds them is informal and
football-oriented. In Brazil, membership in a club is important; it
offers social facilities and contacts as well as opportunities for many
sports at many levels.

Finally, class is still an overt feature of the Brazilian situation.
There are upper class clubs such as Fluminense, which carefully sets
membership and was the last to accept black players, and lower class
clubs such as Flamengo. This feature is especially true of the big cities,
but less so of a smaller city such as Curitiba where the club boasts of its
"family" atmosphere.

C. *Conclusions*

Urbanization is a complex social process. The change in social
relations which it involves includes spatial, social, and economic dimensions. Urban societies are generally characterized by high density
living, factory employment, and a pattern of social stratification derived from that employment. Thus, "urbanization," in its most significant sense, means something very close to "modernization." Its meaning is also close, in a strict, etymological sense, to "civilization," but,
paradoxically, "civilization" in its more common and moral sense can
be the exact opposite of urbanization. It was a characteristic remark of
many observers of the early stage of urbanization that there was a
decline of civilization, a return to barbarous levels of ignorance and
immorality.

Organized, professional sports with a mass following are peculiar-
ly appropriate recreational patterns for modern, urban societies. Association football is the most widespread of these sports; we can
reasonably describe it as the paradigm case. Football is so deeply
significant in the workings of such societies that it is logically impro-
per to assess its effects. If we ask "does sport make any difference to
the overall development of society?", we are committed to a counter-
factual hypothetical speculation about what social relations would be

like in a modern society without sport. This question cannot be answered any more than could a parallel question about whether parties make any difference to the overall development of modern politics. In each case the institution is so deeply ingrained in the process that we cannot detach the one from the other in order to distinguish causes and effects. And, of course, we have no "control experiments," no modern, urban societies from which the institutions of organized sport and organized parties are absent.

A thesis about sport which is commonly expressed and is a useful clarification to consider, is that it serves as an "opiate of the masses." While this exact phrase is only used, to my knowledge, by Dumazedier,[43] and then without commitment, opiate *theories* are commonplace. Austin Whitlock, the owner of a football club in Harold Brighouse's 1913 Lancashire comedy "The Game," said that "Employers of men all know . . . that good football is the antidote to strikes."[44] In 1926, Leon Trotsky predicted that ". . . the revolution will inevitably arouse a tremendous fervor in the British working class, that fervor which has been so artificially restrained and repressed with the aid of social training, the Church, the Press, and has been drawn off into artificial channels with the aid of boxing, football, racing and other forms of sport."[45] Half a century later we find Ralph Miliband arguing that "[the existence of capitalist 'relations of production'] as a daily fact breeds frustrations which seek compensation and release in many different ways, most of them by no means conducive to the development of class-consciousness. One of these ways is undoubtedly sport, or rather spectator and commercialized sport, some forms of which have assumed a central place in working-class life. For instance, vast numbers of people in the countries of advanced capitalism turn out on Saturdays and Sundays to watch soccer being played."[46] In Brazil, Antonio Texeira has offered more precise figures about the palliative effect of (successful) football on industrial workers: "In the weeks that the Corinthians (the most popular team in the city) win, production in São Paulo rises 12.3%. In the weeks in which the Corinthians lose, the number of accidents at work increases by 15.3%."[47]

In considering the status of the "opiate" thesis, it is best to distinguish two versions. First, there is a "strong" version in which the dominant class appears as the controllers and organizers of the development of mass sport. The implication of my argument about the transitional stage in the development of football is that for the most part this thesis is historically false. Admittedly, there were cases both abroad and in England of capitalists organizing football clubs with a fairly clear notion of the social advantages of their existence. West Ham United seems to have been a fairly clear case in England. It is also to be noted that the Football Association could be used as an instrument of social control: A striking case occured in 1914 when the Association was instrumental in recruiting 500,000 soldiers in the first few months of the war.

However, the majority of evidence refutes this thesis. Football clubs were founded to play football, not to pacify plebians. Remarkably quickly, the working classes themselves took over the game. Even where the game was organized from above for reasons of principle and interest, it was the demand or need from below which caused it to spread, change, and develop. Some social institutions have been organized by dominant classes for the diversion and emasculation of the energies of the subordinate class; these include the Roman circus and possibly modern Youth Clubs. But Youth Clubs survive only so long as they are organized from above, whereas organized sport is self-sustaining.

Second, a "weaker" thesis is one in which the dominant class is posited as the beneficiary of the institution of football which has the latent function of maintaining its position. Here the thesis is not false; rather it is meaningless in any strict logical or empirical sense. Modern football coexists with many regimes, from Brazil to England to the Soviet Union. As an antidote to revolution, its potency cannot be measured. What goes on in the stadium of Dynamo Kiev seems remarkably similar to what happens in Ibrox Park, the home of Glasgow Rangers. It is precisely those developed urban societies to which mass sport is functionally most appropriate (and in which it is empirically most common) which have shown very low propensities to "revolution," in any strict sense, in the last century.

It follows that the hegemonic thesis is itself meaningless. Whether one envisages organized sport as a legitimate expression, or as a subtle repression, of working-class emotions depends upon philosophical and moral premises which are not susceptible to argument. The same is true of many other institutions of "advanced capitalism," for instance, universal suffrage. It is interesting to note that Miliband prevaricates on the subject when he argues that "[t]he nature of this [cultural fallout from sport] is not quite as obviously negative as Marxists are often tempted to assume. The subject lends itself to simplistic and prim-sounding attitudes, which are often over-compensated by hearty demagogic-populist ones."[48]

Having rejected the opiate thesis, it remains to state clearly what I am positively arguing about football. My thesis has two aspects, the first general and functional, the second particular and historical. Generally, modern football represents the adaptation to modern urban conditions of recreational institutions which express emotional needs that are present in all human societies. The institution is thus appropriate to all modern urban societies regardless of their prevailing ideology or class structure. Particularly, the evolution of modern football in Victorian England was such a process of adaptation. In its relations to other social forces it was an integral part of a general stabilization of social conditions and an improvement in the quality of social life which had as their concomitant the substantial incorporation of the working class into the mainstream of English life.

Those are the bare bones of the argument. To give them flesh one must move away from abstraction towards the subjective realities of how people actually react to football. In short, we must try to develop an understanding of what football *means* to its players and spectators. Many of the most profound emotions it engenders seem to be common to both the traditional and modern game. First, a sense of loyalty and identity is developed. One writer remarked in the *Spectator* in 1712 that "At the Seasons of Football and Cock-fighting," many parishes "reassume their national Hatred to each other. My Tenant in the Country is verily persuaded, that the Parish of the Enemy hath not one honest man in it."[49] Many young Burnley fans are still similarly persuaded about Blackburn Rovers and Manchester United. Second, the game is a focus for our need for myths, heroes, and continuities. Just as many observers of the ancient game noted that it gave rise to myths and legends of great durability, so I was brought up on tales of feats performed by James, Gallacher, Bastin and Hulme long before I was born. Finally, football is an outlet for our communal emotions of freedom and solidarity, just as it was in feudal society. It is not too far-fetched to say that sporting emotions represent a "communitas" or *Gemeinschaft* dimension in modern societies in which normal productive and legal relations are on an impersonal and rational basis. The outlets of collective emotion can take many forms, from community singing to violence, but in whatever form, important rituals are maintained. It follows from my analysis that the "hooligan" element in English soccer is not something endemic only in our "sick" society, but represents an element in any society. It must be dealt with not, as is fashionably argued, by attacking mythical "causes" such as unemployment, but by increasingly sophisticated techniques of social control. It was there in the feudal villages and when Darwen played Blackburn Rovers in 1880. Like the poor, it is always with us.

The modern game is a compromise between ancient emotions and modern industrial and urban society. This compromise is partly functional: Games take limited time and use limited space to absorb and involve vast numbers of people. But the compromise also has a cultural dimension: The ancient values of the peasant are constrained by the needs of an industrial society for discipline and control, and by the bourgeois concept of religion. As a result, English football is a game in which "discipline" is thought to be the important virtue and professional football is still not played on Sundays. The compromised forces are acutely evident at an English League or Cup match when a referee penalizes one of the home team's players for dissent. The "hooligan" element sing lustily, communally, and aggressively, "The Referee's a bastard," while a more staid element of the crowd "tut tuts" the player's action on rational grounds. "The fool!", they say, "he should know there is nothing to be gained from criticizing the referee."

My argument that modern football can only be understood in terms of what it *means* to players and spectators, and that its meaning can only be understood in terms of emotions whose anthropology predates modern society, clearly fits the case of the development of football in Lancashire. It has often been argued that a surprising number of practices and traditions survived from pre-industrial Lancashire into the industrial society. Both the broad development of the game (Lancashire has always been an important area for modern football) and its detailed progress from industrial village to town to city support the argument. Football rapidly became part of the working class culture of the region.

Nobody has better expressed the meaning of football than J.B. Priestley in his description of the fictitious Bruddesford United. Marvelling at how 35,000 men can afford a shilling to watch the game in times of hardship, he asserts that:

> For a shilling the Bruddesford United A.F.C. offered you Conflict and Art; it turned you into a critic, happy in your judgment of fine points . . . it turned you into a partisan . . . watching a ball shape Iliads and Odysseys for you . . . . And what is more, it turned you into a member of a new community, all brothers together for an hour and a half . . . . To say that these men paid their shillings to watch twenty-two hirelings kick a ball is merely to say that a violin is wood and catgut, that *Hamlet* is so much paper and ink.[50]

APPENDIX

Some Main Dates in the Transition to Modern Football

1845: first written rules at Rugby School
1846: first written rules at Cambridge University
1857: Sheffield football club formed
1862: Notts County F.C. formed
1863: formation of the Football Association
1866: first representative match, London versus Sheffield
1871: first Football Association Challenge Cup competition
1874: first 'Varsity Match', Oxford versus Cambridge
1878: Lancashire Football Association formed
1882: first British international championship
1883: first predominantly working-class team to win the F.A. Cup (Blackburn Olympic 2, Old Etonians 1, after extra time)
1885: legitimacy of professionalism recognised by the Football Association
1888: formation of the Football League
1892: introduction of a second division to the Football League, with promotion and relegation between divisions based on test matches.

NOTES

1. B. SEEBOHM ROWNTREE & G.R. LAVERS, ENGLISH LIFE AND LEISURE, A SOCIAL STUDY 136 (London: Longmans, Green & Co., 1951).

2. H.J. DYOS & MICHAEL WOLFF, eds., 1 & 2 THE VICTORIAN CITY: IMAGES AND REALITIES (London & Boston: Routledge & Kegan Paul, 1973).

3. B. SEEBOHM ROWNTREE & G.R. LAVERS, *supra* note 1, at 136.

4. R.N. RUNDLE, BRITIAN'S ECONOMIC AND SOCIAL DEVELOPMENT FROM 1700 TO THE PRESENT DAY (London: University of London Press, 1973).

5. For recent attempts to analyze the implications of modern sport, see JAMES WALRIN, THE PEOPLE'S GAME (London: Allen Lane, 1975); *Sport and Leisure in Victorian Society*, 21 VICTORIAN STUDIES (University of Sussex, 1976). In addition, a conference has been held on *The Making of Sporting Traditions* (Univ. of New South Wales, July 1977).

6. Dumazedier, *Leisure*, DAVID L. SILLS, ed., 9 INTERNATIONAL ENCYCLOPAEDIA OF THE SOCIAL SCIENCES 253 (New York: Macmillan & Free Press, 1968).

7. I should qualify the phrase "working class culture". I mean it to be the real, empirically discernible, culture which owes a great deal to pre-industrial society, to consciousness of the national development of England, and to the authoritarianism of the army and of industry. I do not mean a concept of culture abstracted from the role or status of the working class.

8. This was neatly illustrated in late 1914 when the Home Office produced a scheme which would involve the constabulary in checking on the wives of enlisted men to make sure they were faithful to their husbands. The London Times blithely regarded this as a "good idea", but to the Manchester Guardian it was an "insult".

I am indebted to John Osborne of the Department of History, Stanford University, for this example.

9. ARTHUR REDFORD, 2 THE HISTORY OF LOCAL GOVERNMENT IN MANCHESTER 205–241 (New York & London: Longmans, Green & Co., 1940).

10. For instance, Marx wrote that "[t]he carrying of Universal Suffrage in England would . . . be a far more socialistic measure than anything which has been

honoured with that name on the Continent. Its inevitable result, here, is the *political supremacy of the working class*" (emphasis in original). Karl Marx, *The Chartists*, NEW YORK DAILY TRIBUNE (Aug. 25, 1852).

11. CARL BOGGS, GRAMSCI'S MARXISM 36–55 (London: Pluto Press, 1976).

12. RICHARD M. MORSE, FORMAÇÃO HISTÓRICA DE SÃO PAULO (São Paulo: Difusão Européia do Livro, 1970).

13. John Foster, *Nineteenth Century Towns—A Class Dimension*, H.J. DYOS, ed., THE STUDY OF URBAN HISTORY 294 (London & New York: Edward Arnold & St. Martin's Press, 1968).

14. The following dates may prove helpful in tracing the development of English football:

THE FOOTBALL LEAGUE CLUBS OF LANCASHIRE[a]

A. The Surviving Clubs[b]

	Formed	Limited Company	Professional	League Member
Blackburn Rovers	1875	1897	1880	1888
Blackpool	1887	1896	1887	1896
Bolton Wanderers	1874	1895	1880	1888
Burnley	1881	1897	1883	1888
Bury	1885	1897	1885	1894
Everton	1878	1892	1885	1888
Liverpool	1892	1892	1892	1893
Manchester City	1887	1894	1887	1892
Manchester United	1880	1895	1885	1892
Oldham Athletic	1894	1905	1899	1907
Preston North End	1881	1893	1882	1888
Rochdale	1907	1910	1907	1921
Southport	1881	1919	1919	1921
Stockport County	1883	1898	1891	1900
Tranmere Rovers	1881	1920	1912	1921

B. Former League Clubs

	Formed	League Dates
Accrington Stanley	1878	1888-93, 1921-62
Barrow	1901	1921-72
Bootle	1881	1892-93
Darwen	1875	1891-99
Nelson	1882	1921-31
New Brighton	1890	1898-1901, 1923-51
Stalybridge Celtic	1920	1921-23
Wigan Borough	1921	1921-31

a. Lancashire is defined as the three counties of Greater Manchester, Merseyside, and Lancashire defined by the Local Government Act of 1972. This is the administrative unit most closely approximating to the cultural region of Lancashire.

b. In cases where there is a clear continuity of a club which has changed names, the modern name of the club is given with the original date of foundation. For example, Manchester United was founded in 1880 as Newton Heath.

15. It is interesting to note that the Italian name for the game, il calcio, is an indigenous name, one of very few words for the modern game which does not derive from English 'football'.

16. See Francis P. Masoun, Jr., *Football in Medieval England and in Middle English Literature*, 35 AMERICAN HISTORICAL REVIEW 37–38, 40, 42 (—: —, 1929–1930); AUSTIN L. POOLE, ed., 2 MEDIEVAL ENGLAND 625–626 (Oxford, 1958).

17. MANCHESTER COURT LEET — (Manchester: —, 1608).

18. Consult author.

19. ROBERT W. MALCOLMSON, POPULAR RECREATIONS IN ENGLISH SOCIETY 1700–1850, at 101 (London & New York: Cambridge U. Press, 1973).

20. ROBERT A. SLANEY, AN ESSAY ON THE BENEFICIAL DIRECTION OF RURAL EXPENDITURE — (London: —, 1824).

21. HENRY ZOUCH, HINTS RESPECTING THE PUBLIC POLICE 6–7 (London: —, 1786).

22. Quoted in ROBERT W. MALCOLMSON, *supra* note 19, at 105.

23. ANON., SOME ACCOUNTS OF THE HAMLET OF EAST BURNHAM, CO. BUCKS., BY A LATER RESIDENT 45n (London: —, 1858).

24. WILLIAM HOWITT, THE RURAL LIFE OF ENGLAND 527 (London: Longman, Orme, Brown, Green & Longmans, 2nd ed., 1840).

25. MALCOLMSON, *supra* note 19, at 141–142.

26. Theodore Walrond, *Thomas Arnold*, LESLIE STEPHEN, ed., 2 DICTIONARY OF NATIONAL BIOGRAPHY 113 (New York & London: Macmillan & Smith, Elder & Co., 1885).

27. CLARENDON COMMISSION REPORT — (Oxford: Clarendon Press, —).

28. J.W. Fidler, *On the Sports Field*, J.L. SPENCER, ed., THE ROYAL GRAMMAR SCHOOL LANCASTER, QUINCENTENARY COMMEMORATIVE VOLUME 53 (Edinburgh: Lancaster Royal Grammar School, 1969).

29. Sir Harold Wilson's frequent attempts to identify with football and footballers are of some significance in this light.

30. HARRY BERRY, A CENTURY OF SOCCER, 1875–1975 at 9 (Burnley: — Blackburn Rovers Football Club, 1975).

31. *Id.*, at 11.

32. Olympic, incidentally, have a curious place in the history of the game. When they won the cup in 1883, it was against all the odds and caused surprise and consternation among the Rovers. Rovers had simply never taken Olympic seriously as competition and had beaten them regularly.

33. See GEORGE W. KEETON, THE FOOTBALL REVOLUTION: A STUDY OF THE CHANGING PATTERN OF ASSOCIATION FOOTBALL 52 (Newton Abbot, England: David & Charles, 1972).

34. Quoted in BERRY, *supra* note 30, at 21–22.

35. Berry considers the involvement of directors of cotton mills in the Rovers club to be evidence of the working-class roots of the game. BERRY, *supra* note 30. Such a view reinforces the argument that class was a very different concept in Lancashire from what it was in London.

36.   FOUNDATION DATES OF SOME LEADING BRAZILIAN CLUBS

1895	Flamengo
1898	Vasco da Gama
1902	Botafogo
1908	Atletico Mineiro
1912	Santos
1914	Palmeiras
1921	Cruzeiro
1920	São Paulo

37. It is interesting to note, however, that cricket did put down a few roots in Argentina but none in the rest of South America.

38. JAMES WALVIN, THE PEOPLE'S GAME 98 (London: Allen Lane, 1975).

39. Miller's role is stressed in the account of Brazilian football in JOHN AR-LOTT, ed., OXFORD COMPANION TO WORLD SPORTS AND GAMES 363-4 (New York & London: Oxford University Press, 1975).

40. It must be remembered that slaves were only emancipated in Brazil in 1888.

41. ARLOTT, *supra* note 39, at —.

42. *Id*. at —.

43. Dumazedier, *supra* note 6, at 253.

44. Transcribed by author from performance of play televised by BBC, January 1977.

45. LEON TROTSKY, WHERE IS BRITAIN GOING? 175 (London: Communist Party of Great Britain, 1926).

46. RALPH MILIBAND, MARXISM AND POLITICS 51 (London: Oxford University Press, 1977).

47. Texeira, *A isto se chama religiao*, quoted in Janet Lever, *Soccer as a Brazilian Way of Life*, G.P. STONE, ed., GAMES, SPORT AND POWER 159 (New Brunswick, New Jersey: Transaction Books & Dutton, c1972).

48. Miliband, *supra* note 46, at 52.

49. Consult author.

50. J.B. PRIESTLY, THE GOOD COMPANIONS 3-4 (London: William Heinemann, 1929).

Index